"Perhaps counterintuitively, our perception of public education and our policy choices are influenced by the education sector's relationship with the corporate sector. What that means for education, for students, and for the public is documented in this thoughtful, detailed, and engaging book, which traces the evolution of the corporate classroom and the implications for public policy."

— Erika Shaker, director of education and outreach,
Canadian Centre for Policy Alternatives

"*Captive Audience* should be a wake-up call to parents, policy makers, and pundits alike. Gidney chronicles the rise and spread of a flawed business logic applied to education and the rampant and breathless quest for the latest corporate-sponsored fads, vividly illustrating neoliberalism's structural exploitation of both students and teachers. Running schools like businesses has only solidified a hierarchy of moneyed interests promoting techno-gadgets, STEM, and job-skills idolatry at the expense of civics, the humanities, and the basic hard work required for learning. *Captive Audience* should be required reading for anyone interested in rejecting this corporate onslaught and instead developing schools as centres for human engagement and critical inquiry."

— Deron Boyles, professor of philosophy of education,
Georgia State University

"That we live in a consumer culture is increasingly evident. That this is problematic for education is increasingly incontestable. Tracing the history of school commercialism in Canada through the twentieth century, *Captive Audience* provides a historical account of how commercial interests sought to influence schools so as to create new consumers and promote a positive corporate image."

— Trevor Norris, author of *Consuming Schools: Commercialism and the End of Politics*

"Those troubled by corporate sponsorship, commercial promotion, and the inculcation of consumer preferences in Canada's public schools will welcome the evidence in Catherine Gidney's *Captive Audience*. Her examination of corporate influence on public education raises questions—What purposes does schooling serve? How can equity be maintained?—that each generation must answer."

— Charles Ungerleider, author of *Failing Our Kids: How We Are Ruining Our Public Schools*

"*Captive Audience* is a comprehensive history of the normalization of commercialism in Canadian schools—engagingly written, and disturbing."

— Larry Kuehn, director of research, BC Teachers' Federation

"*Captive Audience* puts the emphasis right where it should be, leaving little doubt about who has taken over our schools and exposing their agenda. Gidney pulls back the corporate shroud to uncover the gnarly and debilitating ties between business and schooling. Our educational system is not autonomous, rather its every facet is increasingly beholden to and shaped by corporate capital. Painful and necessary reading that should be required for all educators and parents."

— Randle W. Nelsen, author of *Degrees of Failure: University Education in Decline*

Captive Audience

Captive Audience

How Corporations Invaded Our Schools

Catherine Gidney

BETWEEN THE LINES
TORONTO

Captive Audience

© 2019 Catherine Gidney

First published in 2019 by
Between the Lines
401 Richmond Street West
Studio 281
Toronto, Ontario M5V 3A8 Canada
1-800-718-7201
www.btlbooks.com

All rights reserved. No part of this publication may be photocopied, reproduced, stored in a retrieval system, or transmitted in any form or by any means, electronic, mechanical, recording, or otherwise, without the written permission of Between the Lines, or (for photocopying in Canada only) Access Copyright, 69 Yonge Street, Suite 1100, Toronto, ON M5E 1K3.

Every reasonable effort has been made to identify copyright holders. Between the Lines would be pleased to have any errors or omissions brought to its attention.

Library and Archives Canada Cataloguing in Publication

Gidney, Catherine (Catherine Anne), 1969–, author
Captive audience : how corporations invaded our schools / Catherine Gidney.

Includes bibliographical references and index.
Issued in print and electronic formats.
ISBN 978-1-77113-426-2 (softcover).—ISBN 978-1-77113-427-9 (EPUB).
ISBN 978-1-77113-428-6 (PDF)

1. Business and education—Canada.   2. Advertising in educational media—Canada.   3. Advertising and children—Canada.
4. Education, Elementary—Canada—Finance.
5. Education, Elementary—Economic aspects—Canada.
6. Corporate sponsorship—Canada.   I. Title.

LC1085.4.C3G53   2019   372.971   C2018-906067-0
                            C2018-906068-9

Cover illustration by Danesh Mohiuddin
Text design by Gordon Robertson
Printed in Canada

We acknowledge for their financial support of our publishing activities: the Government of Canada; the Canada Council for the Arts, which last year invested $153 million to bring the arts to Canadians throughout the country; and the Government of Ontario through the Ontario Arts Council, the Ontario Book Publishers Tax Credit program, and Ontario Creates.

For Alexandra and Emma

Contents

	Introduction	1
1	The "Discriminating and Alert Teacher"? *The Early History of In-School Commercialism*	7
2	"Education Is Too Important to Be Left to the Educators" *The Rise of School-Business Partnerships*	27
3	Tapping the Educational Market *Computers in Classrooms*	47
4	"It's So Pervasive, It's Like Kleenex" *Schools—The Last Frontier of Advertising*	65
5	Youth News Network or "You're Nuts to Say No" *The Struggle over Classroom Commercialism*	87
6	Building Brand Loyalty *Vending Machines, Fast Food Outlets, and Junk Food*	105
7	"All We're Trying to Do Is Help Youngsters" *The Politics of Raising Funds*	127
	Conclusion	151
	Acknowledgements	159
	Notes	161
	Index	205

Introduction

> A school is not simply a building, or an organizational
> convenience. It is not simply a place where teachers come to teach.
> It teaches in its own right, and very powerfully. We cannot afford
> to ignore its political content, for the reality is that the whole
> school is a vehicle of political education.
>
> — KEN OSBORNE[1]

Over the course of two years in the late 1990s, Vancouver's Sir Wilfrid Laurier Annex Elementary School assigned its Grade 3 and 4 students the task of conceptualizing and designing two new product ideas for White Spot, a well-established British Columbia restaurant chain. As part of a "creative thinking" component of the class, they came up with "Zippy pizza burgers," which became a feature on the kids' menu, and a birthday party concept, both of which they pitched to the company through a corporate presentation. In 2004 Home Depot donated playground equipment to Lynn Valley Elementary School in North Vancouver. The parent-volunteers who helped install the equipment received Home Depot shirts and hats, and the students, who were allowed to view the construction project during class time, received "temporary Home Depot tattoos." The ribbon-cutting ceremony included children singing "the 'Home Depot song'"—a ditty quickly written by one of the teachers. A year later, kindergarten students in the Vancouver school district returned home with a health board–approved flyer on dental hygiene that included a number of maze puzzles, each of which ended at a tube of Crest toothpaste. Schools received five cents for each flyer handed to a student.[2]

While these examples are taken from schools in and around Vancouver, they are familiar experiences for students, parents, teachers, school administrators, and board trustees across Canada. Corporate partnerships with schools have proliferated since the 1990s, encouraged by government agencies and often supported by parents or board members. As a result, corporations and their advertising agents have found it easier to gain entry into the schoolroom.

"What's the problem?" you might ask. After all, business is a part of our social and political landscape. Companies not only create jobs and employ parents as well as, eventually, their children, but are also staffed by parents who want to support their children's schools. They can help provide innovative programs that engage students and equipment not otherwise available, including playground structures and computers. They support public health initiatives, breakfast programs, and literacy campaigns. All this is true. These endeavours can be beneficial to schools and children. And yet, such practices are often accompanied by a level of commercialism that should give pause to concerned citizens.

While school commercialism has existed for over a century, it intensified in the 1990s after a decade of fiscal restraint and increased application of business models to the education system. This intensification was due, as well, to the growing expectations placed on educators to provide the most up-to-date equipment, facilities, pedagogy, and support, and to provide it for everyone. Such expectations are not necessarily undesirable, but they have meant a massive increase in the scope and cost of provincial education systems. The technological revolution of the 1980s placed an additional burden on those systems when they were already experiencing the effects of significant fiscal restraint. At the same time, the 1980s and 1990s saw the children of baby boomers, often referred to as Generation Y, reach school age, increasing the stress on existing educational structures and offering up a new consumer market.

School commercialism, then, is not simply the by-product of business owners and employees wanting to help their children or of the philanthropic bounty of corporations. The form it takes today is also a direct result of the demand for new, varied, and sometimes expensive educational programming, slowing investments in education, contracting support for public sector services in favour of private enterprise, and the increasing application of business models to schools. Added to these influences is the determination of advertisers, marketing firms, and corporations to secure new marketing opportunities.

Introduction 3

In the 1990s and early 2000s, the level of commercialization and corporatization in schools reached unprecedented heights.[3] Much broader mandates stretched resources more thinly and left school trustees, school administrators, teachers, and parents with difficult decisions about how to finance the programs and support the students they cared so deeply about. These individuals faced tough questions about how to fund athletic and music programs, provide books for libraries, and make available a host of new technologies. Turning to corporations often provided funding not available elsewhere—a decision repeatedly justified on the grounds that it involved no more advertising than what children were exposed to at home or in the community. Those opposed, however, decried the unyielding onslaught of commercialism into all aspects of children's lives.

At issue was not just how to pay for individual programs and activities, but concerns about the changing nature of society, particularly the substantial acceleration of consumerism. In the twentieth century, the North American economy was transformed from one based on production to one of consumption. Prosperity became increasingly linked to mass consumerism and citizenship to buying goods. Over time, the acquisition of goods beyond the needs of subsistence came to shape individual values, aims, and goals. Individuals began to tie their identity and success to their material possessions. They invested in consumer goods the power to satisfy both physical and spiritual needs and desires. Advertising and marketing agencies became powerful brokers, fuelling those desires and reshaping societal conceptions of basic material needs.[4]

Sociologists and other academics studying the impact of consumer culture on children have argued that it is detrimental both to the individual child and to the broader culture. Children are particularly susceptible to commercial messages. Those under five years of age generally cannot differentiate between advertising and regular programming; even those in early grade school have difficulty comprehending that commercials present selective material in order to sell a product. Only around the age of eight or nine do they begin to understand that ads are meant to sell products and are not always truthful. Still, for a host of reasons related to youth culture, marketing methods, and a desire for inclusion, they, along with much older children, continue to be highly susceptible to marketing campaigns.[5]

Children often relate to commercials in the same way they do to television programs. They bond over them, integrate them into their conversations and social life, identify with the characters rather than seeing these as constructed for marketing purposes, and retain, over long periods, minute details from the advertisements. Significant numbers also purchase the goods that they see advertised or convince their parents to make these purchases for them.[6] While television viewing has declined over the past two decades, sedentary screen time has risen dramatically, accompanied by new sites and forms of advertising.[7]

Cultural critics Shirley Steinberg and Joe Kincheloe emphasize the link between consumption and identity formation and argue that "to some degree we are what we consume." Personal identity, they note, is forged in a variety of ways—through family and community values and peer culture, but also one's "internalization of values promoted by" consumer and popular culture. In fact, "popular culture provides children with intense emotional experiences often unmatched in any other phase of their lives." "It is not surprising," they conclude, "that such energy and intensity exert powerful influences on self-definition, on the ways children choose to organize their lives."[8]

This is worrisome given that researchers have found that advertising and television commercials encourage gender role, social, and racial stereotyping, foster narrow visions of physical appearance, sexuality, social behaviour, and identity, and place a significant emphasis on materialism.[9] After a survey of children in the Boston area in the early years of the twenty-first century, Juliet Schor concluded that "high consumer involvement is a significant cause of depression, anxiety, low self-esteem, and psychosomatic complaints."[10] Critics forcefully argue that consumer culture is not value-neutral and that many of the messages conveyed are harmful to children. The ideals presented in television programming and other media focus attention on possessions, material goods, brands, and obtaining the money necessary to consume goods. Such views encourage adults and children alike to believe that one's self-expression, identity, and self-fulfilment can be achieved through consumption, while promoting discontent when material expectations are not fulfilled.[11]

Advertising aimed at children also often associates happiness and pleasure with consumption in general and with Big Food and fast food in particular, fuelling poor eating habits and contributing to low standards of health. Children's advocates have, for some time, been raising the alarm about the increasing numbers of children who are overweight or obese. We know that children have become less active as a result of increased access to television, video games, and other media, and that these forms of communication feed off advertising that encourages the consumption of unhealthy foods. In combination, this is a deadly formula.[12] As Schor argues of American children, "the bottom line on the culture they're being raised in is that it's a lot more pernicious than most adults have been willing to admit."[13]

The integration of an activity such as menu development for a restaurant chain into school curricula, which seems on the surface to be simply a creative way to increase student interest in their learning, naturalizes children's participation in fast-food culture. It reinforces a creative engagement with that culture rather than inserting a critical stance regarding fast food consumption. (After all, these kids were not doing product development for a new, appealing, vegetable dish.) Equally, be it through this type of assignment, the singing of a song to celebrate a corporate donation, or a flyer sent home promoting a specific brand of toothpaste, commercialism in schools abounds, so much a part of the school landscape that its underlying message often goes unquestioned. Students are its captive, and captivated, audience.

Debates over school commercialism have significant implications for the children who spend much of their day in the classroom. Questions about how to allocate resources and what we, as a society, believe our schools should provide are not simply about educational funding priorities but at root concern the nature of our society. They raise profound issues. What is the purpose of schooling? Who should pay for it? How should it be regulated? And what types of citizens should schools help create? The following pages explore the history of school commercialism—in particular, the spread of branded messages and advertising within school walls. Understanding the history of that phenomenon can help us think about what we want for our children's future.

1

The "Discriminating and Alert Teacher"?

The Early History of In-School Commercialism

IN THE 1940S AND 1950S, whole generations of students learned geography while salivating over chocolate bars. Throughout this period the Neilson's Chocolate company provided Canadian schools with two maps, one of Canada and one of the world, each boasting images of chocolate bars in each corner and banners at the top and bottom that read, in large letters, "Neilson's Jersey Milk, 'The best Milk Chocolate made,'" and "Jersey Milk . . . 'Made from Fresh Milk Daily.'" While Neilson's funded these maps, Copp Clark, a publishing company, distributed them to schools free of charge on condition that they be "used as received." As if anticipating resistance, the publisher noted that the chocolate bars appeared in "corners where they do not interfere in any way with the usefulness of the Map," which would only be made available "if you will agree not to obliterate the advertising." By the early 1950s, Neilson's had successfully disseminated some fifty-five thousand copies of each map, reaching roughly 60 percent of Canadian classrooms.[1]

Although particularly innovative and successful, Neilson's was not alone in attempting to insert advertising into Canadian classrooms or to entice teachers, and through them, children and their parents, to purchase branded products. Though still uneven in its reach and influence, by the 1950s consumer culture shaped the lives of most North Americans. Despite the austerity and material deprivation experienced by many during the

Neilson's Map of Canada. Adam Cross, Personal Collection.

depression years of the 1930s and war years of the early 1940s, Canadian society became increasingly embedded in a culture of consumerism. In the mid-1930s, political rhetoric framed the depression "as a crisis, not of scarcity, but of surplus, where the principal challenges were related to the distribution and consumption rather than the production of goods."[2] Already by that decade politicians could be heard linking consumption, rather than the more traditional value of production, with "the moral and social progress of society."[3] Despite the rhetoric of scarcity, consumer spending surged during the war.[4] In the United States, strategies for postwar reconstruction included securing democracy and prosperity through the encouragement of mass consumption. This trend toward mass consumption could equally be seen reaching into Canadian society in the 1950s and 1960s.[5]

Through the first half of the twentieth century, children and adolescents became increasingly integrated into this culture of consumption. In the nineteenth and into the twentieth century, manufacturers and advertisers most often targeted the sale of children's goods at mothers or parents more generally. Far-sighted companies, however, had also begun to turn their eyes to children, especially those of the middle class, as consumers. This corresponded to a re-evaluation of the value of children and their place in the family. As urban professional and business families began limiting family size, they also paid greater attention to each child. Family ties became based less on children's economic contributions and more on sentimental and emotional bonds. At the same time, childrearing practices gradually shifted from an emphasis on strict parental discipline and filial obedience toward guidance, affection, and a greater degree of respect for children's opinions. By the 1920s and 1930s, advertising reflected these new family patterns, acknowledging the usefulness of gaining parents' attention through advertising directed at children. Advertisers also recognized that parents would often defer to their children's demands.[6]

Children themselves became consumers in various ways. At the turn of the twentieth century, manufacturers began to produce a greater variety of dolls, introduced teddy bears and other stuffed animals, and developed a range of sports equipment and books directed at children. Youth increasingly secured spending money of their own. Childrearing experts began to advocate allowances to teach children both financial restraint and wise consumption. By the 1920s and 1930s, adolescents and young adults had enough pocket money to buy candy, attend the movies, or purchase the latest fashions.[7]

These decades also marked the rising influence of peer culture among youth, particularly within school. The gradual removal of children from the process of direct production and a re-orientation in ideas about childhood that stressed guidance and nurture reinforced the importance of informal and formal education.[8] Beginning in the mid-nineteenth century and continuing through the twentieth century, larger numbers of children attended school and for longer periods of time.[9] Schools became central sites of socialization, with youth spending increasing amounts of time under the direction of teachers and with their peer group.[10]

This process of age segregation occurred simultaneously within various industries that began to subdivide the youth consumer market. The clothing industry was one of the first to do so, creating a children's division and then carving out a distinct teenaged market. Girls, who usually accompanied their mothers prior to the 1920s, became increasingly independent, shopping alone or with their peers. By the 1940s teenage girls' fashions had become a major national market. In Canada, as elsewhere, department stores expanded rapidly in the first few decades of the twentieth century. By the eve of the Second World War, store executives recognized teenagers as independent consumers and began to cultivate this group as a potential new market niche.[11]

The segmentation of the youth market that occurred early within the clothing market would soon spread to other industries. The sentimentalization of childhood and the conceptualization of childhood and adolescence as stages on the road to adulthood would further differentiate consumers. Companies and advertising agencies saw the potential of youth markets and increasingly pitched their products both through, and to, children and teens. As authorities imposed compulsory schooling and extended it for longer periods, companies focused on schools as a unique site where they could gain children's attention.

Early Forms of Commercialism

One of the earliest and most long-lasting methods by which companies obtained access to schools took the form of corporate-designed and sponsored teaching aids. Giveaway schemes gained popularity in the 1880s, with, for example, companies inserting full-colour trading cards featuring birds or animals in packaged goods, or advertising in magazines and newspapers the offer of free booklets and samples obtained by mail. As R. D. Gidney and I have demonstrated extensively in a previous article, this practice became common over the first half of the twentieth century. From at least the early 1920s, companies placed advertisements in teachers' professional magazines and journals for various types of materials that could be used as teaching aids. In doing so, they aimed to enrich classroom resources, and in the process, promote their products among teachers, pupils, and parents alike. Teachers drew frequently on these handouts. Localized studies in the United States from the 1930s to the 1950s found that upward of 85 percent of teachers made use of this type of resource. Similar statistics do not exist for the Canadian context, yet there is clear evidence of such material appearing on classroom walls and in the educational press.[12]

Producing the teaching aids cost money, so not surprisingly they were available, nearly exclusively, from national or international firms with substantial resources, mostly those with major advertising departments or even distinct educational resource divisions. Two kinds of organizations were involved: most commonly, individual firms selling particular products, but also trade associations promoting the virtues of an industry. In the 1920s Colgate and Lifebuoy advertised the most frequently. In the next decade, recurring ads appeared from Shredded Wheat, Bristol-Myers,

The "Discriminating and Alert Teacher"?

and Canadian Industries Limited (CIL), which manufactured a variety of products, including paint, plastics, and fertilizers. Canadian Cellucotton (Kotex and Kleenex), Nonspi (a deodorant), and the American Can Company joined this group in the 1940s. Through the postwar years, many of the same companies continued to advertise, as did new entrants including the oil, banking, and insurance industries. All of the materials had one thing in common: they were clearly branded, either with a company logo or with the product's brand name, and usually both.

Many of the materials were booklets, wall charts, and posters useful for social science, science, and health classes, describing a product from its natural state through its transformation during the manufacturing process. For example, Salada provided a booklet titled "The Story of the Tea Plant," Shredded Wheat produced a wall chart titled "The Story of Wheat," and Canadian Sugar Factories offered a poster on the sugar beet. A number of companies combined all of these methods into one comprehensive package. For instance, Bristol-Myers, the maker of Ipana toothpaste, ran an ad for its "5-Way Plan" that included a teacher's manual, a wall chart, a score-card, a tooth-brushing model, and individual and class certificates.

Ipana Tooth Paste campaign, *A.T.A. Magazine* 30, no. 2 (October 1949), 36–37. Republished with permission of Bristol-Myers Squibb.

Offered as a "popular" and, with its "carefully-plotted programme," easy method of teaching "modern dental care," the classroom teachings in "the correct method of brushing teeth and massaging gums" also reinforced "regular home care" through daily scoring and encouraged class involvement, with the awarding of a "Giant Certificate" once the "entire class qualifies."[13]

From the late 1940s, classroom advertising also embraced film. For example, up to that point Canadian Cellucotton provided an instruction manual titled "This is Why," a "jumbo size Menstrual Physiology chart," and a booklet for students titled "As One Girl to Another." Starting in the 1940s, however, it also offered to loan, through its education department, the Walt Disney productions "The Story of Menstruation" and "How To Catch a Cold." Shell advertised a series of colour films on oil and related subjects, and CIL offered films on various chemical processes. Imperial Oil provided a package of five booklets, three filmstrips, and ten films.

At times, companies provided materials about issues of public concern. In the US, Metropolitan Life Insurance had a long history of involvement in educational matters, promoting a variety of social programs, from business English classes for its employees in 1909 to public health campaigns, to English-language primers for immigrants in the 1920s. Recognizing the correlation between health education and longevity, the company combined altruism and self-interest to provide health literature. In 1924 it set its sights on schoolchildren through the creation of its Advisory Educational Group, composed of educators from the US and Canada who "served a consulting role, helping the company to extend its educational activity" to produce a variety of pamphlets and films strips on health matters aimed at children.[14] Similarly, in the late 1930s *The School* reported that "the life insurance companies of Ontario recently supplied 5,000 sets of health posters, entitled *What to Eat to be Healthy*," distributed by Department of Education inspectors.[15]

While some corporations attempted to introduce their teaching aids into the classroom by appealing to teachers, others focused more directly on students. In the 1940s and continuing into the 1950s major department stores such as Eaton's and Simpsons gained entry into some urban schools through organizations aimed at high school students. Eaton's, for example, developed a Junior Council for girls and Junior Executive for boys while Simpson's created a Collegiate Club.

Eaton's began soliciting teenaged girls' opinions through focus groups in 1939, developing clubs the following year. Company executives chose the all-round student, someone with solid marks but who was also a leader in extra-curricular activities, a trendsetter respected by his or her peers.[16] In doing so, they replicated an employment pattern in which they selected employees not only for their skills but also "to increase the worth of the store's product and image."[17] Meeting on Saturdays, students shared their opinions on merchandise, helped plan window displays, and even aided in the development of contest-based advertising campaigns. Katharine Rollwagen's work on Eaton's points to the ways in which the company used the councils to keep on top of changing teenage fashions, to draw high school students into its stores, to foster customer loyalty, and to gain "a direct line to Canada's urban high school students."[18] Eaton's executives recognized teenagers as independent consumers in their own right.

Although these clubs existed outside school hours, Eaton's executives made use of the emerging teenage culture of the high school. To gain access to that market, they solicited staff assistance in selecting potential club members and required their authorization for student participation. To curry favour, they also offered a number of services to schools. For instance, in Toronto, Eaton's staff printed class timetables and distributed these to students at the start of the school year. Eaton's also "created a Band Box—a portable sound system equipped with current popular recordings" that Junior Executive members could reserve and use free of charge for school dances. In addition, the company "printed tickets, posters, and programmes free of charge for school events." Each of these initiatives prominently featured the name of the department store.[19]

Eaton's was not the only company to gain entry into schools through students' extracurricular activities or by means of handouts to students and teachers. In the 1940s and 1950s, various banks and credit unions provided textbook dust covers with their logo boldly displayed—a useful service to keep expensive books clean but also one that placed a corporate name in front of a young audience day in and day out.[20] Corporate and business support also enabled the publication of student yearbooks and, indirectly, the existence of clubs devoted to that activity. An examination of yearbooks from Northern Vocational School and Oakwood Collegiate Institute in Toronto reveals that from early on such publications depended on advertising. These yearbooks contained four to eight pages of ads, mainly from local businesses such as sporting goods stores, shoe stores, jewellers, and optometrists. Eaton's and Simpsons also regularly featured in these publications from the 1930s through the 1950s. In addition, in the postwar period larger corporations such as the Imperial Bank of Canada,

"Eaton's Junior Reps.," *The Norvoc*, yearbook of Northern Vocational School, Toronto, 1948, Toronto District School Board Museum and Archives. Republished with permission of Cadillac Fairview Corporation.

Bell Canada, Confederation Life of Canada, Royal Bank, Pepsi-Cola, and Coca-Cola began to sponsor these initiatives.[21]

Corporations also curried favour with students, parents, and teachers by supporting a variety of school excursions and extramural learning initiatives. In 1935, for instance, the Canadian Pacific Railway arranged for over four hundred Ontario teachers and children from London and St. Thomas to enjoy an all-day trip to Toronto to visit the parliament buildings, the Royal Ontario Museum, and the Ontario Art Gallery. Similarly, in 1956 the Consolidated Mining and Smelting Company (Cominco) offered two open days for teachers in and around Trail, Rossland, and Castlegar school districts in British Columbia at which they introduced teachers to their operations and in the evening provided dinner for attendees and their spouses. Some companies also supported courses or programs to further teachers' training. In 1948–49 Imperial Oil donated $5,000 to a national "Teacher Exchange" program facilitating exchanges to the US and Britain. In the 1950s, teachers' magazines advertised all-expenses-paid Shell Merit Fellowships for high school chemistry, physics, and math teachers—fellowships to be held at Stanford University's School of Education to further teachers' education in their field.[22]

While many corporations had to use a circuitous route to reach teachers or students, some occasionally gained access more directly. The creation of school banks is a case in point. By the late nineteenth century, Europe, Great Britain, and the United States all boasted school savings-bank movements. Canada established the Dominion Penny Bank Act in 1906, creating a central depository in Ottawa to accept schoolchildren's pennies. This program gained swift attention. In 1906, 44 schools in two urban centres participated, depositing over $50,000. By 1913, 222 schools in 31 centres in Ontario had deposited just over $200,000.[23] Support for this initiative remained strong after the Second World War, though now credit unions and banks took the lead. In 1947, for example, a teacher in Caraquet, New Brunswick, wrote effusively about the creation of a caisse scolaire, with all materials furnished by a branch of the local Caisse populaire.[24] Though slower off the mark, in the late 1960s the Canadian Imperial Bank of Commerce (CIBC) began to implement some student-staffed branches in secondary schools.[25]

Essay and poster contests provided another means of placing particular issues or organizations in front of children and the broader community. In the early 1930s the *Globe*, concerned about students' writing abilities, established an essay competition with a cash prize for students on the topic of "What I Learned from C.N.E. Exhibits," encouraging teachers to take up the challenge as a classroom competition, which they reportedly did in large numbers.[26] In the early 1960s, the Fraser Valley Tourist Association in British Columbia promoted essay and poster contests on local heritage for high school students that, with the co-operation of principals, were held in local schools. The best essays received a cash prize from the Bank of Montreal and were "publicized through purchased advertising space in newspapers and on the radio." In choosing the best posters, the association looked for designs that could be easily adapted to a billboard, stationery, or chest buttons.[27]

In the 1960s and 1970s, some of the sites and forms of advertising began to change. Advertising in teachers' magazines for free teaching aids either disappeared or declined significantly, likely because of the changing economic climate after the middle of the century. As teachers' salaries rose, association fees could be raised, ensuring the sustainability of professional magazines without the need for advertising. The consolidation of school boards in this period, the increase in provincial government grants, and the introduction of equalization formulas to ensure better financing for schools across various districts all enabled boards to provide adequate libraries and classroom materials without recourse to as much commercial advertising.[28] The creation of department of education curriculum services providing aid with a variety of lesson planning may also have played a role in reducing the need for supplementary commercial materials. These decades also witnessed a broad critique of commercial culture, reinforcing these trends.

Still, in the late 1970s and early 1980s, new forms of advertising and innovative corporate materials appeared with the introduction of high school marketing and consumer education courses. Robert J. Clegg Ltd., a Toronto marketing company, created a Student Family Pack, with samples of eight to ten products, which was valued at between eight and twelve dollars and offered to students at an 80 percent discount. The company aimed its product at marketing teachers, with the intent of creating a project they could use to teach students the principles of advertising, sales, and market research, with proceeds from the sale of the packs financing the classroom endeavour. In 1976 the company distributed sixty thousand such packs to about 160 Ontario high schools.[29] The company had thus discovered a new and innovative way to distribute product samples to teens and their parents.

Consumer education courses developed in the 1980s with the intent to educate and empower students about the marketplace. Many of these types of courses became focused on creating better consumers, as opposed to developing citizens able to negotiate or make demands of market forces. Business interests found these types of courses particularly easy to penetrate. British Columbia instituted a compulsory course as early as 1982, and in that same year, Junior Achievement offered materials and speakers, on request, through a program titled Project Business. Active at first in only a few Vancouver classrooms, in just four years it could be found in two hundred schools covering fifteen school districts.[30]

Students were also exposed to new sites of commercialism. In 1978 the *Globe and Mail* reported on regular tours by Toronto schoolchildren of McDonald's restaurants. Students received free hamburgers on the tour and a coupon for fries that could be redeemed on a return visit. McDonald's also appealed to teachers by sponsoring films on topics such as ecology, bicycle safety, and home safety. One showing of the ecology film at Withrow Public School in Toronto was accompanied by free litter bags that contained a voucher for fries.[31]

While new forms and sites of commercialism appeared in the 1970s, they formed part of a decades-old pattern. Whether through teachers or directly to students, advertisers, marketing firms, and corporate educational departments found a variety of ways to place branded products or corporate names in front of students. Still, to gain access to schools, these types of materials had to be used by teachers and endorsed by school administrators. Maps had to be hung on walls, teaching aids ordered, school excursions organized. Why did at least some teachers turn to these corporate offers?

The Draw of Corporate Material and Sponsorship

Corporate material and sponsorship appealed to educators for both economic and pedagogical reasons. Teachers worked in cash-strapped schools. Squeezed in the 1920s by the pressures of enrolment growth, hit hard financially by the depression of the 1930s and then the Second World War, even many of Canada's larger urban school boards had limited resources for classroom libraries, maps, or globes, while provincially approved textbooks were often badly outdated or inadequate without supplementary resources. Moreover, the gap between the resources available in urban and rural areas was enormous. Depending on the decade and the province in question, anywhere from 30 to 50 percent of Canadian children attended one- and two-room rural schools. Most of the budget to run these schools was eaten up by teachers' salaries, and whatever was left over went mainly to fuel, maintenance, and janitorial services (if any). There was not much left for classroom resources.

In 1937, the Alberta school inspector responsible for the Camrose district drafted a composite portrait of the average one-room school in his area, based on the written responses of his teachers to a questionnaire that included a canvass of classroom resources. These schools had on average twenty-two students across eight grades. While the classroom would have a blackboard, desks, a small cupboard, a work table, a pencil sharpener, a handbell, a yardstick, a flag, and an old globe, it contained no clock, measuring sets, or illustrative charts. There might well be no framed pictures. It might possess only a couple of maps and only twenty to thirty books suitable for a particular grade. Across the country, there were individual rural schools better off than these, and many much worse off; but there was nothing especially atypical about those in the Camrose inspectorate.[32]

Many teachers found that beyond textbooks, corporate materials proved to be one of the few ways of obtaining information. The author of a 1935 article on school display cases noted that schools had limited resources for creating displays for classes such as geography or chemistry and suggested that "collections of minerals, industrial products, models and charts, or pictures, can be accumulated so as to give these subjects more meaning." Samples, the article continued, could be obtained from companies such as Canadian Industries Limited, the Canadian Salt Company, or the Gypsum Lime and Alabastine Company.[33] Similarly, in 1946, B. C. C. Evoy of the Health Education Division of the Department of Public Health for Alberta encouraged teachers to draw on the department's "Health Kits" containing up-to-date information prepared for schools. He had been a classroom teacher earlier in his career and had found it difficult to locate information for his health lessons. He explained:

> I gathered together a certain amount of source material. These consisted of a copy or two of some out-dated textbooks, an almanac which might well be considered rather partial to a certain well-advertised line of pills, and some medical books, which required constant translation before the material provided could be passed on to my pupils. Add to this a selection of pamphlets thoughtfully prepared by an insurance company and you have the limit of my resources.[34]

More than simply providing basic information, corporate materials and sponsored events appeared to offer pedagogical advantages. From at least the early 1920s, Normal School instructors, senior Department of Education officials in nearly every province, the provincial inspectorate and urban supervisors, and editorials and articles in the educational press all emphasized the need to move beyond lessons based solely on textbooks, rote memorization, and exercises based on problems abstracted from real life. Instead they urged teachers to use "enterprise methods"—hands-on activities and problem-solving methods—and to secure a rich fund of classroom materials. These, they argued, constituted best practice. For example, in 1936–37 the Department of Education in Alberta introduced its "enterprise" curriculum in which "teachers are recommended to obtain copies of pamphlets or booklets describing industrial processes and products, and also to obtain where possible any displays of such products." The program aimed to bring children "into contact with what is going on in Canada today."[35]

The branded teaching aids did not exist in a vacuum, and the boundaries between them and other sorts of supplementary material were blurred. Aside from materials available directly from departments of education, free posters, wall charts, maps, pamphlets, sample products, and films were also available from other branches of government, both provincial and federal, and from a variety of nonprofit agencies like the Red Cross.[36] In 1937, for instance, the Dairy and Cold Storage Branch of the Dominion Department of Agriculture offered free pamphlets on topics such as "School Lunches" and how to use milk. During the Second World War, the National War Finance Committee offered a War Savings Kit titled "Canadian Schools at War" to stimulate interest in buying War Savings Stamps. At the same time, CBC provided school broadcasts just before lunch hour on topics such as "Heroes of Canada"—a series on historical figures from regions across the country.[37]

Teachers' magazines rarely differentiated between these types of materials. In 1952 the New Brunswick teachers' magazine, the *Educational Review* published a list commonly found in similar publications elsewhere, titled, "Valuable Information and Where to Obtain It..." that included not only corporate-sponsored pamphlets but also ones published by not-for-profit think-tanks and various government bureaus.[38] There was only a thin line, or sometimes none at all, between an Ontario or Alberta government agency trumpeting provincial mining or forestry resources through a wall chart and one from INCO or Imperial Oil; between the Woman's Christian

Temperance Union's posters and leaflets on "Alcohol Education" and similar material from Bristol-Myers or Lifebuoy on healthy minds and bodies.[39] It was not difficult, in other words, for teachers to see the commercial materials as but one useful resource among many for the classroom.

Knowing the need for resources, corporations and their advertising agents carefully crafted their materials to fit within the curricula. They successfully carved out two distinct niches: specialist subject instruction in the high school such as home economics, commercial, and science classes; and those subjects in Grades 4 to 10 where textbooks were notoriously inadequate and supplementary classroom resources thinnest—health instruction, social studies, and general science.

Many educators and administrators, in turn, explicitly endorsed commercial material due to the lack of alternatives, the perceived usefulness of corporate-sponsored resources, and the turn toward "hands-on" methods. In 1950, for example, the Ontario Department of Education recommended the Disney and Kimberly-Clark film "The Story of Menstruation" as part of the Grade 9 curriculum for physical education.[40] Two years earlier, Alberta's Chief Superintendent of Schools had asked members of the High School Curriculum Committee to evaluate the educational material offered by Canadian Industries Limited (CIL). The committee recommended "that the Department take fullest advantage of the offer. The general feeling was that all the advertising material that the CIL puts out is invariably educational and would be of the greatest value in the classroom, especially for chemistry." The committee also suggested that CIL should "prepare a catalogue of available materials and send it out to schools."[41] In 1949 the Saskatchewan Department of Education reported that it had deposited in its library three films from Imperial Oil: "Search Unending," "Oil in Canada" and "Loon's Necklace." They were available for loan and considered "excellent for classroom use."[42]

Individual teachers also encouraged adoption of this material, with some penning articles in the educational press. In 1936 Mary Douglas, a teacher in a Kitchener, Ontario, high school, described the benefits of the project method for geography classes. Every year her students undertook a topic of their own choosing. They had to write to a company for samples, pictures, and booklets or, if a local company, students would do a site visit, becoming acquainted with that part of the business world.[43] Similarly, after offering his own list of companies, one teacher advised that "if you are searching for special material for . . . a special project write to the most widely advertised companies who will generally send plenty of illustrative material and sometimes samples if you clearly state your purpose."[44] In a 1942 article in *The School*, a teacher at Empress Public School in London, Ontario, detailed his use of films from the Kellogg Company of Canada and the Fry-Cadbury Company "to show how farm products are used in the manufacture of other products" as part of Grade 8 class lessons on Ontario history and resource development.[45]

In the late 1970s, teachers continued to allude to these pedagogical methods when defending school trips to McDonald's. Mary Gomes, as part of her religious and social studies program, took her combined Grade 3/4 class from St. Monica Catholic School in Toronto on a side trip to McDonald's after an excursion to Mount Pleasant Cemetery, stating "I could quote you a paragraph right out of my religion core curriculum that says to go out to the community and see what is going on. As far as I'm concerned, McDonald's is part of the community." Betsy Borden of Rosedale Public School took her class of Grade 4 and 5 students to the fast food outlet, using "the occasion to get the children thinking about what they saw" and holding a debate "on the pros and cons of fast food restaurants." Her principal added, "the children initially gained a lesson in economy and math by learning about profits and losses in their visits to McDonald's."[46]

Businesses, of course, did what they could to encourage such support. Many of the advertising campaigns appealed to teachers' desire to improve the lives of their students and by extension their students' families. In the US in the 1920s, for example, Cream of Wheat developed a package for teachers that included "an instruction manual, graded contest devices, prizes, and breakfast charts free of charge." The month-long program ended with teachers sending home to mothers a card "affirming that their children had eaten a hot breakfast cereal three times a week." The campaign drew on national concerns at the time about children's malnourishment and the need for a healthy citizenry.[47] Similarly, Colgate developed an ad focused on the benefits of dental hygiene to help the "laggard" holding back the rest of the class. "Better teeth," the ad told teachers, would result in "brighter minds."[48] It took little imagination to conclude that bad health habits arose in the home and by helping their students, teachers could aid their families and improve the public health of the nation.

Similar rationales underpinned other commercial educational initiatives. Field trips, some companies argued, broadened children's experiences. School banks, maintained others, could help inculcate the value of thrift. Eaton's stressed the educational benefits to students of its Junior Council and Junior Executive groups. The company's executives emphasized that the motivation for sustaining this initiative was more than simply self-interest, providing important opportunities for students to gain familiarity with retail operations and facilitating exchange with, and a chance to learn from, business executives. The company framed these activities within the pedagogical desires of the period for more experiential learning and vocational training.[49]

Teachers' attempts to keep their lessons interesting and relevant, and educators' desires to see progressive educational methods implemented in the classroom, combined with the poverty of many Canadian classrooms and school districts to create an opening for a variety of organizations and corporations to gain access to the classroom. In some cases this put products directly in children's hands. In others, it ensured the prominent display of corporate names, resulting in indirect endorsements. Many educators willingly used this material. Others, however, forcefully opposed such practices.

"Hucksters in the Classroom"

In the late 1920s, some educators raised concerns about encroaching commercialism in schools. The US National Education Association (NEA), for instance, issued a *Report of the Committee on Propaganda in the Schools* in 1929 recommending that state departments of education set up guidelines concerning the use of corporate-sponsored teaching aids and to train teachers to be aware of the pitfalls of such resources. It did not advocate the complete exclusion of this kind of material but rather careful selection. However, the committee suggested that schools would be less reliant on these sources if they were provided with adequate funding.[50] The NEA's warning about corporate material constituted part of an emerging consumer movement that would gain force in the 1930s as citizens confronted the effects of corporate price fixing and the dumping of surplus food at a time of economic hardship. Social critics, including parent-teacher associations, also focused attention on the increasing amount of food advertising on the radio directed toward children, taking aim at its biased nutritional information, promotion of unhealthy products, and undue influence.[51]

Criticism of the impact of advertising on society and in particular on children re-emerged in the 1950s. Vance Packard, in his best-selling book, *The Hidden Persuaders*, revealed advertisers' and marketeers' use of the latest psychological theories to manipulate consumers. In particular, he noted that it had become commonly recognized that if companies could sell children on their brand name, "they will insist that their parents buy no other."[52] Concern over the free "tidal wave of instructional materials" aimed at schools in this period led the American Association of School Administrators to issue a pamphlet titled *Choosing Free Materials for Use in the Schools*. Like the report by the NEA, it did not condemn the use of commercial teaching aids but warned against using such materials as a complete package rather than as supplemental to other resources. It also provided advice on how to develop policies that "will set up safeguards against the school becoming the agents of those who seek to warp the minds of our children to their own selfish ends."[53]

In the United States, the issue of commercial materials in schools re-emerged in the 1970s. This formed part of both a broader North American consumer movement seeking to empower and protect consumers that gained force in the 1960s and 1970s and the development of countercultural anti-consumerist impulses that would have far-reaching influence.[54] In California, for example, a number of individuals formed an organization named "Vigilance in Public Education" after they discovered that an elementary school mathematics resource series used examples that included Twinkies, Tootsie Rolls, McDonald's, and KFC. Titled *Mathematics Around Us*, the series had no corporate sponsors but rather was the effort by authors and publishers attempting to make math relevant to students' lives. In 1977, as a result of the work by that citizens' group, California developed "guidelines to proscribe the use of state-adopted textbooks for grades K-8 which depict brand names, corporate logos or selected food products of low nutritional value."[55] In 1979 Sheila Harty, working for the Center for Study of Responsive Law in Washington, DC, brought broad public attention to the issue by raising the alarm in a report titled *Hucksters in the Classroom: A Review of Industry Propaganda in Schools*.

Although no such major reports on commercialism seem to exist in Canada, a few educators and administrators did raise their voices against this type of activity. In 1925 New Brunswick's superintendent of education included the following injunction in his annual report: "As the schools are a good advertising medium, they are sought to be exploited from every side. . . . The schools should not be an open forum, and their use, for such purposes, should be refused."[56] In 1929, John Popkin, Chairman of the Brandon School Board, condemned the variety of advertising schemes directed at schools:

This is an age of advertising, and vast sums of money are spent yearly by commercial firms for this purpose. The public schools offer a very attractive field for the advertiser, particularly when that advertising takes the form of some free gift or the opportunity to secure something for nothing . . . while advertising is a perfectly legitimate method of securing business, school authorities cannot permit the schools to be used for that purpose. . . . A whole day's work in the school may be absolutely lost by the intrusion into the routine of an exciting advertising proposal. The safe plan is to hold to fixed prohibitory rules on school-house exploitation.[57]

Although encouraging the use of commercial teaching aids, one Alberta inspector also acknowledged the perils of commercialism when he suggested that the material could be of use to the "discriminating and alert teacher."[58] Though the department would change its mind a couple of years later, in 1945 Alberta's Deputy Minister of Education responded to a circular from the Canadian Education Association about the use of "printed matter and films to be prepared by industrial corporations," stating that he was not prepared to introduce this sort of material or encourage its preparation due to the current level of "strife in industrial centres."[59] Several decades later, in 1972, when the New Books editor of the *BC Teacher* suggested that teachers could draw on a host of corporate materials to supplement their regular teaching resources, he received a fervent reply from the Peace Action League opposing the use of such material in classrooms, along with a number of letters expressing the same opinion.[60]

Equally, when credit unions began to make inroads in some school districts in the 1940s, some expressed doubts. In January 1948, one Coquitlam district trustee brought forward to her Board a proposal from the Coquitlam Credit Union to give talks to students on the importance of having a savings program. After discussion, the Board decided to follow the advice of the Superintendent of Education, concluding that "it was unwise to instigate money transactions within the classroom." A month later a member of the BC Credit Union League spoke to the Board directly, this time presenting the idea for the creation of "Savings Clubs." Again the Board declined the proposal on the grounds that "it was difficult to determine various types of activity which may be operated within school buildings so that of necessity any activity of the Credit Union League must be carried on outside of school hours."[61]

Given such responses, businesses clearly recognized that they had to tread lightly in attempting to open school doors to their products. Corporate tie-ins to the aims of the curriculum or values taught in the school provide a clear indication that educators were particular about the material they used. Hence, Eaton's executives carefully tiptoed around school and board policies. In 1947 the superintendent of the Toronto District School Board informed Jack Brockie, the organizer of the junior clubs program, that his board had a policy prohibiting teachers from circulating advertisements in class. Brockie, as a skilled organizer, cultivated relationships with principals and superintendents, using these to legitimize Eaton's endeavours, ensure favourable reviews to provide to school boards resistant to the clubs, and gain advice on how to secure and maintain access to schools. Eaton's learned to pitch its message. It also cultivated goodwill among educators. In acknowledgement of Eaton's past helpfulness to the district, Toronto's superintendent willingly stretched the rules for Eaton's, allowing Brockie to send promotional materials to principals.[62] Brockie, like representatives and advertisers for other companies, tested the boundaries of educators' acceptance or disapproval of school commercialism, constantly searching for new doors through which they could legitimately enter.

Conclusion

From the 1920s to the 1970s protests against various attempts by corporations to gain access to North American schools occurred, but in piecemeal form. This was particularly true in the 1920s and 1930s and again in the 1970s, periods that witnessed the emergence of broader-based consumer movements. Still, outright condemnation was limited. Teachers needed resources. School administrators and departments of education encouraged teachers to draw on a wide variety of materials. And teachers' professional magazines and their colleagues endorsed the use of all available supplementary sources. As a result, corporate material and corporate-sponsored events became one means of enriching the classroom and activities of the school.

Companies in turn began to perceive schoolchildren as a large—potentially very large—captive audience who could be exposed to a brand name, in some cases day in, day out, for months or even years at a time. For corporations, schools appeared to be a good way to build a future market of loyal consumers. They could draw on the authority of the school, and the teacher in particular, to entice children, and potentially their parents, to become long-term consumers of their products. In gaining children's attention, corporations also hoped to influence the immediate purchases of Canadian families. Directing attention toward schools was an innovative campaign in the attempt to increase market share. How to gain entry and maintain a long-term influence was another question.

Still, in the first three-quarters of the twentieth century, corporate advertisers and marketeers gained a solid foothold within schools. From chocolate bars on school maps, bars of soap handed out for health lessons, films produced and distributed by corporate sponsors, yearbooks financed through advertising, dust-jackets with bank logos, timetables with department store runners, to class projects selling product samples, children and young adults experienced myriad forms of commercialism in schools. That exposure, however, would come to seem significantly less substantial in comparison to the veritable tsunami of commercialism that would develop over the course of subsequent decades.

2

"Education Is Too Important to Be Left to the Educators"

The Rise of School-Business Partnerships

IN 1985 Betty Ozvoldik, a business teacher at George S. Henry Secondary School in North York, Ontario, came across a Gulf Canada ad requesting ideas from the public about how the company could provide aid to the education system. Intrigued by the opportunity, staff at the school met with company officials to devise a one-year trial program, the first of its kind in North York. The company, by that point subsumed into Petro-Canada, provided speakers, tours of its refinery and research centre, and science awards valued at $1,000. In return, the school band offered concerts for the company's employees.[1]

Other Canadian school boards also tentatively began to develop these kinds of partnerships with corporations and community groups in the mid-1980s, a phenomenon that would explode in the subsequent two decades. Three years after Ozvoldik's initiative, North York schools boasted seventeen such arrangements. Similar growth occurred elsewhere in Ontario. In the greater Ottawa area, school-business partnerships began in 1987, expanding to over fifty by 1995. The Etobicoke Board of Education was slightly slower off the mark but quickly emerged as a leader in these types of programs. Starting with three business-community agreements in 1995, only two years later it had established more than 550 such relationships. In that same year, Edmonton's public school system had 23 partnerships and its Catholic counterpart just over 40, while the Calgary board had developed some 215 such arrangements, and aimed to have all schools partnered with a business by the year 2000. Such was the momentum for these endeavours that some school boards began hiring full-time employees simply to oversee and develop business partnerships.[2]

How had schools gone from fairly limited forms of in-school commercialism and corporate presence in the 1950s and 1960s to situations in which their boards forged multiple partnerships? What sorts of relationships did these consist of? And what were some of the benefits and pitfalls? This chapter examines these questions. The growth of school-business alliances was intricately connected to the provision of computers in classrooms—the focus of the next chapter. To appreciate that phenomenon, it is important first to understand the economic and ideological context that encouraged the turn toward partnerships more generally.

The Financial Context

The period from the mid-1950s to the early 1980s witnessed a significant financial investment by provincial governments in their education systems, with a particular rise in funding from 1960 to 1974.[3] This paralleled a broader expansion of government-financed health and welfare programs, all underwritten by a period of economic growth that extended from the end of the Second World War until the early 1970s. The general prosperity of the period increased public willingness to support the expansion of the welfare state and public services. Moreover, growing public belief in the importance of education, along with a "baby boom" from roughly 1946 to 1965, focused attention on schooling. At the local level, an increasing portion of property taxes went to fund schools. Provincial governments too allocated a greater percentage of their budgets to education, taking on a larger share of the operating costs in order to offer innovative new programs and build the new schools necessary to house the baby boom generation.[4]

Beginning with the energy crisis of 1973, however, the next two decades brought high inflation, low rates of economic growth, and significant levels of unemployment, as well as recessions in the mid-1970s and from 1981 to 1983. Economic growth returned from 1983 to 1989, but the country entered another deep recession in 1990, with only very slow recovery after that. This was a period of general uncertainty and anxiety as unemployment rates rose and family income remained below its 1988 rates. In addition, there were fears about the economy over the longer term. The late 1980s and early 1990s witnessed a period of industrial and corporate restructuring designed to reduce costs and increase productivity to meet international competition in a more global economy. This process hit blue-collar, white-collar, and managerial workers hard. Companies eliminated jobs and shifted hiring priorities toward low-skilled and low-paying or part-time positions.[5]

Despite this economic context, schools faced greater expectations regarding whom they should educate and how. A push toward universal education increased the number of students graduating from high school. An ideological emphasis on flexibility and choice enabled the provision of more and different types of courses. Alternative schools, francophone schools, French immersion, kindergarten, and a variety of special education programs became common school options. In addition, in the early 1990s provincial governments mandated lower class sizes and increased support services such as psychologists and teachers' aids, while urban school boards provided more extensive ESL programs. The extension of universal education brought greater egalitarianism to the school system but also social and economic pressures to provide for the diversity of the student body.[6]

Education was not alone in expanding its provisions. Other public institutions such as hospitals and social services also began to provide more extensive and diverse programs. As a result, public expenditures soared during the 1970s and 1980s. Spending on education rose over the course of these decades, with per-pupil spending doubling (in constant dollars) between 1971 and 2000 (though a significant amount of this was due to a steep drop in school enrolments in the 1970s and early 1980s).[7] Education was, however, becoming less of a priority, with Canadian provincial spending accounting for, on average, 30 percent of budgets in 1971 and only 20 percent in the 1990s—a trend that continued, with spending accounting for 16 percent of provincial budgets in 2010.[8] In the 1990s, Canadian expenditure per pupil virtually flatlined before beginning to rise again in the first years of the twenty-first century.[9] In the 1970s and 1980s, in short, spending on public services increased dramatically while at the same time the economy experienced severe inflation followed by recession. By the 1990s, both health and debt reduction became overriding government concerns.

The economic impact on education spending proved significant. In the 1970s and 1980s, government spending on education kept pace with inflation.[10] Still, in an effort to contain debt, provincial governments reduced their grants to school boards, placing more of the burden on local taxpayers. For example, from the mid-1970s to the mid-1980s, provincial grants in Alberta declined from 81 to 64 percent and in Ontario from 62 to 48 percent. These governments also searched for efficiencies, from larger class sizes to salary rollbacks.[11]

By the 1990s, however, most provinces were caught in an expenditure/revenue trap. Spending on schools slowed significantly, with some provinces moderately affected and others quite severely.[12] From 1993 to 1998 Manitoba's Progressive Conservative government either froze or reduced provincial funding every year.[13] In Alberta, Ralph Klein's Progressive Conservatives reduced average per-student spending by 14.6 percent between 1993 and 1997, slashing programs generally and halving funds for kindergarten.[14] Once Mike Harris's Tories gained power in Ontario in 1995, they focused on containing the ballooning deficit. For education, this meant a reduction in the operating grant of 22.7 percent, with cuts to be found outside the classroom, in administration, support services, teacher preparation time, salaries and benefits.[15] At the same time, governments began restructuring school funding formulas in an attempt to provide more equitable funding across school districts. The result, however, was often a significant reduction in funding for large urban boards of anywhere from 3 to 10 percent.[16]

For departments of education, school administrators, and trustees, the problem of gaining control over budgets was multifaceted. A period of fiscal restraint encouraged the reduction of provincial grants. They had fewer funds because grants were tied to enrolments, which were in decline. At the same time, they faced increasing costs for items over which school boards had little control, such as heat and teacher salaries. Salaries were increasing as a generally young workforce in the 1970s became more experienced and moved up the salary grid. The expansion of school programs, especially provincially imposed programs, without adequate funding also increased costs. As a result, school administrators and boards looked for efficiencies, offering retirement packages, reducing full-time appointments, or cutting support staff as well as budgets in areas where they had more flexibility such as library and music programs. Provinces also began experimenting with what they perceived as cost-saving measures such as P3 schools (public-private partnership schools) built with private money and leased back to the province.[17]

What did this mean in practical terms? Two examples. Ontario saw its expenditures per pupil drop from 1992 to 1995 before almost returning to 1992 levels in 1998. Between 1993 and 1996 the Huron County School Board, one of the poorest in Ontario, had to cut its budget from $66 to $58 million, despite stable enrolments. It did so in a number of ways, including busing students to central locations for expensive programs such as computer studies; trimming senior staff; utilizing school facilities in order to sell off separate Board offices; sharing social workers with the local Children's Aid Society; using para-professionals rather than teachers as assistants in kindergarten classes or libraries; creating revenue-generation through the sale of computers to students; and not replacing old textbooks.[18]

In Alberta, education spending appeared to increase slowly in the 1990s, but in real dollars, per-student expenditure decreased. Even though Alberta began to experience budget surpluses from 1996 to 1998, and its politicians to speak of a re-investment in education, per-pupil spending was 12 percent less in 1998 than when Klein took office in 1993.[19] Dawn Walton, in an article in the *Globe and Mail,* nicely captured the resulting transformation in working conditions between the 1980s and 1990s. Paraphrasing one Alberta teacher, she wrote, "The 1980s, now that was an exciting time to be an educator.... Specialists were available to work with gifted children; teaching teams were not unusual; librarians who specialized in children's books were common; and other specialists were available to work with teachers." In contrast, that teacher stated, "In the nineties, it was awful. Teachers were having to be everything and do everything on their own."[20] The Edmonton Public Teachers' Local found that teachers' major complaint in the mid-1990s was their increased workload, followed by the reduction in professional support services from social workers to psychologists and librarians to curriculum co-ordinators, and the increasing complexity in the composition of their classes.[21]

By the 1990s, then, teachers were feeling the effects of the reprioritization of funds away from education. School boards and provincial governments who had encouraged the rapid expansion of the education system at mid-century began to trim spending significantly by the 1980s and 1990s. Still, expectations remained high that the school system could cater to, and provide for, a wide variety of student needs and social demands. In the 1990s, those expectations would outstrip schools' ability to meet, let alone exceed, them.

The Ideological Context

The financial retrenchment of the 1980s and 1990s was a direct response to a worsening economic climate. However, it was also undergirded by an emerging ideological shift away from significant government spending on social welfare and toward smaller government, less state regulation, unfettered markets, the application of business models of efficiency and productivity to the public sector, and the privatization of public assets and services. This neoliberal ideology was already emerging in the 1960s but gained increasing traction in subsequent decades. It underpinned a process of capitalist restructuring from the 1980s on that resulted in an increasingly global economy shaped by the finance sector and driven by the growth in information technology. The inability of North American society to establish leadership in this new form of capitalism gave force to a general condemnation of public school systems aimed at both the nature of schooling and the resulting product.[22]

This critique was particularly forceful in the United States. In the 1980s corporate America began to portray itself as a knight in shining armour that could rescue what it perceived as a failing school system. Business leaders decried the financial and organizational inefficiency of schools as well as the nature and quality of education being provided. Although they played little part in the 1960s and 1970s in helping to set educational policy, by the early 1980s corporate leaders began to link low education standards to America's declining economy.[23] The 1983 report of the National Commission on Excellence in Education, *A Nation at Risk*, stated the issue succinctly: "Our once unchallenged preeminence in commerce, industry, science, and technological innovation is being overtaken by competitors throughout the world. . . . The educational foundations of our society are presently being eroded by a rising tide of mediocrity that threatens our very future as a Nation and a people."[24] The blame for America's loss of competitive edge was thus placed squarely on the public school system. The solutions proposed included "stiffer graduation requirements, tougher tests, greater teacher accountability, school restructuring, more advanced technology in classrooms, vouchers, better undergraduate education, and a general improvement in school efficiency."[25] Such reform aimed to create a more efficient and productive school system that would be able to produce a workforce to meet new economic realities.

Concerns about economic competitiveness were not the only worries about the school system. Civil rights advocates in the 1970s and 1980s condemned the increasing streaming of African American and Hispanic youth into vocational schools. Social critics noted the overrepresentation of poorer children in special education and vocational programs. Widespread concern could be heard regarding low achievement levels and lack of school accountability. General discontent, from both the political right and left, along with continuing belief in schools as vehicles of social reform, evolved, educational historian William Reese argues, "into competing schemes to make schools more competitive and private alternatives more tenable."[26]

For business leaders, *A Nation at Risk* became a rallying cry for quick and extensive engagement with all levels of the education system.[27] The Committee for Economic Development, which was established in 1942 as a nonpartisan, business-led research and policy group interested in promoting long-term economic growth, had long emphasized the responsibility of the private sector to engage with educational issues. In the 1980s it became increasingly vocal, asserting, in particular, that its "study of productivity trends showed that the decline of educational standards in the United States . . . is linked to the nation's flagging economic competitiveness."[28] As a result, in 1985 it produced *Investing in Our Children: Business and the Public Schools*, a report that highlighted problems within the education system and reaffirmed the need for private sector involvement in educational reform. The organization followed up that report with a second one, released in 1988 as *American Business and the Public School: Case Studies of Corporate Involvement in Public Education*, that provided models for successful school-business partnerships.[29] Businesses seemed keen to respond. In the US these partnerships rose from 17 percent of schools in 1984 to 51 percent in 1990.[30] One commentator writing in the late 1980s noted that "the participation of the business community has developed so widely and deeply that now it is almost assumed, and the policies adopted bear the mark of business interests in clear standards and accountability."[31]

Criticism of public schools could also be heard in Canada. In the late 1980s and early 1990s the media, government reports, public commentators, and some parents lambasted the school system, dissatisfied with what they perceived to be economic inefficiencies, declining standards and the lack of preparation of students for life beyond high school. As in the US, governments at all levels found themselves struggling to come to terms with competitive global markets, the new area of information technology, and the need to maintain a high-wage economy while under pressure to cut spending. Government officials and school administrators faced the dilemma of needing to develop efficiencies within the school system while responding to a cry for a more highly trained workforce that was innovative, creative, flexible, and open to, and adept at, new technologies.[32]

School administrators, educational officials, and politicians also faced a barrage of criticism from vocal parent groups dissatisfied with a system that seemed unresponsive to their children's needs, their desire for greater involvement in their children's education, or their concerns about the lack of curricular content and standards as well as the impenetrability of ministry statements regarding those standards.[33] Following the American lead, proposed solutions emphasized free-market rationales that favoured privatization of government services and individual choice, including, in the sphere of education, such things as support for charter schools, tax credit programs for private schooling, and the growth of public-private partnerships in building schools. Reformers also advocated standardized testing, a curriculum relevant to the work world, a strong emphasis on STEM (science, technology, engineering, and mathematics), greater public accountability, and improved efficiency along the lines of business managerial practices.[34]

The concerns of the period are nicely encapsulated in a 1987 *Globe and Mail* article by Graham Orpwood, a Toronto policy and planning consultant in science and education, which is worth quoting at length. Orpwood wrote, "Canadians are losing confidence in the capacity of their elementary and secondary schools to prepare young people for the changing world economy." He went on,

> The industrial community, especially in the technology-intensive sectors, is concerned because its future competitiveness depends, in large part, on the quality of the people it will be able to hire. Parents are concerned because they fear for their children's employability in an economy in which many jobs seem to lead nowhere. Students are concerned because many of their school courses seem to be irrelevant, boring and unchallenging. Governments are concerned because the education bill keeps mounting while little progress is apparently being made toward resolving this crisis of confidence.

Orpwood aimed some of his criticism at a lack of curricular reform and reiterated complaints that could be heard as far back as the 1920s: "Students of all ages, but particularly those in the more senior grades, still read pre-digested information from textbooks, perform repetitive mathematical exercises, copy notes off chalkboards into notebooks, [and] memorize information."[35]

Orpwood's attack, however, did not arise from a desire for a more progressive pedagogy, but rather from a belief that schools did not train students for the skills needed in the new marketplace—the information economy. As he put it, "businesses require their employees to be creative and innovative, to question rather than accept handed-down opinions, to have strong interpersonal and communications skills and to be highly motivated toward achieving corporate and personal goals. . . . The best and perhaps the only place to learn the skills of work is at work." Co-op education programs provided one means of linking schools and industry. But Orpwood also wanted to see more extensive connections between schools and business. He continued, "Education is too important to be left to the educators. Schools need to be a part of society, not apart from it. . . . And schools must recognize that they can meet the challenge of educating for tomorrow only by entering a partnership with the rest of society today."[36]

The business community reiterated these concerns. According to a 1993 Gallup Poll, almost 60 percent of Canadian business leaders believed "the private sector should be actively involved in framing educational policy and shaping curriculum standards."[37] A different poll taken that year reflected public unease over the quality of education, with 46 percent feeling that it was worse than twenty-five years earlier.[38] Whether Canadians felt this constituted an educational crisis is unclear. While numerous polls suggested widespread dissatisfaction, a 1990 Decima poll undertaken for the Canadian Education Association suggested that the Canadian public might be less worried about the education system than corporate leaders or media commentators, with 81 percent giving the system a C or higher for postsecondary education preparation and 79 percent for workforce preparation.[39] Though there might be much room for improvement, this was not a failing grade.[40] Still, public dissatisfaction helped sustain and fuel the rhetoric of school failure. Rattled by the economic changes and technological revolution of the 1980s and 1990s, many elements of the business community revved up demands that the education system place greater emphasis on producing graduates with the skills needed for the workplace of the future.[41] In the American context, these demands also became a justification for corporate "influence on and presence in schools."[42]

That presence could already be seen in Canadian universities. In the early 1980s, university and corporate leaders began sitting down together to investigate ways to co-operate. The Corporate-Higher Education Forum, established in 1983, brought together on a semi-regular basis most Canadian university presidents and top executives from a number of major Canadian corporations and subsidiaries. The Forum's first publication focused on the need for universities "to be tuned more closely to the needs of the marketplace, in order to facilitate economic recovery and a successful transition into the emerging 'high-tech' society."[43] The developing consensus in the 1980s was that universities should orient themselves to the "needs of the economy," produce students able to contribute to high-tech industries and encourage research that would bolster Canada's ability to compete in the new global marketplace.[44]

By the late 1980s a flurry of reports began to appear from corporate Canada and government departments focusing on human resources and Canadian industry and linking the importance of learning to economic vitality and prosperity.[45] These reports revealed significant concerns about Canadians' lack of preparation for participation in a changing economy as well as the ability of the "existing learning system" to provide the appropriate training.[46] They drew attention to an estimated high school dropout rate of almost 30 percent and literacy rates suggesting that nearly 40 percent of Canadian adults struggled to read. In addition to urging improvement in Canadians' basic level of education, the reports raised concerns about Canadians' lack of advanced skills, particularly in mathematics, science, and technology. Proposed solutions included improved vocational training, greater emphasis on co-operative programs, increased career counselling, and exposure to the workplace. Schools should become more flexible, less bureaucratic, and more relevant and responsive. The education system should provide school choice, establish clear benchmarks, measure performance, and professionalize teaching to weed out poor pedagogical methods and recognize good practices. At the same time, many of the reports emphasized the need to control costs and reduce duplication of services.[47]

Partnerships became perceived as a means by which "to link various elements of the learning system together."[48] As a report by the Economic Council of Canada noted, partnerships

> hold out the prospect of direct communication between teachers and employers; for students, they can lead to improved information

about the nature of work and employment prospects. . . . Teachers and students gain valuable knowledge about the labour market, while employers assure themselves of adequate supplies of relevant skills enhanced by an exchange of personnel, by "mentoring," by loans or donations of equipment, or by work experience for students through cooperative or apprenticeship programs.[49]

Partnerships, in short, became a key element in the revamping and restructuring of an education system that would be able to produce a workforce able to fill the needs of the economy.

These reports reinforced some of the work already being undertaken by business to develop relationships with schools. In 1990 the Conference Board of Canada established the National Business and Education Centre, later renamed the Education and Learning Department, to reflect the "growing recognition that education-business partnerships make important contributions to Canada's overall competitiveness and prosperity." The Education and Learning wing of the Board worked to promote "mutually beneficial, cooperative relationships" by creating guidelines and resources.[50] In addition, the Board sponsored an annual competition to recognize the best business-education partnerships.[51] In 1997 it published an *IdeaBook*, co-sponsored with the Royal Bank, Human Resources Development Canada, Canada Post, and members of the National Business and Education Centre, in order to highlight some of the most successful business-education partnerships.[52] In that same year, Charles Ivey organized the first Annual Canadian Education Industry Summit. Reporting on the following year's event, Erika Shaker noted that, according to Ivey, "the summit was a forum for enterprising educational institutions and investors alike to benefit from a climate of 'government cutbacks, and the onset of competitive mentalities and demanding stakeholders.'" Speaking at the summit, the federal Minister of International Trade, Sergio Marchi, argued that government had a responsibility to promote the emerging "education industry" both at home and abroad just as it would for any other field.[53]

Education administrators at all levels responded positively to the overtures of the corporate world. In 1993, for example, the B.C. Ministry of Education's Curriculum Development Branch invited business leaders to participate in its curriculum development committees as reviewers, turning to the Business Council of British Columbia to provide names of possible volunteers.[54] At its 1997 meeting, the Council of Ministers of Education, which brought together provincial education ministers, asked senior business leaders to meet with them and attend an exploratory session on methods of co-operation—the first of its kind.[55] Commentators at the time and later noted that many departments of education and school administrators had become more open to applying a free-market approach to education, encouraging not only school-business partnerships but also the use of corporate funding.[56] Tracking this trend, Maude Barlow and Heather-jane Robertson demonstrated in their 1995 book, *Class Warfare*, that corporate language such as "downsizing, value-added, productivity, return on investment, [and] total quality" permeated "education-policy documents written at every level."[57] The emphases and language of business could be seen percolating throughout education systems.

Defining and Forging Partnerships

The idea of linking business and community expertise and resources to schools was not new. In the 1970s and 1980s, school boards began promoting co-op programs, job shadowing, and exposure of students to different workplaces—an attempt to enable teens to gain some work experience and keep schooling relevant. Following on the success of these initiatives, in the mid-1980s businesses began to promote Adopt-a-School programs in which students could learn about a business and receive some work training while the school would offer something in return such as French courses for employees or space for meetings.[58] Some of these programs turned into friendly relationships whereby schools, linked to a number of businesses, could secure additional resources. Such initiatives, however, also gave rise to the idea of partnerships—an attempt to bring business and community groups more centrally into the education system by pairing the skills of local businesses to the needs of individual schools.

The intent of partnerships was to move away from a sponsorship model in which educators requested money for one project or another, to longer-term, mutually beneficial relationships. When Ian Barrett was hired in the early 1990s by the Etobicoke Board of Education to develop partnerships, what he found was "an 'adopt-a-school program'" that he believed "was basically organized begging," involving "going to businesses cap-in-hand to see how much could be squeezed out of them." Instead, he pursued a model that brought schools together with a business, community group, or government agency in a way that would benefit both parties. If schools gained needed resources from business, he argued, they could "help the business . . . improve their bottom line."⁵⁹ Etobicoke's handbook on partnerships suggested that "for students, the partnerships can offer unique educational experiences, access to state of the art equipment and workplace training. For businesses, the partnerships can provide promotional opportunities, access to school gyms, computer labs and student labour."⁶⁰

By the time Barrett started working for the Etobicoke school board, he could draw from a variety of existing programs. For example, in the mid-1980s Hewlett-Packard established an extensive arrangement with the York Region Board of Education. Students worked for school credits at the local office "doing everything from writing computer software programs and secretarial work to repairing defective products and vacuuming company cars." In addition, the company provided tours, speakers for professional development days, talks for teachers and administrators on "effective decision making and developing good interview skills," and scholarships. It also set up "business labs" containing older equipment no longer needed by the company. In return, the school offered "educational upgrading in the form of French courses" as well as "recreational facilities and space for conferences." The terms of this deal also went so far as to allow a company representative to sit on school advisory committees and provide "input into the content of courses given in the schools." By the late 1980s, Hewlett-Packard had a national training manager promoting its partnership programs to teachers during professional development days.⁶¹

Comparable arrangements occurred elsewhere. In 1987 Bell Northern Research partnered with Earl of March Secondary School in Kanata, Ontario. As a result of this agreement, a number of high school students planned and executed the company's summer and Christmas parties. Traditionally the company had hired additional staff for this work, but under the new arrangement it paid the school for the students' time, with the money raised being put toward supplies and equipment for various student extracurricular activities. In addition, the company provided space to exhibit student artwork and hosted band performances. Similarly, in 1993 Harcourt Brace, a leading publisher of educational materials, developed a partnership with an Etobicoke school. Students were able to attend sessions on editing and gain exposure to that workplace, and the publisher provided the school with several computers and spelling resource materials. It also gained access to the school and expertise of the teachers, who "assisted the publisher by giving them feedback on unpublished language and social studies materials" and tested the materials in their classes. In 1995 students at Kipling Collegiate Institute organized a Christmas party for the Matsushita Electrics Company, which had donated cameras and other equipment. Students at that school also had the opportunity to attend in-house seminars at Bell Mobility on topics such as managing one's time and the skill of report writing.[62]

The Conference Board of Canada produced an *IdeaBook* in 1997 to highlight and model what it considered to be some of the most laudable programs. For example, spurred by the declining numbers of youth considering mining as a career path, the Director of Education Programs for the Mining Association of B.C. entered into a partnership with the Director of Community Services, School District No. 43 (Coquitlam). The partnership aimed to encourage "student learning in the geo-science, minerals and mining technology areas through curriculum materials, work-experience placements and field trips." Though the program was funded by industry, teachers wrote and developed the lesson plans. According to the *IdeaBook*, more than 1,500 teachers had used these resources, thus exposing over 125,000 students in BC to the topics of geoscience and mining. The *IdeaBook* considered this endeavour a successful partnership: it provided "new perspectives for teachers" while at the same time assisting "in developing a competitive workforce."[63]

Other partnerships described in the *IdeaBook* included the forestry industry and the banking sector. In 1994, J. D. Irving Ltd. and the New Brunswick Department of Education developed a forestry materials kit for every school and arranged for tours of forest operations for teachers and students, both of which could supplement existing curricula. The *IdeaBook* noted the advantages of the partnership for schools as a "focus on skills and forestry career opportunities" and "better understanding of the forest and the practices, challenges and opportunities within the forest industry"; in turn, for business it "increases interest and awareness of forestry practices" and "enhances corporate/community image." In the same year, Dawn Hicks, department head of Business Studies and Cooperative Education at St. James Collegiate in Winnipeg, forged a partnership with Ian Dark, the general manager of Astra Credit Union. Together they envisioned "a student-driven partnership" delivering "real world financial experience within a school environment." The students of the school learned to "organize and operate their own distinct credit union—developing community leadership skills, real world employment skills and personal financial strategies." The *IdeaBook* listed education gains for students as "enhancement of employability skills" and awareness of "their personal capabilities," while those for business included "development of skilled potential employees" and "opportunity for employees to interact with [the] educational community."[64]

As business promoters encouraged the development of school-business partnerships, some school administrators responded by popularizing these ideas among teachers. The Coquitlam school district issued a booklet titled *Partners in Education* that offered examples of the types of opportunities afforded by these relationships. Members of the local business community could provide expertise such as running Junior Achievement classes, keeping teachers and students informed about workplace skills and needs, teaching interview skills, or consulting on grant writing, public relations issues, or computer needs. Perhaps a sign of the times, the pamphlet also suggested that these local connections could lead to "summer jobs for teachers." Schools, on the other hand, could contribute to developing relationships with business by helping out with company holiday parties or by recognizing and publicizing the relationship through articles in the school newspaper, through business appreciation days, or by inviting the media to events sponsored by the partner. They could also open up their classrooms or facilities for use by company employees or for company events.[65] For the school district, building these types of partnerships offered the possibility of long-term relationships that would bring resources and skills into schools and develop broad support for educational endeavours in the community.

As the 1990s progressed, partnerships advanced well beyond corporate provision of curriculum materials or the exchange of band concerts for used computer equipment. Private academies and programs began to appear within some public schools.[66] For example, Charles E. London Secondary School in Richmond, BC, near the Vancouver International Airport, partnered with Canadian Airlines to provide the school's aviation course with "equipment, professional expertise and career placement opportunities."[67] Local business also became a site of schooling. In 1995, the Catholic School Board in Edmonton set up a course in advanced auto mechanics in a local car dealership.[68] Business and schools thus joined forces to offer specialized programs not otherwise available.

"Looking for . . . Sweet Deals"

These kinds of partnerships could offer students exposure to the business world, knowledge of possible job or career opportunities, and a means of developing organizational and corporate skills. They could provide schools with access to financial resources, equipment, volunteer mentors or tutors, guest speakers, and resource materials. Jack Shapiro, a principal at Rideau High School in the Carleton Board of Education, told the *Ottawa Citizen* that he believed principals would be at the forefront of the move toward partnerships: "I think education has to go that way because school boards just don't have enough money any more to do all these things.... And where the business community can help and it wants to help—gosh, I'm looking for anyone if I can get some sweet deals that will benefit the kids."[69] Proponents of such partnerships also argued that they were about more than bolstering inadequate government funding. Linda Rainsberry, an educator turned journalist, noted that they provided "strategic alliances" through which "students can learn real world skills with up-to-the-minute equipment." She continued, "Adobe, Sun Microsystems, Pearson and Fluke all want to be held to the highest standards of business excellence. For each of them, engagement with educators represents their corporate investment in the future of skilled Canadian workers."[70] Rainsberry was not alone in expressing such opinions. The co-ordinator of the Calgary public board's partnership programs argued, "We're getting away from the notion that learning must only take place inside the four walls of a classroom inside a school.... The workplace has become an extension of the classroom, and we see that as very, very positive."[71]

Still, at times, the rhetoric that partnerships provided more than sponsorship seemed forced. When Carol Parker, chair of the Carleton Board of Education, defended this new form of corporate-school relationship, she referred to Rideau High Schools' partnership with Pepsi. In that arrangement, the company donated products to sell in the school and in return the company gained occasional access to classrooms for its meetings. Her argument: "It's the difference between sponsorship, which provides the students with something the company is trying to sell, and a business partnership.... And my preference certainly at the moment is for a business partnership where the benefits go both ways."[72]

Concern about partnerships was common by the 1990s, particularly over the lack of monitoring or regulation. The Saskatchewan Federation of Home and School Associations recognized this problem early on. In 1992, in reaction to the federal government's encouragement of business and education partnerships, its Board of Directors developed resolutions requesting that the Ministry of Education regulate "acceptable behaviour for business in education" and "take steps to restrict and monitor business advertising in schools, limiting this advertising to presenting only the name and nature of the business."[73] Three years later the BC Teachers' Federation (BCTF) developed a "Statement of Ethical Standards for Business-Education Partnerships" that stressed, among other things, the need for these relationships to enhance education, that they be developed with full consultation of all stakeholders, that their continuation undergo constant re-evaluation, and that they not exploit the school or contribute to inequities within the school system. The BCTF guidelines also proposed that corporate logos should not appear in educational materials or on school grounds.[74]

But most provinces did not have guidelines or policies regarding partnerships in the late 1990s, and teachers' associations continued to demand their development into the twenty-first century.[75] In 2006 Erika Shaker and Bernie Froese-Germain noted that provinces such as Ontario, Alberta, BC, and Saskatchewan, along with the Northwest Territories, had left school-business relationships in the hands of school boards. Where departments of education had stepped in, they often allowed significant wiggle room. Shaker and Froese-Germain pointed in particular to the case of New Brunswick, where the policy "requires sponsor name recognition to be 'discrete and proper' (clearly open to interpretation) and the suggestion that 'classrooms shall be *generally* 'ad free.'"[76]

One of the ways that business learned to alleviate concerns was by bringing educators into the creative process. This was certainly not a new method. In 1980 B.C. Hydro developed teacher kits for various grades about the production of energy, drawing on the help of over thirty "teacher-volunteers." An advertisement in the *BC Teacher* carefully stressed that "special care has been taken to avoid any suspicion of 'hucksters in the classroom.'"[77] Over fifteen years later, John Gregory, an education consultant, told a *Globe and Mail* columnist, "You have to get teachers involved from the beginning" and develop projects that address student and teacher needs. "If you don't," he continued, "you are spinning your wheels." Gregory oversaw projects that fell at the intersection of the corporate and education sectors. His company, for example, had recently helped bring Hewlett-Packard (Canada) together with teachers to create a math and computer workbook, aimed at girls in Grades 4 to 6, that would meet the curriculum mandates of a number of provinces.[78]

The Conference Board of Canada worked hard to create a roadmap for successful, mutually beneficial relationships between business and schools, eventually developing a document titled "Ethical Guidelines for Education-Business Partnerships." The guidelines stated that "ethical partnerships safeguard learners' interests, build trust and mutual respect, regulate themselves, and make informed decisions that benefit everyone involved." In an attempt to ease critics' concerns that partnerships undermined a publicly funded school system, the document stressed that corporations "allocate resources to complement and not replace funding for education." Acknowledging that the aims of business and schools did not always mesh, it also warned participants to "identify and manage potential conflicts between business and education needs and objectives."[79]

However, partnerships involving the development of curriculum material could still raise serious concerns about content selection. For example, in 1997 the Brewers Association of Canada provided funding for an educational resource on alcohol for thirteen- to fourteen-year-olds to be developed by representatives from the New Brunswick Department of Education, the University of New Brunswick, the Department of Health, a local multi-media company, and the provincial telephone corporation. The project was administered by a private consultant, with the dean of the UNB Faculty of Education as project manager. Linda Eyre, a member of that faculty, "was asked to write the Anglophone resource." Eyre, who was eventually dropped from the project, ostensibly due to lack of funds, became critical of the venture on the grounds that despite the Brewer Association's hands-off position, it actually directed the thrust of the resource as "responsible drinking." The material provided "technical information about alcohol," emphasized responsible decision-making, and addressed the issue of drinking and driving, but it avoided the topic of alcoholism and "excluded information about how alcohol works socially, economically, politically, and globally."[80] The end product, she argued, "served the interests of project partners" rather than students, positioning the Brewers Association as a good corporate citizen and placing the blame for alcohol problems on the individual—in this case, the problem student drinker—rather than on the broader social context.[81]

Francine Dube, of the *Ottawa Citizen*, reported on the use of a corporate-sponsored school resource on the history of Hull, Quebec. She discovered that "Grade 3 children attending Commission scolaire Ouatouais-Hull schools in West Quebec learn about Hull from a book funded and written in co-operation with the City of Hull, E. B. Eddy Ltd., and Les Caisses populaires Desjardins." She noted:

> Page 14 is the Les Caisses populaires Desjardins page, featuring a picture of the credit union, circa 1938, and pictures of six modern

ones. It is accompanied by several exercises. What does the photo of yesteryear tell you about the role that Caisses populaires played in the development of Hull? Find these Caisses on a map of the city of Hull. Is there a Caisses populaire in your neighborhood? If so, which one?[82]

Thus, in this case, children learnt about the origins of their city through the eyes of Les Caisses populaires Desjardins, a history lesson wrapped in blatant advertising.

Critics at the time also raised issues about partnerships' use of free student labour. In numerous cases, these relationships involved an exchange of services such as tutoring and instructing in return for a school band or choir playing at a company function.[83] Commentators also pointed out that partnerships provided a legitimate means for businesses to gain free advertising for their product or brand and to promote themselves as good corporate citizens. As one article noted, "The students, their families and staff at the school also end up doing a good marketing job for Hewlett-Packard because of the close relationship with the company."[84] In contrast to the win-win philosophy underwriting school-business partnerships, some parents wondered about the loss of an ethic of philanthropy. George Tsallas, an Etobicoke father who was not unsupportive of business-education partnerships, commented to *Today's Parent*,

> I see a tendency to expose the students to the business world that has to do only with money and profit. I'd like to see a balance, children getting involved with fields where there is a service provided without the consideration of a return on the investment—so that they know that this counts in our society too. We want to develop people of integrity, with a sense of social values and responsibilities.[85]

Conclusion

Whatever the perceived benefits and pitfalls of partnerships, they quickly became rooted within Canada's school systems. The effects of inflation in the 1970s and 1980s and stagnant funding in the 1990s, along with the growing influence of neoliberal approaches to governance, meant that school administrators and many educators looked favourably on corporate or community funding opportunities. The general rhetoric linking education to economic prosperity, which also emphasized STEM and twenty-first-century skills as the means to increase global competitiveness, occurred at a time when governments were looking to reduce their investments in social services, leaving a gap for corporate involvement. Elements of the business community, in turn, began to perceive themselves as a source of leadership in educational affairs. School boards began hiring part-time or full-time co-ordinators to create and promote partnerships. Educational consultants appeared who focused their attention on brokering these partnerships between schools or boards and business and other groups. Economic challenges and new ideological emphases encouraged the application of business management practices and styles to the education system and a closer relationship between the private and public sectors.

Partnerships thus became seen as a means of closing funding gaps, maintaining a diverse and enriching curriculum, and continuing to offer new and innovative programming. They provided a means for schools to obtain specific resources and develop long-term relationships with businesses that in the best of cases could contribute not just materials but know-how not otherwise available. Yet in numerous instances they also involved the free labour of students and teachers, the commodification of students' existing activities (such as band performances), opportunities for blatant advertising, and industry oversight and direction in curriculum materials. Indeed, the turn to partnerships would fuel a hitherto unparalleled level of commercialism in public education.

3

Tapping the Educational Market

Computers in Classrooms

*I*N 1990 the newly built River Oaks Public School in Oakville, Ontario, opened its doors. A model school, wired for the twenty-first century, it had originated in a 1987 partnership between the Halton Board of Education, the Ontario Ministry of Education, and Apple Canada. From the beginning, the principal, Gerry Smith, also developed partnerships between his school and a number of other companies such as Microsoft, Northern Telecom, and Bell Canada. By 1993, the school boasted 240 Macintosh computers for its 670 students, a ratio of roughly one computer to every three students, in contrast to a Canadian average of one computer to every twelve students.[1] Teachers also had access to a personal computer, voice mail, the nascent Internet, and e-mail. Apple provided some of the computers for free and offered others at significantly reduced rates. Other companies contributed "CD-ROMs, electronic keyboards, robotics equipment, desktop video publishing, computerized sewing machines and other specialized tools."[2] River Oaks was not unique. Similar projects appeared elsewhere—for example, IBM partnered with a new high school in Montgomery Village, Orangeville, and Burnaby South, in Burnaby, BC, and Apple with Saint Helen's Separate School in Windsor.

These schools became beacons for the future of education. Many business leaders, lamenting the state of the North American economy and the education system as a contributing factor, believed that greater use of computer technology in schools offered the possibility of an educational transformation that would help stimulate North American leadership in the new, technology-based global economy. The 1993 vision statement of the Conference Board of Canada's National Council on Education, which included senior education administrators as well as business leaders, suggested that the education system could be reinvigorated by using "technology to raise student and teacher productivity and expand access to learning."[3] Focused on improving the education system for national prosperity, the Conference Board of Canada became a big supporter of STEM. Some educators agreed. Jeremy Meharg, a school superintendent in Burnaby, BC, remarked about corporate involvement in the high-tech facilities being built into Burnaby South in 1993: "They are getting involved in changing the way education is delivered: They are part of the revolution in education that is going on right now."[4]

In the 1990s, computer technology symbolized a new direction in the economy in labour skill needs and knowledge; those at the front of this revolution wanted schools to adjust to the times in order to produce the most able citizens. By the first decade of the new millennium, this idea had solidified around the importance of twenty-first-century skills, with an emphasis on changing "the structures, processes and practices of schools, teachers and students along more high-tech, networked and 'innovative' lines."[5] In the 1980s and 1990s, however, the question on everyone's mind was how to spread the innovations from a few cherry-picked schools to all educational institutions. To examine that issue, this chapter briefly reviews developments in educational technology and then focuses on three case studies: the creation of the ICON computer in Ontario; the development of SchoolNet, a national program to connect schools to the Internet; and the New Brunswick Dedicated Notebook Computer Research Project, aimed at providing students with personal laptops.

Education and Modernity

Excitement over the possibilities of technology for educational purposes is certainly not new. In 1922, American inventor and businessman Thomas Edison had stated, "I believe that the motion picture is destined to revolutionize our educational system and that in a few years it will supplant largely, if not entirely, the use of textbooks."[6] This enthusiasm would extend to radio and later television. Larry Cuban, an American historian of educational technology, notes that proponents held up the integration of each new development into the classroom as "a symbol of progressive teaching approaches." "In the 1920s and 1930s," he argues, "the black window shades, silver screen, and 16mm projector lent an aura of modernity and innovativeness to classrooms."[7] Radio and television would likewise come to embody modernity; advocates of these new forms of communication perceived them as a means of exposing students to the broader world, providing students with access to expertise, instilling excitement into teaching, and contributing to interest-based learning.

In Canada too, departments of education paid attention to new technologies and investigated ways of incorporating these innovations into teaching. School authorities explored the uses of radio and film. In Ontario in the 1940s, the Department of Education and the CBC co-operated to produce radio broadcasts on a variety of subjects from music to social studies to health. In the 1950s, most Alberta classrooms had a radio and made use of programming from one to three times a week. Departments of education worked to set up bureaus for audio-visual aids from which teachers could borrow film strips, and provincial governments and school boards invested in sound and film projectors. Access to this technology was often more limited than to radios. In one rural Manitoba school division, for instance, 84 percent of classrooms made use of radios while only 50 percent utilized projectors.[8] As television appeared, educational authorities in Canada, as elsewhere, quickly explored the potential of educational television, developing pre-recorded programs that could be aired through closed-circuit systems.[9]

Computer advocates reflected the enthusiasm of other proponents of technology. In the early 1970s Ivan Illich, a philosopher, theologian, and critic of Western society, saw computers as central to deschooling, whereby interested "networkers of learners" would come together "and schools and teachers would simply wither away."[10] In the 1980s Seymour Papert, a mathematician and computer scientist at the Massachusetts Institute of Technology, boldly declared: "There won't be schools in the future. The computer will blow up the school."[11] Similar sentiments, though perhaps not as extreme, circulated widely. Early advocates argued vigorously for the ability of educational computing to encourage child-centred classrooms, contribute to motivation and creativity, and enable lifelong learning.[12] Computers, as with other forms of technology, became linked to modernity, progress, and individual and social development.

Earlier forms of technology, however, such as radio, film, and television, ultimately had little impact on the nature of teaching. Some teachers certainly integrated the use of this technology into their classrooms. In the US, according to a 1946 National Education Association survey, approximately 37 percent of elementary teachers frequently used film in their class and 32 percent occasionally, rates that declined to 20 and 29 percent respectively at the senior high school level. The Canadian statistics noted earlier suggest similar rates of use. Still, Cuban suggests that teachers employed this technology mainly in an infrequent and limited way.[13] Enthusiasts believed that computers would be different but that belief, like Edison's about the motion picture, was held entirely on faith.

An Emerging Market

In the 1970s and 1980s, the reality of widespread computer use in schools was still to come. An affordable microcomputer was invented only in the mid-1970s. By the early 1980s, however, computer companies were already exploring the personal computer market and envisioning future returns from the educational arena. Apple, Commodore, Radio Shack, and IBM all began developing both hardware and software for classroom use. Just as corporations in the 1930s and 1940s had attempted to insert their brands into schools in the hope of gaining lifelong customers, so too did computer companies expect that students trained on a particular machine would be more likely to purchase that brand. And this was big business. The educational computer market experienced rapid growth. For example, in the early 1980s just over 250 computers existed in all of Alberta's schools; by 1985 that number had increased to over 16,000. In Ontario, the number of computers in schools rose from 649 in 1980 to 6,000 in 1982 and 60,000 in 1986, or roughly one computer per thirty students.[14] As a result, computer purchases held out the possibility of significant revenue. Writing in the *Globe and Mail* in 1983, Brian Milner noted that many provinces hoped to achieve one computer per ten students, a figure that in Ontario alone would result in an estimated $300 million in sales.[15]

Computer companies fought for leadership in this educational market. Commodore Business Machines led the way, accounting for some 70 to 85 percent of sales in Ontario. Apple lagged behind in most of the Canadian market but became the frontrunner in Alberta, with 95 percent of schools opting for its machines after the Department of Education endorsed Apple purchases because of the availability of software. To gain access to the emerging market, companies offered significant discounts. Commodore, for instance, developed a three-for-the-cost-of-two deal while Apple provided some products at cost.[16]

Apple became particularly creative in selling its wares to schools. In 1994, Gayle Long, national marketing and channel manager for Apple Canada, noted that the technological innovation at River Oaks was provided in part through the Apple Canada Education Foundation. Established in 1983, that organization, consisting of educators and other appointees, worked at arm's length from the company to select key submissions seeking Foundation support.[17] In publicizing this information, Long declared, "education has always been the cornerstone of Apple." By 1986 approximately 40 percent of the Canadian branch's revenue resulted from school sales.[18]

In the 1980s, then, as computer companies vied for larger shares of the market, the education sector became a prime target, perceived as crucial both in and of itself, and also a significant potential source of future customers. But while Apple, Commodore, and IBM fought over education contracts, some provincial governments developed their own dreams of harnessing that sector to stimulate local industry. In the early part of the decade, these companies' market share risked erosion from just such an Ontario project.

The "Bionic Beaver"

In 1981, Bette Stephenson, Minister of Education for the Progressive Conservative government in Ontario, launched a Computers in Education program aimed at seeing a microcomputer on the desk of every student within the decade. That government had high hopes that Ontarians' access to computer technology, via the education system, could bolster the province's economy. In 1985, Larry Grossman, the Provincial Treasurer of Ontario who later became the leader of the Ontario Conservative Party, declared,

> Technology offers young people the chance to get into new jobs, and allows our businesses to compete with other countries and regain jobs that have been lost. . . . If we do things properly, we have a chance to take thousands of people off welfare and help them break out of a cycle of welfare dependency. We can make them part of the

communication and technology age, and they don't have to go to expensive private schools to do that. That's why there is a great sense of urgency to put computers in the schools.[19]

The government envisioned Canadian companies working together to design a computer specifically made for use in Canadian classrooms and thus better than anything that international firms could provide. Overall, the intent was to aid Canadian industry, develop software with Canadian cultural content, and provide the best educational microcomputer possible.[20]

Business was key to the Ontario Ministry of Education plan from the start. The government began its explorations into educational computing through private meetings that included the Canadian Advanced Technology Association (CATA), a group of private computer hardware and software manufacturers; the Ministry of Industry and Trade; the Ministry of Transportation and Communication; and the Ministry of Education's experts. Stephenson's announcement of the development of an educational computer occurred at a meeting sponsored by, among others, the Durham Board of Education's Business and Industry Liaison Committee for Oshawa and the Oshawa Chamber of Commerce. The ministry then asked CATA, in consultation with a variety of government departments, professional associations, and computer experts, to establish specifications for a computer.[21]

In the early 1980s, the Ontario Ministry of Industry and Trade helped set up Canadian Educational Microprocessor Corp. or CEM Corp., based in Toronto. While nearly twenty companies expressed initial interest in participating in this consortium, most backed out as a result of financial woes and/or disorganization within the corporation, with Meridian Technologies of Toronto eventually taking a controlling interest. By 1983 the government had committed $10 million to purchase machines and $5 million to produce software; it also promised a grant of between 50 and 80 percent per machine depending on the size of the school board.[22] The result of this process was the ICON, nicknamed the "Bionic Beaver."

The first ICON machines did not appear until 1984. Because of the delays in the Computers for Education program, school boards went ahead with their own buying programs. By 1985 there were approximately twenty thousand computers in Ontario schools, with only 20 percent being ICONs.[23] And the ICON was expensive. Jonathan Chevreau of the *Globe and Mail* noted that the machine was advanced but came with

"Bionic Beaver" ICON computer. Courtesy of Personal Computer Museum, Brantford, Ontario.

a high price tag. "The argument," he stated, "is about whether schools should buy many cheaper microcomputers, giving students ready access to computer time, or a state-of-the-art machine that may result in limited access."[24] The ICON also came with little software. In fact, from the start of the Ontario program, critics had argued that the focus should be on investing in software rather than hardware.[25]

Although the ICON was the first computer to meet Ministry of Education specifications for approval, IBM issued its Ontario government-approved computer, named Ednet, in 1986. IBM had turned its eye to the school market as its sales in mainframes and personal computers for business slowed. According to one reporter,

> IBM appears to be launching a well-orchestrated assault on the education market, even though its efforts may have only a marginal effect on the bottom line in the next year or two.... IBM is donating its computers to schools and also offering deep discounts. In addition it has 105 employees in academic information systems across Canada, solely responsible for marketing to education groups.... When IBM is not meeting teachers, it is mailing them its glossy magazine, *Classroom Connections*, billed as a "channel for dialogue between educators and IBM Canada."[26]

IBM's Ednet, however, was incompatible with the ICON. As a result, the government had to spend $260,000 to make just five ICON software programs usable on Ednet. In 1988 Douglas Archer, the Ontario Auditor General, wrote a scathing review of the whole program, highlighting this waste in particular. He also pointed out that the initiative had cost $131 million, almost $50 million of that in the previous year alone, but that only $72,000 had been spent on teacher training. In that year the Ontario government, following Archer's recommendation to scrap the program, opened up the educational computer market.[27]

The Technological Push of the 1990s: SchoolNet

By the early 1990s, schools with computers were already finding them out of date. In BC, for example, computers lacked the necessary processing capacity "to run integrated software packages using windows and mouse techniques."[28] Moreover, in most schools in Canada, upward of 70 percent of computers remained in labs rather than being integrated into regular classrooms. Yet the push to keep computers up to date and make them accessible remained as relevant as ever. Governments continued to funnel money into computer purchases. In 1995, the BC government announced a $100 million five-year School Technology Plan aimed at achieving one computer for every three high school students and one per six pupils at the elementary level. School districts continued to try and raise money for computers. After the King's County District School Board in Nova Scotia prioritized the need for computers in its twenty-two schools, board members, administrative staff, superintendents, and directors of education all participated in fundraising by knocking on doors, raising $50,000 for its "Futures Fund."[29] In order to win fifteen Macintosh computers, along with installation, maintenance and training, from AGT, part of Telus Communications, Alberta schools competed in a government scavenger hunt in which they had to submit twenty items such as "letters from parents explaining why they chose the school for their children, cards from students thanking volunteers, pictures of families and an elected official at the school, old report cards and proof of a public display of students' 'works.'"[30] Computer companies also continued to pour money into educational institutions in order to expand their market. IBM Canada spent $60 million over ten years in about forty partnerships in Canada. Although Apple was quick off the mark in establishing its education foundation, in

1994 IBM Canada launched EduQuest Canada.[31] By the 1990s, however, there was no longer just a perceived need to have computers in classrooms but also to link them up to the nascent information highway.

In the early 1990s, Industry Canada's Science Promotion Directorate helped fund SchoolNet, a program to connect schools, as well as libraries, hospitals, and universities, to the Internet. SchoolNet was the brainchild of six engineering students from Carleton University who had been helping to develop Ottawa's FreeNet system. In 1992 they established Ingenia Communications Corp. and convinced Industry Canada to sponsor a project to connect twelve schools in the Ottawa area to the emerging net. Using the Freenet system along with some old Industry Canada computers, the young company piloted what would eventually result in the creation of SchoolNet, in the process launching itself as a major Internet consulting firm.[32] Connecting schools to the Internet, however, required a communications infrastructure. SchoolNet partnered with Stentor, an alliance of telephone companies, who could provide the necessary wiring. Launched in 1993, by the end of the school year the program had linked some three thousand schools to the nascent information highway. By 1998, 85 percent of schools were connected to the Internet.[33]

Industry Canada's mandate at the time was to promote economic competitiveness, in particular, by fostering scientific research and encouraging the diffusion of technology. In the 1990s it recognized the need to help develop and stimulate the use of the emerging Internet in order to position Canada well within the new knowledge-based global economy.[34] At the same time, business leaders and IT companies advised Conservative and Liberal governments alike that increasing the emphasis on STEM in education was a primary means by which to do so.[35] In 1994, for instance, the Information Technology Association of Canada (ITAC), a telecommunications and computer industry lobby group, issued an *Education Statement* that pressed for a "complete restructuring of the classroom curriculum to permit the full integration of information technology in the delivery of education."[36] SchoolNet thus became one way in which successive federal governments could visibly satisfy such demands.

As a collaborative program between Industry Canada, provincial or territorial ministries of education, and the private sector, SchoolNet's mandate extended well beyond connecting schools to the Internet. Its goal was also to foster excitement about Internet use and encourage students to think about the field of information technology as a career possibility. It did so through two initiatives: GrassRoots and the DirecPC

SchoolNet promotional pamphlet.
Republished with permission of Innovation, Science and Economic Development Canada.

Satellite Program. The former provided grants to teachers in order to facilitate the creation of relevant and useful web-based projects. The latter enabled rural and remote schools to connect to the Internet via satellite. This allowed schools that previously had only a single telephone line to provide workstations at which multiple students could access the Internet.[37]

Given the problem of covering remote distances, SchoolNet ran into cost issues almost immediately. In 1995, newspaper reports noted that a number of rural school boards—especially in Nova Scotia—had disconnected School-Net because of long-distance charges of up to $10,000 a year. In contrast, schools in large urban centres often had access to a free net node allowing them to connect to the Internet for approximately $300 a year. In some cases, provincial governments stepped in to aid struggling school districts. At a cost of $5 million a year, the Ontario government rented "trunk lines from Bell Canada so that out-of-the-way schools" could access the Internet. Manitoba, however, enforced "equalization," so that rural and urban schools shared telecommunication costs.[38]

Despite these problems, the federal government funnelled significant funds into the program—between $25 million and $35 million in the first four years and close to $130 million between 1995 and 2001.[39] But corporate funding was also central to the viability of SchoolNet. Telecommunications companies played a major role in investing in the program as well as contributing independently to hook up schools and universities to the information highway. Microsoft was a founding partner in Grass-Roots, providing $1 million over the subsequent three years. When that partnership ended, AOL Canada stepped in to provide a similar amount, an announcement that was webcast live. Corporations such as Cisco Systems, Imperial Oil, Esso, and CN provided additional support.[40]

SchoolNet had multiple aims: to connect schools to the Internet, to stimulate interest in computer use, and to encourage the development of Internet-related educational resources. At root, though, its goal was to create student interest in gaining skills that would allow their participation in the emerging high-tech industry. It would not take long, however, before the SchoolNet project became obsolete. While provincial ministries saw its usefulness in stimulating school access to the Internet, they quickly raised concerns about the quality and usefulness of grassroots-initiated programming.[41] That problem became particularly apparent with the increasing sophistication of the World Wide Web. Though providing an active platform for schools in the second half of the 1990s and early years of the twenty-first century, SchoolNet soon became outmoded as a result of the rapid pace of technological innovation.

Laptops for Kids: New Brunswick's Dedicated Notebook Computer Research Project

The technological leaps in information technology in the late 1990s, along with the declining cost of personal devices, soon led to renewed enthusiasm for student access to computers. One idea that caught educators' and the public's attention was that of providing students with their own laptops that they could use at school and home. In 2001 the premier of New Brunswick, Bernard Lord, attended the New England Governors and Eastern Canadian Premiers Conference, where he learnt about a school laptop program being put in place in Maine.[42] In 1999 Maine had a budget surplus of $50 million. The governor of that state, Angus King, pushed through the state legislature a "laptops for kids" plan, with seventh and eighth graders and their teachers receiving Apple laptops for use at home and school in 2002 and 2003. The Maine Learning Technology Initiative, as it was coined, made Maine one of the first states "to offer universal laptop distribution to an entire grade of middle-schoolers." The Maine legislature provided $30 million for the initiative while the Bill and Melinda Gates Foundation provided $7 million. Contracts with Apple came to $90 million. In addition to the computers, these included various technical supports, from software updates to asset management, including aid from a local team of company employees.[43] The initiative aimed to use technology to improve academic standards as well as the state's economic position, both areas in which Maine ranked in the bottom third of US states.

In Canada, these types of programs had begun to make their way into private schools in the late 1990s and some school boards in the first years of the new millennium.[44] Providing such an initiative for a whole province was a massive undertaking. On his return from the New England conference, Lord asked the Department of Education to look into the creation of a similar venture for New Brunswick.[45] The province had already been primed for such an experiment. As Premier from 1987 to 1997, Frank McKenna had worked tirelessly to develop the infrastructure for the information highway and attract IT business to the province. Like so many others drawn to the possibilities of IT, he felt the industry could modernize New Brunswick's workforce and renew the economy. As part of this effort, his government had introduced basic computer competency for high school graduation in 1994 (a first in Canada), had connected all schools to the Internet by 1995, and had begun investigating ways to integrate technology into all levels of schooling.[46]

As with SchoolNet, rural schools had difficulty sustaining these endeavours financially past the pilot phase. In an early trial, Southern Victoria High School in Perth-Andover received two hundred computers for its five hundred students along with a high-speed Internet connection; however, with the completion of the program, the school was left with some modern equipment but found itself unable to pay the $9,000 a year Internet bill. In an article for the *National Post*, David Akin reported that

> the ongoing operational costs of the computers means other areas of Southern Vic's budget have had to shrink. Some shop classes, including automotive shop, have been closed, partly as a result of shrinking demand and a shortage of qualified teachers, but also in response to budget shortfalls. . . . Many schools, including Southern Vic, have taken to selling education or computer services to the local community to generate some extra revenue to pay for operations.

Akin argued that "staff who spend time on these revenue-generating services may have less time to teach."[47]

Still, the idea of implementing a program like Maine's in New Brunswick fit with almost fifteen years of political rhetoric regarding the impulse of technological innovations for economic development. The result was the two-year Dedicated Notebook Computer Research Project. The pilot program started with six schools providing notebook computers to Grade

7 students in January 2005, with an expansion to Grade 8 students in those schools the following September. Among other things, it aimed "to enrich teaching and learning practices to support the skills required to succeed in the global knowledge economy"; to improve teacher and student competency in technology; and "to impact positively on student motivation and achievement."[48] Its implementation involved several private sector partners. Hewlett-Packard (Canada) donated just over five hundred notebook computers in return for which the department agreed to purchase any new Intel-based machines from that manufacturer. Telecommunications giant Aliant offered Internet access while Microsoft Canada provided software and funds for the province's independent evaluation report.[49]

Before the independent assessors even released their final report on the project, the Lord government launched its Notebook Initiative. In March 2006 the government announced that all teachers in the province would be given notebooks. Schools that had participated in the test round continued with their programs while other middle schools needed to apply to become part of the initiative.[50] Despite the reported academic success of the program, the cost was substantial, and New Brunswick did not have Maine's budget surplus. When the Liberals came to power in that same year, the new education minister at first put a hold on the initiative, later continuing it only in schools where it was already in place.[51] This was not uncommon. Even as one-to-one programs became increasingly popular in the US and Canada, some school districts began scaling back because of the cost. For example, Grade 6 and 7 students in the Peace River North school district in BC had had laptops since 2001, one of the oldest programs in that province. By 2008 trustees had opted to have students borrow computers from the library rather than providing personal devices—a move resulting in more than $2 million in savings.[52]

Contemporary Assessments of Classroom Computer Use

New Brunswick's notebook program, SchoolNet, and the development of the ICON all illuminate the continual push since the 1980s to increase students' access to computers and related technology. This enthusiasm for computers began well before their full evaluation as a useful educational tool. Pilot projects often received favourable, and even enthusiastic, reviews. The report on laptop use commissioned by the New Brunswick Department of Education, for instance, found the project to be a success.[53] One independent reviewer told a reporter from the *Times and Transcript* (Moncton):

> The observation after one and a half years is that students and teachers that have laptops in their classroom are meeting and exceeding all the requirements of the curriculum. . . . But beyond that we are seeing a huge impact on attendance, behavior and achievement. This is an enormous tool to enhancing the learning environment.[54]

A case study of the same program, undertaken by the Canadian Education Association (CEA) at the request of Hewlett-Packard Canada, noted similar positive outcomes, stating that "findings from this and a growing number of studies of similar initiatives have demonstrated positive impacts of specific uses of technology on student engagement and motivation, and in creating more inclusive learning environments."[55] These assessments conformed to that of the Maine program. One of the primary evaluators at the University of Maine noted,

> What the research has shown to date is that learners are much more engaged than they otherwise had been. . . . It's a little early to determine a cause-and-effect in terms of the access of the computers and achievement outcomes, but we're certainly seeing learning engagement very high. And that, we think, is going to lead to heightened achievement.[56]

Such assessments were not unusual. Based on qualitative evidence, one-to-one computer initiatives generally received positive endorsements, with students and teachers often reporting "that learning has become more student-centered, students are more engaged in learning, and that collaboration among and between students and teachers has increased." Most of the studies also noted standardized test scores were somewhat improved. Still, in 2008 the Abell Foundation, a Maryland nonprofit organization focused on supporting positive community change, issued the results of a study of a number of these major initiatives in the US in which it claimed, "there is not yet conclusive evidence that personal laptop use leads to gains in student achievement."[57] In fact, according to Bryan Goodwin, vice-president of communications for McRel, a nonprofit, nonpartisan educational research and development organization, the research on one-to-one computer initiatives indicated that the outcomes were mixed. He noted that while Maine saw student writing scores improve, a similar program in Texas revealed slightly lower scores than those recorded prior to implementation. Reflecting on these results, Goodwin concluded, "Rather than being a cure-all or silver bullet, one-to-one programs may simply amplify what's already occurring—for better or worse—in classrooms, schools, and districts."[58]

Whether computers proved useful or not, the rhetoric around educational computing emphasized the inevitability of computers in the classroom, thereby marginalizing critics and wider public debate.[59] Heather-jane Robertson, for example, has argued that the tech industry has "artificially stimulated the appetite for those materials to the point where schools believe they cannot function without them or that the public will cease to support schools unless they have lots of technology."[60] This was not just a problem in Canada. "Pressed by parents, business leaders, public officials, and computer vendors," Larry Cuban contends, "few school boards and administrators can resist the tidal wave of opinion in favor of electronic solutions to education's age-old problems. The questions asked are seldom *whether* to move ahead with new technology but how, under what conditions, and to what degree."[61] Chris Bigum notes of the Australian context, "In the rush to put computer studies into the curriculum, the debate about whether such study belongs in schools did not take place."[62]

Some critics believed that the heavy investment in computers came at the expense of vulnerable programs such as art, music, and early childhood education. Others claimed that the emphasis on technology occurred at the cost of smaller class size, better teacher salaries, and building improvements.[63] Jan Eastman, president of the Canadian Teachers' Federation, speaking at that organization's general meeting in 1998, noted that computer technology was costing schools up to a third of their budget. She stated, "We've got the government and business pushing an electronic curriculum" but "the merits of the Internet on education are not proven."[64] Underlying some of these concerns could be found apprehension about the growing emphasis on schooling as preparation for employment. Proponents of new information technologies made broad, and vague, claims about the skills computers could impart—claims that sat uneasily with many teachers' vision of the purpose of education.

Whatever they felt was lost in the leap onto the technological bandwagon; critics found it near impossible to counter the powerful rhetoric in its favour. David Buckingham, a scholar of media education, has argued that computer technology is sold to teachers as "empowering and emancipating." This technology, like previous variants, is seen as a way to engage the disengaged child and bring enthusiasm to the class. Moreover, he notes, trade companies emphasize the "dangers of being 'left behind.'"[65] Technology companies, in their pursuit of innovation and growth, are vested in convincing policy makers, and the public more generally, of the necessity of computer hardware and software for educational excellence. The underlying message is that the good teacher, or equally parent, who wants the best for a child is one who embraces the educational possibilities of computer technology. The corollary is that those opposed to, or even questioning, the benefits of the technology are standing in the way of that child's development.

Conclusion

A culture of inevitability fuelled the belief in the need for computers, and partnerships became the way forward. In 1993, an Ontario elementary school principal put it this way:

> I always hear the argument that if we let a business sponsor our computer lab, the next thing you know our basketball team will be wearing uniforms with Joe's Heating and Plumbing written on them.... I admit there could be a problem, but when you think about it, there's no way we're going to get new computers any other way.[66]

The principal had put his finger on what would become one of the hot button issues of the decade. The problem for many critics, however, would have less to do with local business—Joe's Heating and Plumbing—than the opening up of schools to multinational corporations and the effect this would have in driving educational decision-making.

In the 1980s the emerging belief in the need for educational computing helped push open the doors for school-business partnerships. The continued need over the next decades for new or better technology helped reinforce that trend. As Buckingham notes about the situation in England, "Amid a volatile and rapidly changing economy, education has provided a relatively stable market for technology corporations eager to sustain their profit margins."[67] Corporations linked to technology, be it computer hardware, software, or communications, worked hard to develop model schools and programs that placed technology at the core of twenty-first-century schooling, in the process helping to create, or shore up, their standing within the educational market. As a result, the desire for computers, and the perceived need of them, stoked by technology corporations themselves, would become a decisive factor in the development of school-business partnerships in the 1990s and beyond. This process would in turn open the floodgates for commercialism in schools.

4

"It's So Pervasive, It's Like Kleenex"

Schools—The Last Frontier of Advertising

*I*N THE 1990s the youth market gained momentum as the first members of the baby boom echo became tweens. Though not as large a generation as that of their parents, their numbers would still mark a new level in children's purchasing power, one that had already grown significantly in the previous decades. Nor did it seem to have any limits. In Canada, spending by children aged nine to fourteen increased from an estimated $1.1 billion in 1995 to $2.9 billion in 2005, while purchases by parents topped $20 billion that year.[1] Moreover, sociologists monitoring children's interaction with consumer culture found that this relationship had become more intense, with unstructured play increasingly replaced by shopping and television.[2]

For marketeers this was a period of opportunity. Having just made a pitch to place ads on school buses within the York Region, Donna Eaton told the *Toronto Star* in October 1996, "Schools are really the last frontier in terms of advertising."[3] Not surprisingly, given her position as a marketing executive, Eaton was on the cutting edge of a new advertising trend aimed at pulling open the doors of the schoolhouse. But she was not alone. In 1999 the president of Le Groupe Jeunesse, a Montreal communications firm, told a reporter for *L'actualité* that schools were the cheapest and most effective way of gaining access to children.[4] This chapter examines the varied forms of in-school commercialism that developed in the 1990s and 2000s. The following two chapters focus on two specific cases: Youth News Network, a youth-oriented, news-based commercial television program; and the growing presence of vending machines and fast food franchises. Together, these chapters illustrate not only the breadth of corporate intrusion into schools during this period, but the justifications provided to support that process as well as the extent and limit of protests against commercialism in enacting change.

Corporate Materials in Schools

In the 1990s, teaching aids, crafted to fit into the curriculum, remained an effective means by which corporations gained access to the classroom. This tried-and-true method continued to offer teachers interesting and colourful material to maintain student interest. For example, in a ploy reminiscent of the Lifebuoy campaign of the 1920s and 1930s, Coppertone provided a package to elementary schools that included a "colourful poster, teacher's guide, entry forms for a colouring contest and 32 achievement certificates for the 'Block the Sun, Not the Fun! Education Program,'" all aimed at teaching children about the danger of sunburns and the importance of using a protective sunscreen. Similarly, the Coal Association of Canada offered "a video, pamphlets on 15 coal-related subjects and samples of different kinds of coal," while the Canadian Nuclear Association developed "a teacher's guide, information sheets and a video" on nuclear fission. Or, if they preferred, teachers could obtain an "Environmental Action Pack" from McDonald's Restaurants of Canada.[5]

Corporations sent some of these materials directly to teachers and schools. But they also pitched their packages in other ways. Stuart Tannock, a sociologist interested in the interplay of corporate-sponsored curricula and public education, wrote in 2009,

> I recently sat in on a workshop for pre-service teachers at a Faculty of Education in Ontario, facilitated by the Prospectors and Developers Association of Canada (PDAC) *Mining Matters* program. PDAC is a lobbying group for the Canadian mining industry. *Mining Matters* is a non-profit, charitable organization created by PDAC in the mid-1990s to educate students "about mining's importance to our quality of life" and help the industry "get its message across . . . in competition with a media-savvy environmental movement." The

workshop was a demonstration of *Mining Matters*' new "Discovering Diamonds" comprehensive curriculum kit, filled with lesson plans, activities, mineral and rock samples, maps and other materials, that uses diamond exploration and extraction in the Canadian North as a pedagogical hook to teach Grade 11 and 12 students earth science concepts.[6]

In this case, then, the lobby group gathered together prospective teachers at a point when they would be thinking about curriculum development and lesson planning, presenting them with methods and materials to teach earth sciences that reinforced the perspective of the mining industry.

In addition to the traditional route of providing teaching aids, various corporations continued to find ways to insert their names into the classroom by ostensibly addressing specific educational goals. One of the longest-running American programs for literacy remains the Pizza Hut Book It program. In the US it has been in operation since 1984 and is used by some fifty thousand schools, gaining the praise of President Ronald Reagan in 1988 and including on its advisory board representatives from teachers' unions and the American Library Association.[7] In the program, students and teachers set reading goals, with successful students receiving a coupon allowing them to obtain a free pizza. By the 1990s, Canadian students too could work to secure up to five pizzas, and if all students in a participating class reached the goal, they won a pizza party. Other corporations have also used this model. McDonald's, for example, developed a "Reading Road" program in which students progressing along the "Road" received coupons for various products such as French fries or hamburgers.[8]

Some corporations simply attached their name to literacy programs without providing additional incentives. In 1988, Northern Telecom supported the "Koalaty Kid Program" in the Dufferin-Peel Roman Catholic School Board. The initiative created a support group of parents and other volunteers to encourage reading, a school book club, and weekly assemblies recognizing those achieving reading goals.[9] Other programs fit into schools' literacy aims by providing free books. At the turn of the twenty-first century, for instance, the Toronto Dominion (TD) Bank Financial Group initiated an annual program to provide a high-quality book free to every Grade 1 student across the country. The TD logo originally appeared on the front cover of the book, but in Ontario, after complaints by some school boards, it was moved to the first page, which also featured a letter from the CEO of the corporation.[10]

Similarly, Scholastic Corporation, an online book publisher and distributor that sells direct to schools, promotes its products through monthly book flyers and annual fairs. Teachers receive rewards (or points) based on student sales while school-based events enable librarians to restock library shelves. Parents are encouraged to buy books both to improve their child's reading skills and to provide free materials for the school. While the flyers traditionally focused on book sales, by the twenty-first century they increasingly advertised the sale of toys and other products in an attempt to direct children's attention toward a particular book. In many cases books are made more appealing by an accompanying charm bracelet, necklace, pendant, or figurine, or through the topic being linked to current movies, television characters, or popular toys. In 2003 Nancy Pearson, director of marketing at Scholastic Canada, told the *Ottawa Citizen* that the company took this turn because "there is a lot of competition for children's attention these days, and reading, I think everybody believes fundamentally, is an important thing, but we are trying to appeal to a wide audience." Some kids, she argued, "need a little extra incentive to even pick up the book club [flyer] to look at it, to sort of see, 'oh, there is something in here for me.'"[11]

While companies such as Scholastic focus on reading, others encourage students' financial literacy. As in earlier decades, some of these programs aimed to develop a habit of thrift. In the late 1990s, for instance, the Bank of Montreal set up a branch in the lobby of St. Stanislaus Catholic Elementary School in Edmonton. Through the school, the bank created an account for each student, with an initial deposit of a dollar. School administrators encouraged students to make deposits each week on "Bank Day," with parent volunteers collecting the money. In other cases, programs introduced students to the language of banking and investments. The Bank of Montreal developed a board game called "My Money" for ages 7–10, providing sixteen thousand copies of the game to Canadian schools. As one journalist explained,

> Kids roll the dice and land on squares that might earn them $4 for cutting the grass, or $2 in dividends on First Canadian mutual funds. Players can pay for financial advice from Nesbitt Burns, a subsidiary of the Bank of Montreal, and race to be the first to reach the Investore, the bank's new retail outlet.[12]

The creation of bank branches within schools could also facilitate students' familiarity and practical experience with the routine processes of the industry. When Guy Vezina moved from Quebec to Alberta in 1993 to take up a teaching position at École Maurice-Lavallée, he immediately championed the establishment of a local credit union branch in his school, something that was becoming increasingly common in Quebec. Two years later he succeeded in convincing Capital City Savings and Credit Union to embrace such an initiative so that students could "earn work experience and special-project credits toward their high-school diplomas." Similarly, VanCity Credit Union in BC co-operated with Surrey's Cindrich Elementary School to open a school branch in April 2005. The program was run by Grade 7 students who, after being interviewed by teachers for their positions, made up "the bank's tellers, cash-counters, security and greeters."[13]

Physical education, like financial literacy, has proved to be an easy means by which some corporations have found a way into schools. This is the case, for example, with McDonald's. In 2005, in response to negative publicity, the corporation undertook a renovation of its image. Management changed the menu, offering salads and bottled water as well as the possibility of substituting apple slices for fries in its Happy Meal.[14] Ronald McDonald also had a makeover. Writing about the situation in the United States, Michele Simon notes that "after forty-two years, the mascot traded in his trademark yellow jumpsuit for sportier garb" as the marketing team developed a program, "Passport to Play," to bring nutritional messages to schools. With the opening of the school year, the company then distributed the program "to thirty-one thousand schools and seven million children, designed to 'motivate children to be more active in unique and fun ways during grade school physical education classes.'"[15]

In Canada, the company joined forces with the Canadian Olympic Committee to encourage physical activity in schools. The resulting "Go Active! Olympic Fitness Challenge" included free posters for participating schools, featuring the McDonald's logo at the bottom. The company offered two programs: an in-school presentation and a fitness challenge. In the former, Ronald McDonald visited the school to advise children on the importance of living a balanced, healthy, and active life. As part of the event, students watched a short video featuring a personal message from an Olympic athlete about the importance of staying fit and eating well. The fitness challenge consisted of students being "tested on a series of six exercises in the fall and retested in the spring, aiming for an overall improvement in their fitness levels."[16] By participating in the challenge, schools had the opportunity to earn up to $500 in sports equipment. One Edmonton school that won the equipment also received a visit from Cassie Campbell, captain of the 2006 gold-medal-winning women's hockey team, for an "Olympic Day Run" in which students, donning free t-shirts with the company name and logo on the front and back, jogged alongside her.[17]

Not to be left behind, in 2004 Kellogg Canada and the Dietitians of Canada sponsored an elementary school-level program called "Mission Nutrition" tied into health studies. The following year the company collaborated with Active Healthy Kids Canada, a charitable organization, to initiate "Kidz Count." Inserting pedometers into Rice Krispies, Frosted Flakes, and Fruit Loops cereal boxes, the program encouraged children to engage in twenty minutes of daily physical activity over a two-week period. Although it was aimed at consumers, some schools also took up the program.[18]

While some corporations have found ways to tie their brand directly to an established curricular emphasis, others have focused on a specific issue or "learning event"—initiatives to educate students about a topic of particular societal concern. For example, in 1994 the Sports Network and Shaw Cable partnered with Langford Junior Secondary School in Victoria, BC, to offer Grade 8 students TSN merchandise, such as pins, baseball caps, and sports bags as part of a "Stay-in-School" program. The sports network had piloted such a program the year before at Don Mills Collegiate Institute, a Toronto high school.[19] Similarly, in 2000, McDonald's teamed up with the Fredericton Police Force, using Ronald McDonald for a special presentation about bullying. The vice-principal of Nashwaaksis Memorial School explained that over the past year the school had been focusing on bullying. "We thought that through Ronald McDonald, it could really enforce what we have been doing (encouraging kids to go to an adult or walk away when a bully approaches)." "His way with kids was wonderful," the principal continued, "and he gets that important message across in a way they can remember."[20] Indeed, sponsoring a talk or a poster with a social message became a new means for corporations to gain access to schools. In 2002, Critical Mass Promotions, a company founded the year before and specializing in school washroom marketing, secured space for its posters in thirty-eight Nova Scotia schools. The posters relayed a positive message but included the logo of the corporate sponsor.[21]

Although numerous corporations focused on inserting their materials into classroom activities or placing advertising in hallways or cafeterias, commercialism was not limited to school grounds or the indoors. As we saw in chapter 1, the Canadian Pacific Railway sponsored educational field trips as far back as the 1930s, while in the 1970s some students took outings to their local McDonald's. However, the level of commercialism reached new heights in the first decades of the twenty-first century when field trips to local retail businesses became formally organized through Field Trip Factory, a Chicago company founded in 1993 by a marketing executive, specializing in organizing "free class trips to the stores of its corporate clients." Canadian teachers could avail themselves of the American companies' services. In 2003, for example, kindergarten classes at Britannia Public School in Mississauga took a field trip to the local PetSmart while Grade 1 students at Thorncliffe Elementary School in Edmonton, Alberta, visited a Rona Home & Garden location, where they learned to build a birdhouse for Father's Day.[22]

As Field Trip Factory prospered, it added a Canadian manager tasked with developing partnerships that would fit within the existing provincial curricula. Links to larger grocers and an emphasis on nutrition seemingly provided the most stable opportunities. In 2013 the company facilitated the Ontario launch of Real Food Trips, a partnership between Hellman's Canada and various Loblaws, Real Canadian Superstore, and Zehrs Market outlets, providing three hundred free visits, though schools paid for transportation. During the outing, a store dietician led students through the aisles, teaching various nutritional principles. Field Trip Factory also promoted a media literacy trip for tweens. In 2014 Grade 7 students at Deer Park Public School travelled to Yorkdale Shopping Centre to participate in a program called "Microsoft Tech Talks: Understanding Digital Media," held at the Microsoft store. Topics covered tablet use, Internet safety, video game ratings, and an introduction to Bing (Microsoft's web search engine). Students also used the Xbox for some physical exercise.[23] Corporations have also come to promote these types of trips independently of second parties.

Instead of offering specific learning-based programs, some companies have chosen simply to donate time, money, and resources. Wal-Mart Canada began "adopting" schools in 1994 as part of a campaign to "give back" to the community. A pilot project in a Northern Ontario school in 1998 included store volunteers helping to plant trees as well as uniformed staff providing talks about the retail industry during career day. Similarly, in 2009 one store donated $4,000 worth of trees, providing a border for a school playground located beside a vehicle-congested street in Rothsay, New Brunswick.[24]

Guiding Stars school nutrition kit, 2018, including cloth backpack, star pen, recipe card, and nutritional stars rating guide. Photo: Jeff Crawford.

Corporations have also used schools' needs for funds and parents' desires to fundraise as an entry point into schools. In return for payment, for example, some trustees have experimented with allowing advertising on school property. In the 1990s marketing firms set their sights on the pristine frames of yellow school buses.[25] Some school boards took advantage of financial offers that placed ads on screen-savers.[26] Similarly, in 1998, Terry Fox Secondary School in Port Coquitlam, BC, signed a deal with Nike in which the company sponsored the boy's basketball team and in return the school displayed the company's logo in the gym.[27] Schools have also allowed company names on their school name and field boards.

While fundraising by parents generally occurs outside of school time, their use of incentive programs often allows corporations to gain entry into schools. Scholastic is a good example of this, and perhaps the most successful in terms of inserting itself into school life. But there are others. In the early 1990s, the Real Canadian Superstore developed a promotion

Colpitts Developments Field name board, Bliss Carman Middle School, Fredericton, NB, 2018. Photo: Michael Dawson.

offering schools a chance to win computers once they had submitted shopping receipts up to a particular value from the school community. Campbell Soup Company's "Labels for Education," which had been running in the US since 1974, expanded to Canada in 1998. Similarly, Kellogg's "Education Is Tops" program encouraged students to collect barcodes from Kellogg products in order to win computers and other materials for their schools.[28]

In the 1990s, then, advertising in schools appeared in a variety of forms, from corporate materials to adopt-a-school initiatives and from advertising on school buses to fundraising incentive programs. And its presence was pervasive. A major survey of Canadian schools undertaken in 2006 by the Canadian Centre for Policy Alternatives (CCPA), the Canadian Teachers' Federation, and the Fédération des syndicats de l'enseignment found that of the 3,100 returned questionnaires, 55 percent of secondary schools and 28 percent of elementary schools reported advertising either in the school or on school grounds. These rates varied significantly by province, with a reported low in Quebec of just over 21 percent compared to almost 38 percent in BC and the Prairies. They also ranged by product. Coke and Pepsi comprised the most prominent advertising, with the brand appearing on vending machines, scoreboards, and school signs. Although 64 percent of elementary schools used Scholastic, only 8 percent participated in the Pizza Hut Book It program. Campbell Soup's "Labels for Education" initiative was the most widely cited incentive program in use, but across the country 30 percent of schools, mainly at the elementary level, reported participating in these types of activities, with a high of 36 percent in BC but only 1 percent in Quebec.[29]

While these statistics provide an indication of the breadth and nature of advertising in schools, it is likely that some rates of advertising were considerably higher than those reported in the 2006 survey. In a study undertaken in 2000, the British Columbia Teachers' Federation found that 99 percent of elementary schools participated in Scholastic Book sales. One teacher noted, "It's so pervasive, it's like 'Kleenex.'. . . It's not seen as a brand and therefore not recognized as corporate involvement."[30] That survey also found—at 61 percent—a much higher rate of school involvement with incentive programs. Likewise, the TD Grade One Book Giveaway program reached most school children across the country, with some eight million books distributed in the first fifteen years of the new millennium.[31]

Whatever the precise rates of advertising, it is clear that corporate intrusion into schools became prominent in the 1990s and even more pervasive in the following decade. Offers for corporate-sponsored curriculum material, literacy programs of various sorts, special learning events, field trips, and incentive programs, all inundated schools. While certainly not a new phenomenon, the level of commercialism indicated a crisis within the education system.

Justifications

School administrators, teachers, and parents justified in-school commercialism in a variety of ways. In some cases, they saw it as a means to supplement the existing curriculum or extracurricular activities. Of his school's bank program, the assistant principal, Robert Martin, stated, "I think it's important for kids to learn about saving money, and it's also another way for them to learn to use computers, since that's where we keep the records."[32] Louise Campbell enthusiastically noted of her class's free trip to Rona:

> It's an absolutely wonderful space. The children learn to use a hammer and nail, and to measure things with their fingers. They work on fine motor skills and listening skills. . . . We write thank-you letters to Rona and that's another language experience, and it teaches good manners. The field trip was also complimentary, so it appeals to any of us in tight budget times.[33]

Others believed the advertising to be within acceptable bounds. In defending her board's decision to allow ads on school buses, Peggy Valentine stated, "About a third of our bused students use Calgary transit. . . . If we were so pristine about what young people are exposed to, we would worry about that."[34] Of the Future Leaders Tech Lab in Surrey, BC, named after its Future Shop sponsor, one trustee noted, "We would not want to put up big double arches in elementary school lunchrooms. That would be a little much because that's direct intrusive advertising. This isn't that."[35] Similarly, Michael Cohen, head of communications and marketing for the English Montreal School Board, enthusiastically supported corporate sponsorship but noted that his board would not accept sponsors whose message might conflict with school goals: "We wouldn't have a beer company, we wouldn't have a soft drink company, we wouldn't have McDonald's. Obviously, there's a subliminal message in any of our sponsorship that we are encouraging students to appreciate the sponsor." Instead, the board preferred companies such as First Canadian Financial Services, RBC Royal Bank, the Norshield Development Foundation, and clothing companies such as JCorp International and Point Zero, and drew on these to support events such as career fairs and parent volunteer appreciation evenings or to provide computer technology.[36]

Although some school personnel saw corporate donations and grants as a way of providing for a variety of needs and desires, corporate representatives understood their programs to be a means for companies to give back to the community. Murray Beckley, TSN's Western Canada marketing representative, told the *Times Colonist* that his company's involvement in the "Stay-in-School" program was "a goodwill thing."[37] At the turn of the twenty-first century, one Wal-Mart spokesperson noted of the adopt-a-school program that education was a top priority for Canadians. He argued that the company did not advertise or market its program. Rather, he stated, "What we are getting out of this is the satisfaction of contributing to the schools and to the communities. . . . That's it."[38] In defence of the Superstore "Apples for Classrooms" program, Jane Ebbern, co-ordinator of the initiative, said, "We truly want to put something back into the community."[39] Bob Hissink, senior vice president, Western Region, McDonald's Canada, noted that "The Go Active! Fitness Challenge is one way we are demonstrating our commitment and dedication to encouraging a balanced, active lifestyle among young Canadians."[40]

At times, such justifications could become quite circular. In the late 1990s, Shaw Cable distributed a resource kit to Alberta elementary schools as part of a "TV&Me initiative" with the aim of sparking classroom conversations that would turn children into informed viewers. The kit was created by Concerned Children's Advertisers (CCA), a nonprofit organization representing a number of companies, such as McDonald's and LEGO Canada, that had a significant interest in advertising related to children's programming. Developing out of a partnership between CCA, Shaw, and Heritage Canada, the resource provided short clips that would allow teachers to ignite classroom debate. CCA chairman Michael Aymong noted, "We believe we have a right to market with kids, but we also have a responsibility."[41]

School trustees, administrators, and corporate representatives all drew on the problem of budgetary constraint to defend their actions. In 1996 the chairman of the York Region Board of Education told the *Toronto Star* that the decision to try out school bus ads was an easy one given that, among other things, they had had to eliminate junior kindergarten programs and add portables to schools as a result of cuts in provincial grants.[42] In 2001 Ron Rubadeau, a Kelowna school district superintendent, told a local newspaper reporter that school trustees remained interested in a controversial proposal that would see ads scrolling on electronic announcement displays placed in hallways, for which the school district would receive roughly half a million dollars a year. In defence of the proposed program, Rubadeau explained that the money would be put aside to pay for the coaches, referees, transportation, and other expenses required for extracurricular activities, asking rhetorically, "Do you want to pay a thousand bucks to play basketball?"[43] Among other justifications for the creation of Field Trip Factory, Susan Singer, the founder of the company, stated, "If [a] trip can teach you a life lesson, that really is our mission. Go to the zoo, go to the museum, we love those field trips, but not every child can do that. It's not always accessible, but there is a grocery store, sports store, bank, pet store in your community."[44]

Much like the justifications around partnerships, administrators and corporate representatives argued that corporate-sponsored programs could benefit all parties. "Advertisers are able to reach specific target groups and at the same time provide benefits to the community," Dale Newman, the president of M2000, argued of his firm's proposal to put ads in school buses. "To the extent that this program supports student transportation and generates revenue for education, everyone wins."[45] Speaking for the English Montreal School Board, Michael Cohen put it this way: "Provided it is done in the soft-sell mode, I believe sponsorship and school is a win-win situation.... It's a program that I would like to step up a lot." While school boards obtained sponsors for various events, corporations could gain community goodwill. In making the pitch to corporations, Cohen argued, "If you hook up correctly, between the (32,000) newsletters, the press releases and other publications the school board does, our Web site and just the general interest we generate from the community, I think they have a lot to gain."[46]

Gary Tymoschuk, a Surrey, BC, school trustee expressed a similar view. In 1998 that board entered into an arrangement in which a thousand students attended the opening night of the Guildford SilverCity cinema. The district school received the ticket and concession sale profits in exchange for their participation in the publicity event. Tymoschuk told a *Vancouver Sun* reporter, "We're looking for agreements that are win-win situations. We're looking from our point of view, at the benefits for the school board but we understand that companies have to get benefits as well."[47]

That win-win situation was at times acknowledged quite openly as a means of making customers of Canadian students. Paul Gleason, marketing director for Schering-Plough, the manufacturer of Coppertone, was crystal clear on this issue: "Obviously, we believe education will lead to increased usage of sunscreen and we're hoping that... if the message was brought to them by Coppertone that they would buy Coppertone products."[48] Similarly, Gord Sarafinchan, the manager of an Edmonton Capital City Savings branch, stated, "The way I look at it is that we hope to have the students as full-fledged customers in the future."[49]

Justifications for the use of corporate material in schools ranged widely. Proponents emphasized any number of reasons, from corporate generosity and mutually beneficial arrangements to school budgetary needs and maintaining student interest. While defence of this type of material can certainly be found before the mid-1990s, it was from then on that justifications became more extensive and prominent within the public record. Perhaps not surprisingly, dissent mirrored that pattern.

Dissenting Voices

As in earlier decades, criticism of various forms of commercialism in schools could be heard occasionally in the early 1990s. For example, in 1992 Tom Spears, a journalist with the *Ottawa Citizen*, wrote an extensive and devastating critique of corporations' use of teaching aids in an attempt to portray themselves as environmentally friendly. The package produced by the Coal Association of Canada indicated that "global warming is just a debatable theory and acid rain a smaller threat than environmental groups claim." The Canadian Nuclear Association's information suggested that "coal pollutes through acid rain and greenhouse gases (which cause global warming), while nuclear power is reliable." The material from Inco relayed the message that the company was "spending $500 million to reduce its emissions of sulphur dioxide, the main ingredient in acid rain." Yet, Spears noted, "Inco's nickel smelter at Sudbury is North America's biggest single source of the gas. The materials portray the company as an environmental leader. They don't mention how strongly, and successfully, Inco resisted acid rain controls for more than a decade in the 1970s and 1980s." He added that McDonald's too had jumped on the environmental bandwagon. Despite the company's significant use of disposable packaging, it had produced "an 'Environmental Action Pack'" for elementary school students covering a range of topics including reducing waste.[50]

Some trustees and parents also raised concerns about initiatives that they deemed inappropriate. While some school boards participated in the Superstore "Apples for Classrooms" giveaway, others felt it problematic. One member of the Alberta Home and School Councils' Association wrote:

> The Superstore promotion involving the donation of computers to elementary schools which collected and turned in shopping receipts to a certain value was particularly distasteful. Regardless of the altruistic motives which may have inspired Superstore, the campaign had the appearance of being nothing more than a sleazy attempt to use schools as an advertising tool.[51]

As these two examples demonstrate, opponents of corporate intrusion into schools did exist in the 1980s and early 1990s. Still, public discourse seemed to favour the role of businesses in improving North American schools and embraced the key role of technology in that process. General dissent appears thin in this period. In the last half of the 1990s, anti-corporate activism gained momentum and significant public support as the effects of the economic transformation of the previous decades became broadly felt. Deindustrialization and the flight of industry to developing countries with cheap labour devastated elements of the North American economy. This trend was accompanied by a growing consumer culture based on the exploitation of labour and resources in other areas of the world by multinational corporations. A growing anti-corporate movement responded to revelations of their practices, including human rights abuses and ecological destruction, a movement that would become interconnected by the turn of the twenty-first century with other consumer-based protest, such as the anti-globalization movement, the anti-GMO movement, and the fair trade and slow food movements.

In the mid-1990s a variety of newspaper articles and television reports focused attention on the exploitative labour practices, including violent repression of union activity, child labour, low wages, and treacherous working conditions, that existed in the sweatshops producing much of North America's brand-name clothing, toys, and other goods. According to Naomi Klein, these reports revealed "the obscene disparities of the global economy: corporate executives and celebrities raking in salaries so high they defy comprehension, billions of dollars spent on branding and advertising—all propped up by a system of shantytowns, squalid factories and the misery and trampled expectations" of sweatshop workers, overwhelmingly women and children.[52] In particular, Nike came under attack for its use of child labour in the manufacture of soccer balls and for union crackdowns in factories making sneakers, Mattel and Disney for their links to children working and living in conditions close to slavery, and Wal-Mart for being one of the largest retailers to hold exclusive distribution rights of these products.[53]

Klein argues that the rise of significant anti-corporate activism can be attributed in part to the increasing financial power of multinational corporations, some with larger budgets than small nations. Yet she also surmises that this activism arose in response to corporations' growing cultural influence in the form of branding. Multinationals have sought to sell their brand, rather than a product, and have done so increasingly by having individuals link their identity and culture to that brand. As the corporations promoting that brand are revealed as corrupt, then at least some individuals "feel complicit in their wrongs, both guilty and connected."[54]

As various corporations became more prominent on university campuses, students focused attention on their practices. For example, chapters of United Students Against Sweatshops appeared protesting the use of sweatshops for university apparel.[55] In the late 1990s, students in North America and Britain used university agreements with PepsiCo and Coke to bring attention to those companies' human rights violations and investments in countries under dictatorial rule. In Canada, student protests forced some universities to reveal the details of exclusivity deals with soft drink companies as well as to cancel contracts and put a halt to negotiations.[56]

Similar activities occurred in some schools. Craig and Marc Kielburger brought attention to the issue of child labour first through the creation of Free the Children and later through the establishment of the social enterprise, Me to We. Craig Kielburger became deeply concerned about child labour in 1995 after reading an article in the *Toronto Star* about Iqbal Masih. Kielburger and Masih were both twelve-year-old boys at the time but had grown up in very different circumstances. Masih had worked in virtual slavery in a Pakistani carpet factory from the age of four and was shot and killed in 1995 after becoming the figurehead for the international movement against child labour. With the help of his Grade 7 teacher, Kielburger organized a school club. He then took a trip to India to see conditions in sweatshops for himself. While there, he met with Canadian Prime Minister Jean Chrétien who was in India on business, thus gaining headlines for the issue of child labour. Free the Children, along with other groups such as United Students Against Workshops, helped raise awareness among students about sweatshop conditions and the corporations supporting this form of production. For example, in 1998 when Terry Fox Secondary School in Port Coquitlam, BC, signed its deal with Nike resulting in the company's logo being displayed in the gym, a handful of students protested, objecting to the school's affiliation with a company known for its links to sweatshops, and especially the exploitation of children.[57]

Alongside this anti-corporate activism, social critics and academics paid increasing attention to the marketization and corporatization of education at all levels. This became a particularly prominent issue within universities, where critics raised concerns about academic freedom, the influence of corporations in directing research agendas and the distribution of money, and the diminishing importance placed on pure, undirected inquiry.[58] Some observers also levelled extensive critiques at the emerging corporate culture in schools. In the US, Alex Molnar, an expert in education policy studies, began tracking school commercialism in the 1990s. The Consumers Union issued a cutting report on the topic in 1995. Organizations such as the Center for Commercial-Free Public Education, established in Oakland, California, in 1993, and the Campaign for a Commercial-Free Childhood (CCFC), founded in 2000, have equally brought attention to the issue.[59] In Canada, Maude Barlow and Heather-jane Robertson's *Class Warfare: The Assault on Canadian Public Education*, published in 1994, and Robertson's 1998 book *No More Teachers, No More Books: The Commercialization of Canada's Schools* helped raise public awareness.

Teachers' unions also began to study the topic. In 1995 the Ontario Secondary School Teachers' Federation (OSSTF) produced an analysis of trends in commercialization in Ontario schools, while the British Columbia Teachers' Federation (BCTF) produced a similar type of survey in 2000. Yet in the early years of the new millennium, there was still little information about the nature and extent of commercialism in Canadian schools. In 2006 the Canadian Centre for Policy Alternatives (CCPA), the Canadian Teachers' Federation, and the Fédération des syndicats de l'enseignement continued the work of the OSSTF and BCTF with a major survey, titled *Commercialism in Canadian Schools: Who's Calling the Shots*.[60] The CCPA publicized the results, along with various aspects of the problem in schools and universities, in a special issue on commercialism in its publication *Our Schools, Our Selves*.[61]

Union leaders integrated their critique of commercialism into publicity campaigns designed to garner support for a strong public education system. In the mid-1990s, for instance, the Alberta Teachers' Association (ATA) created the Public Education Action Centre to develop policy statements, position papers, and newspaper ads, thereby bringing awareness to the consequences of the provincial government's agenda and to what they perceived to be an assault on schools. As part of these efforts, they brought in Barlow and Robertson as speakers for their 1995 annual conference.[62] In 2000, as ATA members gathered again at their annual assembly, the Association proclaimed that businesses should not be allowed to sell their products in schools.[63] In that same year, the Coalition for Public Education in BC, composed of various teachers' and public employee unions, university faculty and college educators' associations, and the Canadian Federation of Students, held a conference in Vancouver for all those involved in and concerned about public education, focused on commercialization and corporatization at all levels of the system. A second major conference followed in 2005.[64] As a result, many teachers would come to see increasing commercialism in schools as a consequence of underfunding and an attack on public education.

Parents, too, voiced their concerns about underfunding. In 1996 Annie Kidder organized a demonstration in Toronto at the Ontario legislature after her daughter's school asked parents to raise money for items such as math workbooks that she believed ought to be a basic provision of a publicly funded system. Kidder formed a social action committee at Palmerston Elementary School in Toronto, out of which developed People for Education, now a major charitable organization for the promotion of public education in Ontario.[65] Concerned citizens also brought awareness to the intrusion of commercialism in schools in other ways. Jill Sharpe created the film *Corporations in the Classroom* after her hairdresser complained about Home Depot's involvement in the construction of a North Vancouver elementary school playground.[66]

As corporate intrusion into schools increased, and protest grew, some education ministers and school boards worked to limit commercialism. This was particularly true in Quebec where the education minister at the time, François Legault, was especially vigilant. As Minister of Education from 1998 to 2002, Legault cracked down on a variety of initiatives that he felt contravened the Quebec Consumer Protection Act, which prohibits advertising aimed at children under the age of thirteen, and a clause in the Education Act forbidding school boards from taking part in incentive programs. As a result, companies such as Pizza Hut, the Campbell Soup Company, and Kellogg had to pull their programs in 2000.[67] Other provincial ministries stepped in where commercialism seemed to hit levels unacceptable to the public. For example, in 2006 the New Brunswick Department of Education prohibited the school presentation in which the McDonald's character, Ronald, gave tips on living a healthy and active lifestyle, though it continued to allow the fitness challenge where the mascot did not appear.[68]

Still, many provinces were less interventionist, leaving school boards to develop their own guidelines and policies on commercialism. Some boards began to do so in the late 1990s in reaction to specific issues. In one case, in the mid-1990s, the McDonald's Corporation put forward a proposal to run a high school cafeteria in the Victoria District School Board in BC.

The board turned down that offer on the basis that it had no policy regarding corporate involvement in schools and then began to formulate one. The resulting guidelines proposed that the board only entertain initiatives that, among other things, would support the "quality and relevance of education for learners." In addition, schools could recognize a corporate contribution so long as this did not turn into an advertisement.[69]

Similar resistance could be found in Kelowna, BC. In 1998 a school board trustee suggested that the board should open the doors to advertising in schools. A variety of proposals came up for discussion, from ads on school buses to electronic advertising boards in the hallways. When the local teachers' union notified the board of the BCTF's guidelines for corporate involvement, the board agreed to hold six public meetings to gain input. The district parent advisory council did its own survey and came out strongly against corporate advertising, drawing on guidelines developed by American scholar Alex Molnar. The board accepted many of the guidelines, and determined that advertising in schools would, in general, be prohibited, though it made exceptions for vending machines, publicity for sports teams or tournaments, and the use of logos for identification purposes.[70]

Not surprisingly, school board responsibility for guidelines had a checkerboard effect. For example, in 1998 Calgary school trustees approved a pilot project for computer screen savers containing advertising, produced by Screen Ad Billboards Inc. of Brampton, Ontario. In Edmonton, on the other hand, the proposal did not even reach trustees, failing to pass a screening process by district officials.[71] Different responses equally appeared within municipalities. In 2006 the Edmonton Public School Board generally supported partnerships or sponsorships if they did not undercut public funding and enhanced "the quality and relevance of education for learners," while the Edmonton Catholic Schools Board of Trustees left decisions about these issues to individual principals.[72] Moreover, boards themselves were not always consistent. For example, the York Region District School Board decided in 1995 that schools should not distribute materials with logos, yet participated in the TD Grade One Book Giveaway until 2008.[73]

Much of the dissent regarding school commercialism was accompanied by high levels of anger and frustration. Social critics and activists railed against what they perceived as an attack on public education and more broadly on a Keynesian welfare system that provided support for those most in need. Their anger could be fierce, and it appeared in many places, from teachers' protests to union-organized conferences. It could also be found in parental denunciations. Nicely illustrative is a letter from Christina Kowalewski to the *Vancouver Sun* about the Vancouver Olympic Committee's sponsorship agreement with McDonald's. She wrote,

> If we protected our children's rights as fiercely as Vanoc protects its Olympic trademarks then Vanoc and its sponsorship obligation to McDonald's, disguised as the Go Active Canada interactive school show, would be run out of town. Who gave Vanoc permission to allow McDonald's to target our kids in school? The message is good, but the messenger isn't. Ronald McDonald as the Olympic representation of nutrition and fitness? Is Vanoc already running out of ideas? Here's the real joke. Participating schools can earn up to $500 for sports equipment. I hope school administrators will consult with parents before selling out for a mere $500. If it keeps junk food and the advertising of junk food out of the schools, I'm one parent who would be more than happy to cut a cheque for the cause.[74]

More than anything else, the tone of Kowalewski's letter reflected the frustration of parents, as well as many other critics, who felt that the commercialism pervading schools did not correspond to their idea of the purpose and nature of schooling.

Conclusion

Despite protests by teachers' unions, parents, students, and concerned citizens, corporate materials and sponsorship—like school-business partnerships—grew in the 1990s and first decade of the new millennium. Advertising in schools appeared in a variety of guises, from incentive programs to one-off special presentations and fitness challenges to science and health classes. Corporate-sponsored materials could be found in the classroom, the hallway, and the washroom stall, the cafeteria, the gym, the playground, and on school buses. Commercialism proliferated in all aspects of students' school experience.

Not only did advertising become more prevalent in schools, but in some cases, it changed in nature. It became increasingly tied to multinational corporations. Fast food and soft drink providers burgeoned. And some companies began to promote their own brand rather than a specific product (as when restaurants or banks promoted literacy).

Proponents justified this activity in a number of ways, including a belief in corporate responsibility and creating community goodwill. While some had a clear aim of creating future customers, many more perceived corporations to be in a good position to help schools in financial need. Equally, not all opponents held identical positions. Some maintained a firm ideological stance against what they saw as the growing stranglehold of consumer culture. Many more were simply wary or uneasy about what seemed like blatant advertising. What opponents would come to discover, however, was that in raising their voices against commercialism in individual schools, they were not only taking on local parents, teachers, administrators, or school board trustees, but also some powerful corporations and a cultural context generally supportive of business involvement in schools. These factors would make successful resistance difficult to achieve.

5

Youth News Network or "You're Nuts to Say No"

The Struggle over Classroom Commercialism

*D*URING the 1999/2000 school year, David Brand, an eighteen-year-old student at Meadowvale Secondary School in Mississauga, participated in "Meadowstock," a competition between student bands from the school. During his band's set, Brand appeared on stage wearing a t-shirt sporting the slogan "YNN Stinks!" After the first song Brand yelled out, "So, what does everyone think of YNN?" In response, the crowd booed. Brand's bassist, Andrew McArthur, quoting the World Wrestling Federation's tag team DX, declared, "I have two words for that!" As if on cue an audience member yelled, "It Sucks!" Almost immediately a staff member cut the power to the guitar amplifiers. As the band walked off the stage, the event's staff sponsor informed them of their immediate disqualification. Brand later wrote,

> What angers me the most about all this is not that we were disqualified; what angers me is that when Mrs. Furzer disqualified us because I spoke my mind on something controversial, she demonstrated to every student in that room that they will be punished for voicing their opinions. When the other students hear about what happened,

the same message will be conveyed to them: school is not the place to have an opinion.[1]

What had Brand and his band done to deserve this silencing? They had waded into an ongoing and messy controversy over the school's decision to sign on to Youth News Network (YNN), a commercial venture to provide news programming in schools across Canada. YNN was the brainchild of Roderick MacDonald, a former organizer for the Manitoba Progressive Conservative Party and talk show host in Montreal, who had been promoting his initiative to Canadian schools since 1990. Inspired by the educational possibilities of television technology, and particularly interactive television, MacDonald defended his enterprise on a number of grounds. It would enable students to produce 20 percent of the news material in order to encourage student interest in local and national affairs, improve students' media literacy, and allow students across the country to communicate with each other. YNN promised to provide schools with the necessary satellites and television equipment. In return, it required schools to sign a contract stipulating that the twelve and a half minutes of programming, including the two and a half minutes of commercials financing the enterprise, would be viewed on 90 percent of school days.[2]

Channel One

MacDonald's initiative followed closely on the heels of a similar venture in the United States. In 1990, after a one-year pilot, Ed Winter and Christopher Whittle launched Channel One: in-school commercial programming consisting of ten minutes of news and two minutes of advertising. On signing a contract to show the programming to 90 percent of students for at least 90 percent of the year, a school received a satellite dish and television equipment valued at up to $50,000 for the duration of the contract. By 1991 Channel One could be found in over 8700 schools in forty-seven states. By the mid-1990s it had secured access to 40 percent of American high school students and could sell a thirty-second advertising spot for $200,000.[3]

Not everyone welcomed this endeavour. Many American educators voiced concern about Channel One because it contributed to the commercialization of schools and pitched its message to a captive audience. For this reason, organizations such as the National Education Association, the American Federation of Teachers, the National PTA, the National Association of State Boards of Education, and the Southern Baptist Convention all issued statements opposing the enterprise. The programming itself attracted strong criticism. Aside from the news, which opponents condemned for being light on daily events and heavy on celebrity updates, weather, and lifestyle issues, the commercials focused prominently on junk food, soft drinks, up-coming movies, video games, and personal hygiene products, and were often presented in a manner that made them appear as public service ads. In 1994 Whittle sold Channel One for $250 million.[4]

The Introduction of Commercial Television in Canadian Schools

In 1990, as Channel One was already drawing significant revenue, MacDonald began testing YNN in thirty-one high schools in the Montreal area. MacDonald and his private investors sank three-quarters of a million dollars into the initial project, co-produced by his private production company and a local television station.[5]

The promotional video consisted of several complete programs that included news clips, public service announcements (such as a "stay in school" segment sponsored by Burger King), and corporate commercials, including advertisements for Coca-Cola and Clearasil. One program, for example, started with the Meech Lake Accord, focusing on the location of Meech Lake and providing a definition of a constitution. It then moved on to a story about Quebec and the environment with a student journalist interviewing a First Nations elder attending a hazardous waste commission meeting in Montreal to defend the environment within his traditional lands. The segment next turned to the town of Duncan, BC, where the municipal council had passed a "no swearing" law. A student journalist asked local high school students their opinion of the new law, with most taking a pro–free speech stance. It then ended with a Clearasil ad. A different program began with a factual description of the goods and services tax being brought in by the Conservative government that year. Next it featured a Westmount High School student in Montreal interviewing a Pulse News reporter about the Meech Lake Accord, with the latter focusing on the "Distinct Society" clause. Student journalists then conducted street interviews demonstrating that most people didn't understand the Accord. This was followed by a Government of Canada–sponsored "stay in school" segment and then a brief interview with a group of high-school students discussing drugs and peer pressure. In order to illustrate the future benefits of YNN, the promotional video also included a segment from Channel One that showed an elementary school student using remote technology to steer an underwater craft, part of a scientific endeavour to chart the ocean floor. It then concluded with endorsements from students, a teacher, and a member of the Laurenval School Board in the Greater Montreal area.[6]

After creating the promotional material, MacDonald began the process of encouraging schools to commit to the network. In part he drew on former school administrators to gain access to school boards: a former head of the Peel Board of Education became the marketing director of YNN; a former chief superintendent in Calgary headed lobbying efforts in Alberta; and a former deputy minister for education in New Brunswick helped obtain contracts in that province.[7] By 1991–92 YNN had secured an agreement with the Laurenval School Board and was negotiating contracts with several Catholic high schools in Edmonton and two high schools in the nearby community of St. Albert. By September 1992 Edmonton's public school board trustees had voted in favour of signing a contract with YNN. The Ottawa Secondary School Board did so several months later.[8]

Before YNN even had a chance to launch its programming, however, it met with significant opposition. With the ink fresh on the Laurenval School Board contract, other associations such as the Montreal Island School Council, the Fédération des commissions scolaires du Québec, and the Baldwin-Cartier School Board raised concerns about the venture. Two key complaints emerged: it contravened school nutrition policies, and it interfered with precious class time. One school located within the jurisdiction of the Laurenval School Board even opted out when teachers there voted against it. In 1993 the Montreal Catholic School Commission, Quebec's largest school board, decided not to use YNN. The Protestant School Board of Greater Montreal took a similar position after a public debate revealed both significant parental concern about the use of children as a captive audience and doubts about the ability of teachers to provide meaningful follow-up to the programming.[9]

Controversy also erupted in Edmonton as various schools began negotiations with YNN. The Alberta Ministry of Education refused to ban YNN. Deputy Minister of Education Reno Bosetti felt that the programming could potentially be worthwhile and commercials would not sway the children. At the same time, the ministry decided not to support the broadcasts during class time, initially arguing that YNN did not fit the curriculum and later that the commercials could not be aired during class time. Still, the minister left it to school boards to decide on the issue.[10] Both teachers' organizations and parents voiced their opposition to the network. Louis LaPointe, president of the Catholic teachers' local within the Alberta Teachers' Association, decried YNN as "sickening."[11] Some parents in Edmonton formed a group called Parents Against Commercial TV in Schools, believing "it's wrong for schools to increase the emphasis on advertising in the lives of children when they should be placing more emphasis on literacy and skills."[12] They also opposed the automated monitoring built into the equipment that, as one reporter noted, "measures time, length and volume of YNN broadcasts to classrooms to gauge the number of students reached by YNN and to determine advertising rates."[13] The group used the municipal election to place pressure on trustees. The combination of public outcry and the ministry statement that YNN could not be played during class time led the Edmonton Public School Board to withdraw from its negotiations with YNN.[14]

As in Alberta, opponents of YNN in Ontario often found that they had to take on the network on a board-by-board basis. In 1992 the Ontario Ministry of Education issued a public statement against compulsory viewing of commercial advertising in schools but noted school boards' legal right to decide YNN's fate.[15] It was thus left to concerned teachers, parents, and citizens to fight the issue once a board indicated that it was going ahead with negotiations. In Ontario, as elsewhere, much of the rhetoric around the introduction of YNN into the classroom focused on the way in which students would become a captive audience. Liz Barkley, president of the Ontario Secondary School Teachers' Federation, nicely summed up this position: "It's using the authority of the classroom to pitch your company."[16]

Across Canada, groups spoke out against YNN. The Canadian Conference of Catholic Bishops proclaimed that Catholic schools should not join the program. Home and School Associations and teachers' unions called on ministries of education to oppose the initiative. The Canadian Association of Media Organizations, formed in 1992 to unite provincial groups focused on media literacy, immediately put its resources toward fighting YNN. These varied associations all opposed a commercial venture's colonization of instructional time in schools and condemned the compulsory viewing of commercials as unethical.[17]

For all the criticism, however, there was also continuing support for the project. Regarding the commercial nature of the venture, Edmonton

Public School Board trustee Joan Cowling stated, "I don't get the feeling that we're abandoning our responsibilities at all.... We're really naïve if we think that we're as pure as the driven snow in keeping advertising out of schools."[18] Others perceived YNN as an opportunity. In Calgary, trustees voted five to one to allow eight schools to sign up for a five-year period if parents and teachers approved. Margaret Lounds, chair of the board of trustees, defended the action on the grounds that the board "has to be open to opportunities that are presented," particularly given the economic climate. A local high school instructional technology expert noted that his school had a fourteen-year-old television monitor that it couldn't afford to replace, making the possibility of new monitors in each classroom particularly alluring.[19] Similarly, Lee Rother, a high school teacher in the Laurenval School Board district, stated "It's going to sound like this is a bribe.... But we don't have the money for that kind of equipment."[20]

School trustees also liked the participatory element of the program. Betty-Ann Kealey, chair of the Ottawa Separate School Board, told a reporter from the *Ottawa Citizen* that "It's a whole philosophy—you try to provide the best program you can, and it looked pretty good.... It's news for kids by kids."[21] Some students also endorsed the program. Steven Fouchard and Julian Celms, in "The Student's Page" of the *Ottawa Citizen*, downplayed the impact of the commercials, writing, "Give us a little credit. When test pilots ran in Montreal, students would simply tune out and then tune in after the commercials, much as we do at home." Moreover, they considered the opportunity to view YNN to be "very attractive." As they explained it,

> While the system will link schools to a national network, it can also be used to great advantage within the school. It provides educational programming from such reputable sources as TV Ontario (TVO) and National Geographic. We were shown an experiment in interactive learning broadcast by Channel One . . . in which students were linked by satellite to an undersea expedition as it happened. YNN has the potential to provide this sort of educational interaction.[22]

All of these rationales formed part of the sales pitch for YNN. As John Fraser, YNN head of marketing put it: "Here's a way business and industry can get involved in supporting the school. Profit's not a dirty word to me, and there is a cost in doing this. Just 2.5 minutes a day for advertising and we're not advertising cigarettes or beer." In her *Financial Post* column, Diane Francis endorsed this position, writing, "Anyone in charge of educating our kids must realize that advertising makes our world go around—and pays their wages. Critics ignore the fact that teachers and students use newspapers and periodicals in their classrooms and libraries as references or teaching tools. And more than 50% of any successful publication's space is filled with ads selling everything from booze to bras. . . . There's no doubt," she continued, "YNN offers budget-strapped schools something for nothing and educators shouldn't look this gift horse in the mouth. . . . Educators can exploit YNN to improve their school. To me, YNN should stand for You're Nuts to say No."[23]

Despite such beliefs, YNN had trouble securing contracts, and by November 1992 MacDonald was looking for a new infusion of cash and a permanent home. Facing negative reaction in his home base of Montreal, he approached the city of Halifax, offering to establish YNN's headquarters there and, in the midst of a recession, promising the creation of 155 jobs if the city built a $2.5-million TV studio that the network could lease and if the province provided at least $5 million in grants and loans. Though city council endorsed the deal, the provincial government turned down the proposal. As a result, MacDonald began looking toward Alberta as a possible base.[24] At this point, YNN disappeared from public view.

A New Push for YNN

In the fall of 1997 YNN made a second attempt to gain access to Canadian schools, launching a twenty-week pilot project in five schools located in three provinces: Alberta, Quebec, and Ontario. Lacking success beyond the pilot stage, over the next several years MacDonald worked to re-establish the financial footing for his plan. In 1998 YNN re-emerged as Athena Educational Partners Inc., a subsidiary of Telescene Film Group, a production company based in Montreal. Telescene now envisioned not only a national school television network but, once the equipment was installed, the possibility of expanding plans to include a large-scale distance learning venture. Telescene expected YNN to generate 80 percent of its revenue through advertising.[25]

In 1998 Athena Educational Partners (AEP) launched a new pilot project in Meadowvale Secondary School in Mississauga, Ontario, part of the Peel District School Board. As a test case, the school received over $200,000 worth of equipment, including a satellite dish and twenty-five computers. AEP then initiated a marketing campaign with the intent of securing a full network by fall 1999. Emulating the approach of Channel One, it offered not only free equipment but also maintenance of the technology and technological training for teachers. In order to fend off criticism about the commercial nature of YNN, it also established an advisory board to assess the educational and advertising content of the programming. And it hired Les McLean, professor emeritus at the Ontario Institute for Studies in Education, to provide an independent assessment of the endeavour.[26] Whereas in 1992 MacDonald had pitched YNN to school boards, in this round he went directly to school principals, who, as one newspaper reporter commented, were less beholden to parents and taxpayers.[27] Moreover, the company hired the public relations firm Hill and Knowlton, one of the largest in the world and one that previously had placed its weight behind the tobacco industry, spin-doctored support for the Gulf War, and sanitized the reputation of several governments accused of human rights violations.[28]

In many jurisdictions, educators and concerned citizens once again reacted swiftly to MacDonald's initiatives. In February 1999 the Conference of Catholic Bishops reaffirmed its opposition to the programming, closing the doors of Ontario Catholic schools to YNN. Numerous teachers' unions, home and school associations, and media education organizations publicly opposed the venture. So did citizens' groups such as the Canadian Centre for Policy Alternatives (CCPA) and the Council of Canadians, as well as political parties such as the Ontario Liberals and NDP.[29] By spring 1999, New Brunswick, British Columbia, and Nova Scotia had all rejected the network. In Manitoba, the issue became part of the 1999 election campaign. Gary Doer, the provincial NDP leader, promised to ban commercial sponsorship in classrooms if elected, which would terminate YNN's agreements with eight schools. After winning the election, he informed those schools that they should not sign up after the trial period.[30]

Still, during the first few months of 2000, YNN began trial broadcasts in six schools in five provinces: Alberta, Saskatchewan, Manitoba, Ontario, and Newfoundland.[31] In provinces where individual school boards held the power to decide YNN's fate, the network continued to make headway. This was the case in Saskatchewan, for instance, where seven rural schools signed up.[32] A number of principals found the package attractive enough that they were willing to change the daily schedule to accommodate the programming outside of curriculum time: one school began the day five minutes early and shortened lunch break; another eliminated the afternoon break between classes. By June, fourteen schools were connected to the YNN network. Many more proved interested but YNN did not have the necessary equipment for expansion.[33]

The programming during the pilot project in the early months of 2000 consisted of ninety-five episodes composed of news, public service messages, and commercials. It was much faster-paced and had a hipper style than that offered in 1992. Each episode featured two young Telescene actors covering two stories (one current event and one general interest topic such as job-hunting or self-esteem), who relayed the details and then elicited opinions from students and experts. This was followed by news clips or updates on previous stories, a public service ad, a pop quiz related to the content, and student feedback. Advertisers included "Clear Speech Works (computer software), CMT (country music television), Long and McQuade (musical instruments), Trident (chewing gum), AT&T/Rogers (pagers), United Against Racism [a nonprofit], and the CRB Foundation Heritage Project [later known at the Historica Dominion Institute]."[34]

A typical program, one of the first, featured a piece on a Montreal rally organized by the Canadian Jewish Council to bring attention to the recent electoral success of Jörg Haider, the anti-Semitic leader of the Austrian Freedom Party, and to protest the actions of the more mainstream Austrian People's Party, which had formed a coalition government with Haider's party. The report captured highlights of the rally, showing speakers who compared the formation of the new coalition government to Hitler's rise in power, followed by interviews by student journalists of youth involved in the event. That segment closed with two ads, one for CMT and the other for Long and McQuade. Next came a positive report on the return of sacred artifacts to the Blackfoot nation by the province of Alberta and then a Canadian Heritage moment about Jennie Trout's experience of sexism as one of the first female medical students in Canada. The program ended with a pop quiz on the name of the UNESCO World Heritage site outside Fort McLeod, Alberta—a tie-in to the previous feature on Blackfoot artifacts.[35]

Most of the programming followed this general pattern. Les McLean, YNN's independent evaluator, noted that as the pilot program continued the news features became "shorter and less frequent," with more time being devoted to a single topic and to pop quizzes. In addition, the short messages on social advocacy were gradually replaced by longer ones on topics such as drug abuse, condom use for protection against HIV, and prostitution.[36] The CCPA asked several media literacy specialists to analyze a few of the broadcasts. They found that "at best, the broadcasts were somewhat simplistic, and avoided deeper contextual analysis. At worst, they provided commentary that was leading, and not entirely balanced in exploring alternative perspectives." As an example, they cited a program on Cuba stating that Cubans were frustrated with Castro and desired economic independence and an end to their poverty, but did not mention that Cubans had universal health care and education or that the US blockade had contributed to poverty on the island.[37]

Whatever the benefits or limits of the programming, however, in general neither support for nor opposition to YNN mentioned the actual content material. Instead, debates raged over the commercial nature of the venture, particularly the presence of advertising, teachers' loss of control of classroom time, and corporate intrusion into the classroom.

Renewed Conflict

Opposition to YNN manifested itself in a variety of ways. Two examples, one from Lester B. Pearson School Board in Montreal and the other from Meadowvale Secondary School in Mississauga, Ontario, are particularly illustrative. In Montreal, the controversy took the form of a pitched battle between the minister of education and the school board. In June 1999 Lester B. Pearson School Board voted to allow YNN programming in three locations: Hudson, Beaconsfield, and Macdonald high schools. The chair of the central parents' committee stated that the proposal had overwhelming support from the teachers in those schools while Marcus Tabachnick, the chair of the board, claimed that the governing councils of those schools all supported the programming. Three trustees voted against the proposal, which also met opposition from the president of the Pearson teachers' union as well as from some individual teachers. The approval or rejection of YNN fell within the rights of the school board. However, Quebec Minister of Education François Legault opposed the presence of YNN in classrooms and ordered an internal review of YNN programming. The Education Act prohibited school boards from accepting money, be it a gift or a grant, if that money was in any way tied to commercial solicitation. The review determined that YNN contravened the Act, ostensibly halting the deal between YNN and the Pearson School Board in its tracks. Yet Legault faced the ire of school board officials, who claimed that the decision infringed upon the Board's autonomy. Moreover, Tabachnick argued that there was little difference between YNN and other accepted business endeavours such as Scholastic Books. To sidestep the problem the Lester B. Pearson School Board established a verbal agreement with YNN that programming would only be aired if it included federally sponsored announcements rather than commercial advertising.[38]

The board's actions did not appease Legault, who in September 1999 issued new guidelines to address the debate that had emerged over YNN. Those guidelines, the Montreal *Gazette* reported, prohibited schools from accepting donations where "persons at the school will be subjected to commercial solicitation and encouraged to purchase certain goods or services." Also, while a sponsor could be named, that name could not be accompanied by a logo because "a logo that is very familiar to young people, as small as it may be, may nevertheless incite them to purchase the coveted object."[39] Legault's tenacity on the issue eventually led the school board to drop the project.

While in Quebec the Pearson School Board faced the ire of its minister of education, in the case of Meadowvale, it was parents, students, and teachers who sounded the alarm. In June 1999, despite the controversy surrounding YNN, Meadowvale signed on to the network at the conclusion of its pilot project. In doing so, Janet McDougald, chairperson of the Peel District School Board, told journalist Margaret Wente, "We're supportive of corporate partnerships in general." According to Wente, McDougald saw television advertising as an extension of corporate material that had long pervaded schools: "I don't think we can be naïve enough to think the business world is not interested in attracting young people to their product. It's a matter of personal preference whether you think one logo is more intrusive than another."[40]

As the introductory story about the silencing of David Brand's band indicates, what is most notable at Meadowvale was the attempt by school officials to curtail protest against the programming. Brand and his band were not the only ones to experience the heavy hand of school administrators. The previous year the principal had threatened Lindsay Porter, another student at the school, with suspension after she published and distributed an underground newspaper criticizing YNN, even though her activities occurred off-campus. According to students and teachers, the climate within the school discouraged discussion or criticism of YNN. Once the programming commenced in January 2000, students who did not wish to view it could opt out after writing a paragraph explaining their decision and gaining parental consent. They were then forced to sit in silence at a library carrel for the fifteen minutes of programming.[41] Students and parents reported feeling that the process aimed to discourage opting out and that those who did so were "ostracized and treated unfairly."[42] During the same period, a school superintendent told a parent who was also a teacher in the district that she could not cross Meadowvale school property while she was involved in a campaign against YNN.[43]

Members of Athena Educational Partners, along with some school authorities, also attempted to silence parents and community critics. During the 1998–99 school year the parent-run school council supported the pilot project. Indeed, in her update to the Peel District School Board on the progress of the pilot program, Principal Laurie Pedwell "described her school community's overall reaction as being extremely positive."[44] Opponents recalled a different version of events. One parent reported that they found council unwilling to hear their concerns. When parents opposed to YNN were elected to council the next year, the "meetings became a battleground."[45]

The issue came to a head at Meadowvale in March 2000. It was inflamed, however, by events elsewhere. Even as protests began to be heard at Meadowvale, MacDonald continued to encourage other school districts to support his project. In February 2000, he attended a public meeting about YNN held in Lively, Ontario, a community outside Sudbury and part of the Rainbow District School Board. Several months earlier the principal of Lively District Secondary School reported to the board his intention to pursue a contract with YNN. As a result, the board held an open meeting in order to solicit public opinion. After showing a sample of the programming, MacDonald explained the virtues of the venture. While some supporters of YNN attended the meeting, the reaction was generally hostile. Parents and students voiced their criticisms. So too did the Ontario Secondary School Teachers' Federation (OSSTF) district president and Erika Shaker, education director with the CCPA, who had flown in from Ottawa. A show of hands indicated general opposition to the idea of YNN in the classroom. As a result, the board decided to delay a decision on the matter until the summer.[46]

Soon after, the school council at Meadowvale organized its own information session for parents. Members of the Canadian Association of Media Education Organizations (CAMEO), OSSTF, and the Canadian Teachers' Federation (CTF) also attended. Parents voiced sufficient anger and frustration to convince Principal Pedwell to adjourn the meeting. Parent Mark

Goldstein stated, "This is the first meeting we've ever had on YNN and I'm afraid it's a fait accompli."[47] Pedwell, along with officials from Athena Educational Partners (AEP), reportedly blamed the disintegration of the meeting on "outside agitators."[48] In May 2000 AEP initiated a lawsuit targeting four vocal critics of YNN (two parents of students at the school, one teacher from the district, and the former liberal candidate for the area) as well as a local group, People Against Commercial Television in Schools, requesting $900,000 in damages from each party. AEP accused its critics of defamation resulting in financial losses. The lawsuit effectively silenced those critics.[49]

Despite the various attempts by school authorities and AEP to clamp down on criticism, in late May 2000, about fifty students from Meadowvale initiated their own protest by walking out of school during the fifteen-minute period in which YNN was usually shown. On the same day, the vice-president of marketing of Athena Educational Partners announced that the commercial advertising on YNN would be replaced by sponsored public service announcements—a change intended to indicate that the company was willing to compromise on issues raised by critics who "are rational and make some sense."[50] Athena's change in strategy reflected the deep divisions over their programming. At Meadowvale, 43 percent of students believed the school should eliminate YNN, 27 percent were unsure, and 30 percent were in favour of keeping it. Division also existed among teachers, with 36 percent in support of the venture, 42 percent unsure, and 22 percent opposed. Interestingly, 77 percent of parents supported YNN. Despite all the concerns raised, the Peel District School Board went on to renew its contract with AEP. In the end, however, MacDonald ran out of money, and the venture folded in 2001.[51]

The End of YNN

Why did YNN fail? There are several plausible answers to this question. First, while YNN attempted to emulate Channel One, by the early 1990s there was already a significant body of influential criticism of the American project that was available to Canadian educators and concerned citizens. Studies of Channel One reported little difference in knowledge gained about current events between those students who did or who did not watch the programming. Even a 1993 University of Michigan study commissioned by Channel One found the programming to be of little

Student protest over YNN at Meadowvale Secondary School, Mississauga, Ontario.
Photo: Frank Calleja/*Toronto Star*/Getty Images.

educational significance.⁵² If the programming had little impact, the ads proved deleterious. In his study of two hundred Grade 9 high school students in central Missouri, cultural critic Roy Fox realized that students "found many ways to embrace commercials, to trust them, to view advertisers' motives in a positive, trusting way."⁵³ He discovered that students used the commercials as entertainment, acting them out with each other as well as relaying them to siblings and parents at home; that they used the ads as a means of peer bonding; and that they drew on them as a resource, writing them into class assignments. He noted too that Channel One sold products that were available in school vending machines—soft drinks, juices, chocolate bars, and candy. Other studies showed that schools signing up with Channel One tended to be located in poorer districts with less money for instructional material.⁵⁴ Some American states that banned YNN, or reduced funding for schools employing it, questioned "the legality of selling student time in exchange for free television equipment."⁵⁵ Thus, by the time YNN attempted its 1998 launch, Canadians opposed to the initiative could draw on a significant body of literature criticizing Channel One and look to the lead of American activists against commercial television in schools. And, unlike in the US, they could do so before the programming became entrenched within the school system.

Second, Canadian critics also seemed to have broad public support behind them. For example, an Environics poll conducted on behalf of the Canadian Teachers' Federation in 2000 showed that 92 percent of those surveyed disapproved of advertising on televisions or computers during the school day.⁵⁶ Nothing appeared in Canadian assessments of YNN that might sway public opinion. Canadian reports on YNN came to conclusions similar to those reached in the United States. The study undertaken by the Peel District School Board suggested that "the impact of YNN is neither as positive as its strongest supporters claim, nor as negative as its strongest detractors imply."⁵⁷ Still, it concluded that "exposing students to daily news did not increase students' interest in local and world events, or motivate them to attend to news more often."⁵⁸ Neither teachers nor students felt that students had learnt very much from watching YNN. This was likely in part because 41 percent of teachers did not discuss YNN material with students at all, while most others did not connect the programming to classroom content.⁵⁹ Les McLean, YNN's own evaluator, noted the same problem, finding that teachers made little use of the programming. For example, social science teachers, who might have been best placed to use the newscasts, found them unhelpful because in most cases the programming came on right before students moved to their next class. Nor did the company provide any guidelines or tips on how to use the material. As McLean described the broadcasts, "They have been an add-on, to be tolerated because of the technology but not given any attention by almost all teachers."[60]

Finally, another reason for the failure of YNN may have been financial. Both Erika Shaker and Andrew Nikiforuk have argued that one reason MacDonald had more difficulty inserting YNN into schools than did Channel One is that Canadian school systems are better funded than many of those in the US and that there is less discrepancy between school districts.[61] Of the five schools he examined, Les McLean noted that "the computer laboratory provided by YNN was welcome everywhere, but in only two schools did it make an important difference in the education of the students. The other schools already had adequate computer resources and access to the Internet."[62] MacDonald may also have found it more difficult to gain startup and sponsorship money for his enterprise. Corporations tend to shy away from negative publicity, and the vocal public criticism may well have reduced corporate interest in sponsoring the project. In addition, YNN's shift to sponsored public service announcements in place of direct advertising likely proved less attractive to corporations.

Ultimately it is difficult to determine whether protest against YNN succeeded in halting the venture or whether YNN failed as money dried up. Likely it was some combination of the two. MacDonald initiated the project at a time when the tide against corporate intrusion was high. YNN became a very specific and obvious target upon which activists and educators could focus their attention. Nor did there seem to be broad public support for this type of blatant commercialism imposed during class time.

Conclusion

The public debate over YNN centred on whether children should be held captive to advertising in schools and whether commercialism is harmful to children. While critics condemned the advertising that children would be subjected to, proponents either downplayed its effects or accepted it as an unfortunate cost. Advertising in schools was often seen as no more than what children would be exposed to at home. Indeed, MacDonald continually reiterated this belief about students and advertising: "When a commercial comes on, they recognize it in five seconds and they'll talk to their friends, they do the same thing as they do at home."[63] Still, if the commercials had no impact or were completely ignored, why, one might ask, would corporations bother to insert their advertising in YNN programming?

What is clear is that opponents of the venture expended enormous energy fighting its introduction into Canadian schools. The battle to prevent YNN from gaining permanent access to Canadian classrooms proved to be one of the more successful in which educators and concerned citizens confronted the increasing prevalence of commercialism in the education system. Yet, they had to do so continuously over a decade before the venture failed. Without strong provincial policies, such ventures could pop up over and over again. As the next chapter will show, the fight against commercialism in schools was often beyond the means of local parent groups, teachers' unions, or nonprofit public policy organizations.

6

Building Brand Loyalty

Vending Machines, Fast Food Outlets, and Junk Food

*I*N SEPTEMBER 2003, Cindi Seddon, the new principal of Pitt River Middle School in Port Coquitlam, British Columbia, introduced healthy food into her school cafeteria. Gone were the "McDonald's burgers and fries, KFC and Pizza Hut." Instead, the new menu consisted of "fresh sandwiches, bagels, macaroni and cheese, fruit and milk." In the school's vending machines, Seddon replaced chocolate bars and pop with granola bars and juice. Despite support from staff and parents, and to the shock of the parent advisory council, Coquitlam school district officials soon overruled and reversed these efforts. The district had piloted the idea of school food courts in 1999 and expanded the program thereafter. In doing so, district administrators claimed jurisdiction over school cafeteria policies.[1]

How did junk food become so readily available in schools? It seems that process occurred incrementally. School reformers introduced lunch facilities in the early to mid-twentieth century amid worries about student health, and as more students spent the whole day away from home. In the 1920s and 1930s teachers, dieticians, and health officers in many rural areas attempted to set up regular hot lunch days or programs so that children would receive hot cocoa or soup to supplement packed lunches.[2] During that period, but even more so in the next two decades, cafeterias became more common as a result of a number of phenomena, including school consolidation, longer distances commuted between home and school, refurbishment and modernization of older schools, and construction of new schools to accommodate the baby boom. Educators thus came to see lunchrooms as key elements of their plans to provide a hot, full-service meal.[3]

Cafeteria managers, however, faced the daunting prospect of providing food to students quickly and cheaply. They soon discovered that many children used the cafeteria only as a means to supplement their homemade lunches. The results were often disheartening. In 1976 William Shaver, principal of Glenview Senior Public School in Toronto, noted that with the failure of their hot lunch program his school had gone from providing healthy meals to junk food. As Shaver explained,

> We switched to a system of supplementing what a child brought from home by offering soup and a few desserts. In three or four years this had grown to six beverages, four or five different kinds of ice cream, potato chips, cheesies, popcorn and six or seven varieties of cake and candies.[4]

Cafeteria management dilemmas were not the only factor in increasing children's access to less nutritious food. In the 1940s and early 1950s, the dairy industry introduced chocolate milk into school milk programs, thus offering students a substitute for the more nutritious but less exciting white milk. By at least the 1970s many home and school associations had turned to monthly pizza or hot dog days as school fundraisers.[5] By the 1980s vending machines filled with soft drinks also made their appearance, becoming fairly common in high schools.[6]

This infiltration of less nutritious food into schools did not go unnoticed. Even as the dairy industry introduced chocolate milk, trustees in London, Ontario, and Montreal worked to ban its sale. The issue resulted in several years of debate at the Toronto Board of Education. Recognizing its less nutritious value, by 1949 that Board had in place a policy of selling chocolate milk for a higher price than white milk to discourage sales of the former. In May 1953 the Board's finance committee passed a motion to ban the beverage, an action delayed by the Board as a whole after a presentation by the Canadian Dairy Industry Suppliers' Association that emphasized the "hardship the move would have on the industry." The Board finally approved a ban later that year.[7] But it was really in the 1970s, with the growth of the health food movement, that newspaper reports about unhealthy school food appeared more frequently. In North America, many nutritionists, parents, and concerned citizens raised the issue of junk food in school vending machines and cafeterias. Individual concerns gained political clout in 1975 when the American nonprofit Center for Science in the Public Interest (established in 1971) launched a campaign to eliminate junk food from vending machines.[8]

Early to the mark, Montreal elementary and secondary schools prohibited the sale of junk food in school cafeterias in 1974. In addition, they subsidized the cost of healthier meals. In 1977, the Etobicoke Board of Education removed chocolate bars and soft drinks from school cafeterias. By the early 1980s, Ontario's York Region District School Board had introduced a two-year nutrition program that both directed food service companies to place greater emphasis on healthier food by, for example, only serving fries twice a week, and subsidized healthier fare.[9] Such change did not occur easily. At the Toronto Board of Education, for instance, the school programs committee recommended that items such as "pop, taco chips, potato chips, doughnut-type foods, packaged cakes and cookies" be removed from cafeterias. While some trustees argued that the cost of such a ban would close down cafeterias, others insisted that was not a good enough reason "to justify selling harmful foods." In 1978, after a series of rancorous meetings, the Board finally voted to eliminate chips and pop from high school cafeterias.[10]

The movement for healthier food in schools gained traction within the broader political culture. In the mid-1970s Marc Lalonde, the Minister of National Health and Welfare, issued a report based on a Nutrition Canada survey undertaken between 1970 and 1972 that drew attention to a new health concern—the growing numbers of overweight Canadians. Lalonde voiced support for a preventative health strategy that included higher taxes on junk food.[11] By the early 1980s, provincial ministries of health began reinforcing school nutrition projects. In one Ontario case, the Ministries of Health and Education provided plaques and $1,000 cheques to student councils in "schools most effectively presenting a nutrition program during the year."[12] Moreover, catering companies embraced the political turn toward healthier fare. VS Services Ltd., for instance, secured a contract with the Peel District School Board by developing a program promoting healthy food, something the company hoped would allow them to "realize our market share objective."[13]

Parents, too, encouraged this attention to providing healthy food. For example, the Health and Nutrition Committee of the New Brunswick Federation of Home and School Associations put forward a circular at its 1980 annual meeting "emphasizing the dangers of junk foods," urging principals to eliminate vending machines, and requesting the Department of Education to develop a provincial response. Such demands reflected actions taken at the local level such as that by parents at Grand Manan Elementary School to establish a "health food cart three days per week... to discourage the children from eating 'junk food.'"[14]

Despite these efforts, unhealthy food became widespread in schools. Some school districts did not enforce the policies on their books while others simply ignored the issue.[15] By the 1990s an unhealthy foodscape existed within a great many school districts—a situation that corporations keenly seized upon.

Building Brand Loyalty: Big Food Sets Its Sights on Schools

In the 1990s, as companies searched for new markets and school boards faced continuing financial cuts, the nature and presence of unhealthy food in schools changed substantially. Whereas individual schools had once signed contracts with a particular bottler or vending machine supplier, some school boards began signing multi-million-dollar contracts that pertained to the whole district and often did so behind closed doors. Some districts also began to turn to fast food franchises in order to rejuvenate their cafeterias.

In 1994 the Toronto Board of Education signed a deal with Pepsi-Cola Canada Beverages Ltd. that would pay the board $1.14 million over three years for Pepsi's exclusive right to place its products in school vending machines. As one of the first school boards in Canada to enter into such an agreement, it set the trend for the next two decades.[16] One by one, school boards across Canada faced pressure to join this movement. Not surprisingly, a 2006 survey of commercialism in schools found Coca-Cola and Pepsi to be "the two most prominent corporations in schools," with ads appearing on "scoreboards, clocks, beverage machines... banners, school signs and gym equipment."[17]

In some places this was a process aided by marketing executives. In 1995, Dale Boniface, president of Spectrum Marketing and a former

Leo Hayes High School name sign, Fredericton, New Brunswick, 2018. Photo by author.

employee with Coca-Cola, not only brought the possibility of an exclusivity contract with that company to the attention of the administration at the University of British Columbia (UBC) but then brokered that deal. Spectrum Marketing went on to represent municipalities and universities in similar negotiations across Canada. School districts also began to employ the company to negotiate deals on their behalf. In 1999, both the Maple Ridge-Pitt Meadows and Mission school districts in British Columbia agreed to pay Spectrum its usual fee, an estimated 15 percent commission on sales, once the company had secured a ten-year contract with Coke. University administrators and school boards turned to Spectrum because of Boniface's insider knowledge and their belief that even with the commission, Spectrum could broker a significantly better contract for them than they could on their own. As negotiations began, Coke announced it would no longer negotiate with third parties because, according to one report, all monies should go directly to schools. Despite this blatant attempt to cut out intermediaries, the school boards maintained Spectrum's services, though at a reduced rate of 8 percent as the marketing firm took on an advisory role.[18]

While school board negotiations constituted one trend in the 1990s, another was a move toward secret agreements. The UBC deal raised eyebrows not only because of its exclusivity but also because the university would not release the details of the contract.[19] Two of the largest school boards in Ontario, York Region and Peel District, similarly refused to provide information about their deals. Critics argued that, as public institutions, schools and their boards should be financially accountable to taxpayers, who should have a right to scrutinize the terms of contracts and how money is spent. School boards and soft drink companies frequently claimed that releasing this information would damage their competitive advantage and reduce the ability of both parties to enter into the best agreements.[20] Nor did all administrators believe that schools needed to respond to public concerns. Despite a New Brunswick policy in 2000 requiring transparency regarding fundraising, the principal of Oromocto High School, which had a contract with Coke, bluntly proclaimed, "I really don't feel it is necessary that we should sit here and tell you how much money Oromocto High School receives from any one of our sponsors; that's not the kind of agreements we have with our sponsors."[21]

As school boards began to sign exclusive soft drink contracts, some commentators wondered what would be next. A 1994 editorial in the *London Free Press* asked, "And if Pepsi, why not school lunch rooms run by McDonald's or Burger King?"[22] In fact, this process was already underway. Some American schools turned to fast food franchises as early as the 1970s.[23] Canadian schools embraced this trend more slowly, but in 1993 the Etobicoke Board of Education allowed its schools to introduce such kiosks.[24] As with Coke and Pepsi, the entry of fast food franchises into school cafeterias formed part of corporate efforts to secure consumers for the long term. Discussing the situation in British Columbia in 1998, Gerry Lev, president of Subway Developments for that province, commented, "Non-traditional locations are the way to go.... It won't be too long before you see Subway [sandwich] outlets in high schools here."[25] Indeed, a year later Terry Fox Secondary School, in the Vancouver suburb of Port Coquitlam, became the first in the region to introduce franchises such as Subway, Pizza Hut, Great Canadian Bagel, and Kentucky Fried Chicken.[26] In 2003, voicing what corporate leaders, advertisers, and marketeers had long known, John Alm, CEO of Coca-Cola Enterprises Inc., defended the sale of soft drinks in schools by baldly stating that "the school system is where you build brand loyalty."[27]

"The Thin Edge of the Wedge": Debating Big Food

In the 1990s and 2000s, supporters championed exclusivity contracts as a means of securing significant pots of money. In 2003 individual high schools with contracts could raise $20,000 to $30,000 a year.[28] In Vancouver, Kitsilano Secondary earned about $110,000 on a five-year contract with Coke, and Killarney Secondary, $100,000 on a three-year contract with Pepsi. Individual elementary schools brought in significantly less. At East Chilliwack Elementary School, the Parent Advisory Council stocked Pepsi products and received between $200 and $300 a month. Eastwood Public School in Windsor received $200 every three months from its Coke supplier. Schools in catchments that signed agreements by district may well have seen their revenue increase substantially. For example, the school district for Maple Ridge-Pitt Meadows received $75,000 to $80,000 from sales in its five high schools in 1999 and an estimated $160,000 a year later under an exclusivity contract.[29] In large school boards, where deals made headlines, the revenues seemed staggering. Toronto's 1994 agreement with Pepsi garnered significant public attention for its contract that promised $1.14 million over three years. The Peel District School Board signed a ten-year agreement with Coke in 2000 estimated at $14 million. And in the first years of the twenty-first century, the York Region School Board brokered an estimated $3.7 million, five-year deal with Pepsi that immediately put $700,000 into their coffers simply for installing Pepsi machines.[30]

What these figures mean is difficult to assess. Initial reports indicate that such arrangements helped cover cafeteria costs. Norbert Hartmann, the Toronto School Board's superintendent of business in 1994, suggested that the contract with Pepsi allowed the board to sell milk at cost and fresh fruit at a reasonable price. In some cases, these deals also brought in additional revenue. In that same year, a report on Etobicoke noted that in the first year of the agreement about $30,000 had been turned over to student councils, with 10 percent of the money from vending machine revenue and 4 percent from fast food kiosks. At Terry Fox Secondary School in Port Coquitlam, cafeteria revenue reportedly jumped from $300 to $1,400 a day.[31]

Still, the year the Toronto School Board signed its agreement, it needed to reduce its $647 million budget by $25 million. Thus $1.14 million over three years was but a drop in the bucket in terms of generating revenue.

Similarly, in Maple Ridge-Pitt Meadows the revenue from the estimated $160,000 contract with Coke occurred during a year when the school board figured it faced a $2 million shortfall. The Toronto School Board estimated that its 1994 deal would net about $3 per student—a fairly small amount.[32] While deals with Big Food could not begin to cover the huge shortfalls encountered by school boards at the turn of the century, however, schools had become increasingly reliant on junk food sales, whether through exclusive contracts or not, for sustaining and growing extracurricular programs. As a result, reaction to such arrangements was often mixed.

School trustees justified the negotiation of contracts with soft drink and fast food companies in a variety of ways. They argued that these deals made up for lost revenue after what boards and unions claimed were several decades of provincial cuts. Soft drink funds provided money for items considered necessary for extracurricular activities such as sport team uniforms and electronic scoreboards, as well as for such things as library books, computers, and "fine arts, early literacy, and gifted programs," all of which fell outside the scope of the traditional core curriculum.[33] That position proved useful to corporate executives. Ron McEachern, CEO of Pepsi-Cola Canada, stated of the 1994 agreement with the Toronto Board of Education, "An initiative like this demonstrates the fruitfulness of enterprising innovative partnerships between the public and private sectors. Regarding Canadian education, we are proud to be part of the solution."[34]

Some trustees ideologically supported the financial assistance that private enterprise could provide to schools. David Moll, the Toronto school board chair at the time of the 1994 Pepsi deal, was among the most enthusiastic: "Some people say this is the thin edge of the wedge—well, I say I hope it is. . . . If someone wants to pay us to give us computers, that sounds good to me. Step right up."[35] In other cases, trustees justified the decision on the grounds of providing a desired service to their constituency. In 2003, Holly Butterfield, chair of the Coquitlam school board, defended its support for school food courts not only on financial grounds but also on the basis that students and parents wanted variety in their cafeterias.[36] Others perceived board negotiations with corporations as a beneficial extension of existing practices at individual schools: by representing all of the schools collectively a board would be able to increase the bargaining power of each unit and thus broker the best contract possible. In explaining the introduction of fast food franchises in her school district, a Coquitlam school district community services co-ordinator told a reporter from the *Vancouver Sun* that the district regarded the practice as simply an extension of elementary school hot dog days.[37]

In many cases, school trustees and administrators viewed both types of agreements—those with soft drink companies and those with fast food franchises—as a means to stem the financial hemorrhaging of school cafeterias. Whether the claim of overall cuts was real or not, there was no question that the cafeterias themselves were hurting. Before turning to fast food kiosks, the Etobicoke Board of Education posted a loss in cafeteria costs of $80,000. Similarly, in the late 1990s administrators in the Coquitlam school district contemplated shutting down their cafeterias as a cost-saving measure. School cafeterias faced a number of problems. The custom of bringing lunch from home continued; some students never ate in the cafeteria while others used it only to supplement their lunch, rather than buying a full meal. In Etobicoke, for example, only 30 to 35 percent of students regularly bought lunch from the cafeteria, resulting in low financial returns.[38] Another reason for underuse was the generally poor quality of cafeteria food. Cafeterias also had to compete with local, off-campus vendors. Especially in urban centres, students flowed out of schools at lunchtime to nearby fast-food restaurants or stores such as 7-Eleven. School administrators and trustees thus justified the turn to fast food franchises on the grounds that students preferred such food, private enterprise would be able to offer more choice more profitably, and having these outlets on school grounds would be safer for students.[39]

Contracts with Big Food, however, did not proceed without controversy or protest. School trustees certainly recognized the potential for conflict. Minutes of the Etobicoke Board of Education, for example, indicate that the discussions about changes to cafeterias occurred behind closed doors, in private sessions of meetings of the whole board. Newspaper reports indicate that across the country board meetings on the topic led to extended and confrontational discussions.[40] Trustees also faced the ire of other groups. Teachers' unions proved formidable opponents. Barbara Sargent, president of the Federation of Women Teachers' Associations of Ontario, denounced the 1994 Toronto School Board deal with Pepsi, calling for the cancellation of the contract. Similarly, Kathleen Thomson, president of the Coquitlam Teachers' Association, spoke out against the introduction of fast food franchises in BC school cafeterias.[41] Some unions began their own investigations of commercialism in schools, carrying out surveys, writing reports that they then publicized widely, and demanding bans on junk food in schools.[42]

Students and parents also quickly organized themselves. Protests against the 1994 Toronto deal saw students marching on the board's downtown headquarters, and teachers and parents attended a school board meeting to request that trustees reconsider their decision. They did so again in 2000 and 2004, as the Toronto District School Board considered new contracts with Pepsi-Cola, in both cases requesting delays on votes until wider public consultations had taken place.[43] Such actions were not unusual. When the Maple Ridge-Pitt Meadows school district was considering an exclusive deal with a soft drink company, students involved in the school club Youth for Environmental and Social Justice expressed their discontent at the local school board meeting.[44]

Members of the public also agitated against the secrecy of many of the contracts. This was true for individual schools as well as for school boards. At Walter Murray Collegiate in Saskatoon, where the principal accepted a confidential agreement with Coke on behalf of his school, parents and students expressed their anger over the process. "The school institutions are paid for by taxpayers' funds so we have a right to know the terms of these contracts," one parent argued. "How does the principal account for this money collected from the company?"[45] The principal responded to a two-hundred-name student petition with intransigence. As a result, some students took to selling juice boxes as an alternative, with the money raised donated to charity. Joe Rubin, a senior at the school, told the local newspaper, "I don't agree with these contracts at all and I thought that this would be an interesting way to protest—by providing a healthier alternative at a lower price from a company which isn't Coke."[46]

One of the most prominent cases was that of Nicholas Dodds, a Grade 8 student who protested the ten-year contract with Coca-Cola signed in 2000 by the Peel District School Board by taking his complaint to the Information and Privacy Commissioner of Ontario. Reflecting on the reasons for his actions, Dodds recounted:

> I thought that's not right.... Students are not in schools so that they can be used as a captive audience.... They're not there to be marketed to. I go to a public school. I'm affected by this deal between the board and the company, but somehow I'm denied the right to know what's fully happening in the school.[47]

In 2003 Dodds won his case, forcing the board to open its books. His actions and similar ones elsewhere revealed that deals with soft drink companies were based on projected sales, with cash received tied to specific consumption quotas. If boards did not meet those quotas, the contracts would be extended for several years with no further payment until the quota was met.[48] In essence, the contracts directly encouraged soft drink consumption.

Critics also raised concerns about the potential reduction of freedom of speech resulting from exclusivity contracts. An oft-cited case occurred in the US in March 1998 when students at Greenbrier High School in Evans, Georgia, participated in a number of activities during its Coke Education Day, including wearing red and white clothing and forming a human chain (or billboard) to make the word "Coke." As a photographer took pictures, one student, Mike Cameron, revealed his Pepsi T-shirt, an action that landed him a one-day suspension.[49] A similar event occurred in 2000 in Abbotsford, BC, where a marketing teacher developed a project in which students learned to run a business by selling a product in the school for a week. Some students decided to sell Jones Soda. A Coke representative saw the posters for the product and complained to the vice-principal, who then ordered that the posters be removed. Ultimately the Coke public affairs manager for Western Canada declared the issue a misunderstanding, stating it had no problem with the project. By that time, however, the school's contract with Coke had interfered with the teaching of the marketing class.[50]

Students also spoke out against the belief that fast food was all teenagers wanted to eat. In a letter to the editor of the *Globe and Mail*, Peter Simeon, a student at Martingrove Collegiate Institute in Etobicoke, Ontario, responded to the headline "Board Caters to Teen-age Tastes" with a letter headlined, "Nothing could be further from the truth." He wrote, "Student responses to perpetual Pizza Pizza has [sic] not been 'positive,'" as claimed in the article. Rather, he argued, students eat what is available.[51] Some students who testified before a BC provincial legislative committee stated that they bought junk food because it was cheaper and more available than healthier options. They argued for the need for greater selection, including vegetarian fare, as well as access to fridges and microwaves in order to store and re-heat homemade foods.[52] Heightened awareness of debates about healthy food in schools also led to new forms of student activism. In 2007, three sixteen-year-old students at Bluefield High School in Hampshire, Prince Edward Island, all members of a healthy eating committee and recent attendees at a symposium sponsored by the Eastern School District's Healthy Eating Alliance, spearheaded a shift to stock vending machines with healthy products.[53]

Implications for Student Health

Although some students protested the introduction of fast food franchises in their schools or worked to implement healthier food options, studies of students' eating habits suggest this was not the typical response in North America. A 2004–5 investigation into school food purchases in Ontario, for example, revealed that students bought unhealthy foods in significantly larger quantities than healthy food. The exodus at lunchtime of students in New York City to local food-outlets led the administrators of that school food program to dress up healthy dishes in the guise of fast food in order to compete with vendors off school grounds.[54] In the Canadian context, it may well be that the consumption of high levels of nutritionally poor school food results from the fact that most students bring their lunch from home, using the cafeteria to supplement it.[55] If, as one American commentator has suggested, much of the higher caloric intake in the past thirty years comes not from regular meals but rather from snacking, then placing unhealthy food within easy reach of children all day cannot but add to the problem.[56]

Two examples illustrate the way in which contracts with Big Food contribute to an unhealthy foodscape. As we saw earlier in the case of Pitt River Middle School, such contracts can tie school officials' hands in terms of promoting healthier fare. That case also indicates that once a fast food program is established, it is difficult to eradicate. The Coquitlam school district initially introduced food courts in secondary schools for a variety of reasons, but among them was a desire to keep students on school grounds at lunchtime. However, students at Pitt River had never been allowed to leave school grounds.[57] The district effectively opened up what had been a closed market, in the process providing middle-school students with convenient access to fast foods on a daily basis.

Similarly, contracts with soft-drink companies have linked revenue to consumption. One strategy, resulting from the competitive nature of the industry, is to entice consumers by offering more bang for the buck. In 1998, for example, Edmonton's Old Scona Academic High School changed its allegiance from Pepsi to Coke. Students "benefitted" from that move with a one-dollar, 355ml can of Pepsi replaced by a 600ml bottle of Coke for only twenty-five cents more.[58] Some of the deals have also included multiple bonus cases to be used at fundraisers or school functions, thus encouraging soft-drink consumption. And with the introduction of secret exclusivity contracts, corporations have directly tied payment to consumption quotas.

Neither soft drink companies nor fast food franchises are the sole culprits. Non-branded school cafeterias share the blame. The sugar and fat in cheap, highly processed, and non-nutritious foods, the increased availability and consumption of such foods, along with a lack of exercise, are contributing to an unhealthy generation.[59] The perceived need to rely on food and beverage purchases for fundraising is equally to blame, forcing schools, in the words of sociologist Anthony Winson, "to view their students as customers, and cafeterias and vending machines as profit centers." As one high school activity director told Winson, "All the money you need for student activities walks in the door each day, and walks right out again [to purchase food and drinks] unless you can capture it in the school."[60] Writing about the fight against junk food in the Windsor Catholic school system, Anne Jarvis noted that parent councils raised "thousands of dollars a year feeding students pizza and hot dog lunches." Of her own children's public school experience, she wrote, "Last year, there were fundraising lunches every other week. Often it was pizza or hotdogs, sometimes subs or pasta. Occasionally, bottled water or milk were offered. Pop and chips? Almost always. There was even a doughnut day."[61] As such examples make clear, Big Food is only part of the problem. Yet the competitive marketing of products, the encouragement of consumption, and the accessibility of fast food cannot but contribute to children's ill-health.

"Sugar Seemed to Be the Problem": Bans on Junk Food and Soft Drinks

Cafeteria managers, principals, teachers, and parents have long been aware of children's increasing caloric intake and attraction to sugary products. While large-scale contracts and protests against them often stole the limelight, many observers within these groups had for some time been acting in a variety of ways to eliminate unhealthy food in schools. In the 1990s, for example, Ms. Hilts, the cafeteria manager and dietician at Fellows High School in Pembroke, Ontario, developed a "teen cuisine" program that drew together public health dieticians, teachers, students, and cafeteria workers to develop contests, ads, and surveys that would promote healthy eating. The cafeteria shifted from frying to baking, increased healthy options, and reduced less nutritious ones. Over the course of ten years, the school reduced its daily servings of fries from 150 to 50 pounds. None of this was easily accomplished. As Ms. Hilts explained, "There was a lot of flack when we changed . . . but students definitely are eating healthier now. If the options are there and it's trendy, they'll eat it." Still, the cafeteria remained reliant on junk food. A local newspaper reporter noted, "Sales of junk food actually subsidize the sales of more costly healthier cafeteria foods." Moreover, the reporter explained, while Hilts' "cafeteria still has to turn a profit, she has options other schools might not have. Fellows cafeteria is the only cafeteria in the area run by the school board instead of a private contractor."[62]

Principals and parents at individual schools also took action. In the first few years of the twenty-first century some restricted access to pop machines, limiting availability to the lunch hour or the end of the school day.[63] Others replaced soft drinks with juice and water. According to the *Edmonton Journal*, Principal Brian Horbay of Holden Elementary School in Edmonton

> made the change after noticing kids were becoming lethargic in class. Other teachers found kids to be unmanageable, at times hyper, noisy, jittery. "We noticed peaks and valleys in our ability to work with them easily," said Debra Boyda, the Grade 4 teacher who runs the school canteen. "Sugar seemed to be the problem."[64]

Parents also drove some of the efforts for change. At nearby McKernan Elementary and Junior High School, administrators stopped filling vending machines with soda after one parent questioned the wisdom of the practice, and consultations with other parents revealed general agreement with the change in procedure.[65]

Schools with culinary programs have made significant progress, though again, it is often as the result of the efforts of a particularly energetic teacher. At Stratford Northwestern Secondary School, Paul Finkelstein, a culinary arts teacher, opened the Screaming Avocado Café in 2004 in competition with the regular cafeteria in the school run by Chartwells, a division of Compass Group Canada, a major food service provider. The Café survived through a combination of funding from the Ontario health ministry, selling takeaway meals to teachers, hosting community dinners, and having culinary students cater events. In this way, it was able to offer its junior high students lunch, including a healthy drink, for three dollars. Finkelstein's efforts became an early model that influenced heads of culinary arts programs at other schools.[66]

Concern over the prevalence of junk food in schools also led caterers and parents, sometimes one and the same, to develop their own privatized solutions. Bill Greenan, owner of Thyme Savers Catering in St. Catharine's, Ontario, observed a market niche. Bothered by the use of pizza days and their equivalent for elementary school fundraising, he made a proposal to a number of parent councils for the preparation and delivery of hot lunches three days a week, with a percentage of the sales going directly to the school. Three schools immediately accepted.[67] Similar types of private catering companies have appeared, particularly in more densely populated urban areas.[68] A slightly different variation developed at the high school in Whistler, BC, where parent and school secretary Chris Shoup organized a drive to eliminate junk food by having parents run a daily concession offering a healthy lunch.[69] Thus some individuals and schools developed creative alternatives to fast food cafeterias.

These were local and limited solutions, however; only government junk food bans would have a comprehensive impact. Such bans began to be put in place first in the United States and Europe. In 2002 the Los Angeles United School District unanimously voted to eliminate pop machines from its schools, as did some school districts in the San Francisco area. In September 2005 the Governor of California signed legislation to reduce student access to junk food in schools.[70] Similarly, in 2004, France, which had never allowed vending machines in elementary schools, banned the sale of soft drinks in middle and secondary schools. A year later the British government passed legislation prohibiting "junk food high in fat, salt or sugar" in school canteens.[71]

During that same period, similar policies began to be implemented in Canada. The years from 2000 to 2007 witnessed a variety of surveys and reports by nonprofit organizations, professional nutrition societies, and provincial departments or ministries of health, that consistently found school cafeterias to be nutritionally deficient, or in the words of a January 2007 *Globe and Mail* editorial after it conducted a similar survey, "nutritional wastelands."[72] Dr. Perry Kendall, provincial health officer for BC, called for a ban on junk food in schools in 2003. In 2005 the Ontario Medical Association suggested the need for greater restriction of junk food and increased physical activity for school-aged children, while in Quebec an advisory panel on nutrition issued recommendations such as subsidies for school nutrition programs and the development of zoning laws to prevent fast-food outlets opening near schools.[73] In the same year, provincial health ministers agreed, under the *Integrated Pan-Canadian Healthy Living Strategy*, to develop standards for school nutrition. Some provincial governments then began to restrict the types and amount of junk food and unhealthy drinks sold in vending machines and school cafeterias, and to create healthy food guidelines.[74] Indeed, politicians found it difficult to resist public pressure for healthier school food. In March 2006, Quebec Premier Jean Charest declared that his government would not ban junk food in cafeterias, preferring the educational approach of counselling students on proper nutrition. Under public pressure, the premier later reversed his position, announcing the elimination of soft drinks and fatty foods by January 2008.[75]

As provincial governments in Canada and state legislators in the US began to rethink school food and beverage policies, international organizations were bringing pressure to bear on Big Food companies. In 2005, for instance, the Center for Science in the Public Interest released a significant report, titled *Liquid Candy*, on the harmful effects of soft drinks to Americans, and two years later, with the International Association of Consumer Food Organizations, launched an international "Global Dump Soft Drinks Campaign."[76] The food and beverage industry also faced pressure from activist groups such as the Alliance for a Healthier Generation (composed of the Bill Clinton Foundation and the American Heart Association), the World Heart Federation, and the Campaign For a Commercial-Free Childhood.[77]

Recognizing public discontent with its practices and capitalizing on the turn toward healthy and organic foods, Big Food attempted, in turn, to align itself with its critics. In 2005 the president of the American Beverage Association (ABA), Susan Neely, stated, "Childhood obesity is a serious problem in the U.S. and the responsibility for finding common-sense solutions is shared by everyone, including our industry.... We intend to be part of the solution by increasing the availability of lower-calorie and/or nutritious beverages in schools."[78] ABA's Canadian counterpart, Refreshments Canada, toed this line.[79] Around the same time, ABA and food companies, such as Kraft Foods and Kellogg, announced plans to stop advertising some high fat and sugar products to children under twelve, to limit the use of cartoon characters to market junk food to children, and to develop more healthy product lines.[80] By 2010, PepsiCo had announced that it would voluntarily remove "full-calorie, sweetened drinks from schools in more than 200 countries by 2012." Following Pepsi's lead, though less enthusiastically, Coca-Cola announced a global policy that would discourage the sale of Coke in primary schools unless requested by parents or school districts themselves. (The company did not extend that policy to secondary schools.)[81] Marketing by not marketing had come to be in the best interests of many corporations.

"A Tempest in a Teapot": Championing and Lamenting Bans

The threat of bans, and the bans themselves, did not occur without reaction. Individual schools and parent groups complained about the loss of revenue. When, in 2005, health and education groups in Newfoundland put pressure on the provincial government to remove junk food from schools, a number of larger schools complained about the potential loss of revenue. Parents at Geary Elementary School in New Brunswick, worried about what might follow from implementation of their province's school nutrition policy: they had a volunteer-based hot lunch program, including such items as Kraft dinner and hot dogs, that raised about $10,000 a year for school and sports equipment and helped subsidize field trips.[82]

Public commentary reflected the belief that food consumption was an individual responsibility best regulated by parents. An editorial in the Fredericton *Daily Gleaner*, for example, stated: "We don't need government forcing the issue of nutrition. We need parents who understand that poor nutrition leads to a lifetime of health issues for our young later in life. . . . The schools can teach a balanced lifestyle; it's up to parents to set an example and provide the opportunity for healthy living at home."[83] Trustees who attempted to regulate or eliminate less nutritious foods sometimes faced the ire of those engaged in school fundraising. Joan Courtney, Catholic school board vice-chairwoman in the Windsor area, was caught off guard when she attempted to do so. "I think I've started a tempest in a teapot, I'll tell you," she told a reporter; "I didn't think it would be so intense."[84]

In various places, as governments brought in food and beverage policies, some students leapt at the opportunity to develop their entrepreneurial skills. One newspaper report noted that "two students at Bernice

MacNaughton High School in Moncton, N.B., decided to capitalize on their classmates' cravings by selling soda pop and chips from their lockers. The principal shut down the operation after someone complained about warm pop."[85] In Vancouver, three teens developed a Facebook page to facilitate their sales of candy, chips, and chocolate bars at marked-up prices after the introduction of a policy promoting healthier school food. In that case, much of their profits reportedly went to various charities.[86] Their successful business occurred off school grounds.

Critics of junk food in schools, however, complained about the limited nature of the new food policies. Despite their promises, provinces were often slow to enact change, and many of the measures were partial. For instance, in 2004 the Ontario Ministry of Education issued a memorandum encouraging the provision of healthier food in elementary school vending machines, a recommendation that only became mandatory in 2011. Even in enacting healthy eating policies, many provinces continued to allow non-nutritious food to remain on the menu, though less often than before. After September 2011, the Ontario government banned most nutritionally poor food but still allowed ten special event days a year when the rules did not apply.[87] Similarly, in New Brunswick, schools could still serve foods high in sodium and fat, such as pizza or ice cream, twice a week.[88] Other provinces developed only voluntary nutrition guidelines.[89] Nor did healthy food policies necessarily apply to the fundraising activities of support groups. In New Brunswick, parent groups partnered with local pizza and cupcake companies. In BC, students at one school raised money for their 2013 "After Grad" through Krispy Kreme Doughnuts sales and a dinner at McDonald's, some of the proceeds of which returned to the school.[90]

In addition, critics have found corporations' self-regulation to be something of a mirage. Michele Simon notes that in the United States "from 2003 to 2005, almost every state proposed legislation to address the sale of soda and junk food in public schools," but only twenty-one actually passed bills and of these, ten were "watered down, a result of political lobbying and compromise." She argues that despite strong public support for such bills, "in almost all states where bills fail or are weakened, trade associations and individual companies have a heavy hand in the lobbying."[91] The former, in particular, allow corporations to fight legislation opposed to their interests without fear of damage to their public image. For instance, the Grocery Manufacturers Association, which consists of, among others, Kraft and PepsiCo, "is on record as opposing virtually every state bill across the nation that would restrict the sale of junk food or soda in schools."[92] Their massive resources far outweigh the efforts of nutritionists and nonprofit advocacy groups to improve the school food landscape.

Implementing healthy food policies has its own cost. The financial burden on school districts providing healthier fare has been recognized for some time. In the late 1970s, the Toronto Board of Education shied away from banning junk food, arguing that it would virtually shut down cafeterias and be too costly. When Glenview Senior Public School in Toronto attempted to cut junk food in 1976, sales dropped from $110 to $80 a month.[93] The situation was no different almost forty years later. In 2013 the Auditor General of Ontario reported that the switch to healthier fare resulted in a drop in revenue of between 25 and 45 percent from cafeteria sales and 70 to 85 percent from vending machines, leading newspaper reports and editorials to infer that the policy was a failure.[94] Indeed, it may have contributed to a long-standing crisis that in the Toronto school district resulted in the closure of thirty-two cafeterias.[95]

These revenue declines were not confined to Toronto. Highland Secondary in Comox, BC, witnessed a steep decline from approximately $17,000 a year to $1,000. So too did others in the area. At Mark R. Isfeld Secondary School in Courtenay, BC, the reduction from $18,000 to under $3,000 affected school sports because that revenue traditionally paid for substitute teachers who covered coaches' classes. After one school in Vancouver made the switch, it experienced a drop from $80,000 to $35,000, funds that covered not only sports but also band activities, field trips, and Christmas parties.[96]

The choice to institute and maintain healthier fare is often both financial and ideological. A comparison of two Edmonton schools is apt. In 2004 administrators at Ardrossan Junior Senior High School implemented a healthier cafeteria menu and reduced servings of burgers and fries to three times a week. As a result, sales declined 14 percent and the principal had to divert $6,000 earmarked for academic use to the cafeteria. While the school maintained its healthier fare, it subsequently reinstated daily servings of burgers and fries in order to maintain revenue. At W. P. Wagner High School, administrators also switched to a healthier menu. Fries disappeared four out of five days. Pop machines didn't operate during school hours. And revenue slipped by 15 percent. But the *Edmonton Journal* reported that while "revenue from the Wagner cafeteria helps pay for the school's fitness room, fitness staff, barbecues and other things all students can use," the principal was willing to forgo some revenue in exchange for better student nutrition.[97]

Although the introduction of nutritional policies seems to have led to immediate drops in revenue, further assessment is necessary to determine their long-term financial impact. Early evaluations of school nutrition policies, though, suggest that they may result in an improved diet.[98] Quebec, which has the least penetration of advertising in its schools and the smallest percentage of exclusive contracts with soft drink companies, also boasts the lowest consumption of snack food and pop in Canada. It is perhaps not coincidental that it has legislation restricting advertising toward those under age thirteen and commercial solicitation in schools.[99] This suggests that legislative change can help reduce immediate access to junk food. In the Coquitlam school district in BC, for example, as a result of healthy food legislation and financial losses, fast-food franchises were quietly taken out of schools.[100] While recent policies do not eliminate Big Food from schools, food and beverage corporations have had to replace soft drinks with fruit juices and water and remove some of the high-fat, high-sugar, and processed foods from cafeterias.

Conclusion

If the jury is still out on the profitability and effectiveness of introducing healthy menus into school cafeterias, what is clear is that the anti-corporate and healthy food coalitions ended up parting ways. Unwilling to forego the money generated by vending machines, advocates of healthier food pushed instead for the reduction of less nutritious food in schools. However, while vendors often replaced pop with juice and water, a corporate presence remained. Erika Shaker and Bernie Froese-Germaine have noted that "the direction at the policy level . . . appears to focus more on providing less unhealthy foods rather than on commercialism."[101] Such activities include endorsement of expensive bottled water rather than tap water, ignoring the global perils of the unnecessary use of plastics.

Moreover, while exclusivity or pouring rights and unhealthy cafeterias have come under significant scrutiny, much less attention has focused on parent fundraisers and hot lunch programs that draw on fast food chains. Elementary schools in many jurisdictions now offer lunches provided by companies such as Burger King, Pita Pit, and Great Canadian Bagel Co. In 2016 some New Brunswick schools offered Slush Puppie Plus—meet-

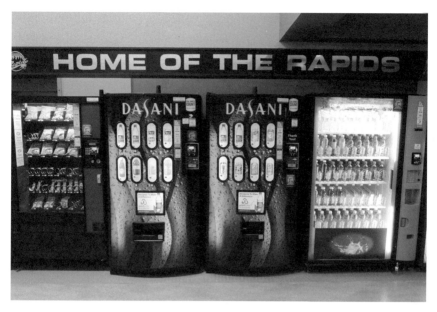

Vending machines at Riverside Secondary School, Port Coquitlam, BC, 2018. Photo: Michael Dawson.

ing nutritional standards in consisting of 99 percent apple juice but still containing twenty-nine grams (seven teaspoons) of sugar.[102] These cases are sometimes justified as a service to parents and sometimes as part of a parent fundraiser. Asked about Burger King's provision of hot lunches to several New Brunswick schools, Aubrey Kirkpatrick, the director of finance and administration for Anglophone East School District, stated, "I know when people see Burger King you have a different mindset. . . . But they do have items that meet the policy and we're happy they're helping to provide schools without cafeterias the opportunity to provide a hot lunch."[103] In allowing such practices, administrators brought corporations into the schools and helped naturalize regular consumption of fast food. Such practices counter provincial efforts to encourage healthy eating practices, including school lessons on nutrition.

Branding, then, continues unabated. Corporations continue to sell their wares in schools, though they offer slightly different products and in different forms. Their job is to find new markets, new ways of marketing their products, and new entry points. Schools are generally ill-placed to fight this process. At the local level, campaigns motivated by widespread concern about the dual emphasis on schools' commercial activities and student health have resulted in mixed success. But public discontent, the work of activists and teachers' unions, the spectre of increasing childhood obesity, the cultural turn toward local and healthy food, and the example set by international precedents have put pressure on provincial governments to develop school policies and guidelines. Those factors may have played a role in halting the spread of fast food franchises in schools and forcing corporations to undertake some policy changes regarding marketing unhealthy food to children. It seems clear, however, that while local action can have a significant impact on public discussion, and sometimes meet with success, government intervention is required to ensure change across school districts.

7

"All We're Trying to Do Is Help Youngsters"

The Politics of Raising Funds

IN THE EARLY YEARS of the twenty-first century, the Ontario government's safety commission informed Ottawa school trustees that playground equipment at some of their district's schools needed to be replaced. The trustees were understandably concerned. Equipment and installation costs could be prohibitive. A simple set of four swings, for example, could cost up to five thousand dollars, close to half the average yearly funds raised by an elementary school. When the trustees gained a meeting with Premier Dalton McGuinty to ask about obtaining funds for the equipment, the Premier's response struck a familiar note. He directed them to Home Depot.[1]

Schools have become perpetual fundraising sites. Students, parents, teachers, school administrators, and trustees are constantly in search of money. Local fundraising questions are usually framed in relation to educational priorities: What does a school need? What can parents do to improve their children's school experience? How can these aims be best achieved? Fundraising is a method of securing resources beyond what is on offer from a school board or provincial ministry of education in order to meet the school community's needs or desires. A community might prioritize, for example, sports equipment and team transportation, or musical instruments, or computers and tablets, and then seek funds in pursuit of these goals. But what of the actual activity of fundraising? How much fundraising should a parent or school district undertake? How much time should be devoted to this process? What resources should be harnessed?

What initiatives should be funded by parents rather than supported through public funds? And what are some of the social and cultural consequences of fundraising activities?

This chapter explores these questions. It does so by briefly examining the changing nature of fundraising initiatives, particularly in the past thirty years. It then looks at three specific forms of fundraising activity: corporate grants and competitions, casinos, and charitable foundations. It focuses primarily on cases that have come under public scrutiny because of their level of commercialism, the nature of their methods, or their novel approach. Finally, this chapter concludes with a consideration of the Learning Partnership, a nonprofit organization that has built a solid national reputation by creating or sponsoring educational programs, a number of which bring business practices, free market ideology, and consumer culture directly and unequivocally into school curricula. All of these examples raise a variety of ethical questions about the practices of fundraising and the methods of program delivery.

The Changing Nature of Fundraising

Parental contribution to the improvement of their children's schools is nothing new. Individually and through Home and School Associations, parents have long provided both labour and financial contributions to improve their local school and to raise money for a variety of purposes. In 1934–35, for example, the Superintendent of Education for Nova Scotia reported,

> At Fox Point, Lunenburg County, a dozen men with their oxen—over a period of three weeks—converted a veritable rock pile into a smooth playground. At Hillsborough, Inverness County, each resident donated one desk-chair (with attached drawer) to replace the old-fashioned school seats. When the planting season interrupted the painting of both interior and exterior of the building, a half-dozen women completed the job![2]

Several years later the superintendent noted that across Nova Scotia, home and school associations had helped improve school buildings, equipment, and grounds, held dental and vaccination clinics, donated musical instruments, hired music teachers, and created study clubs for parents.[3]

In the 1940s and 1950s, on the other side of the country, parent-teacher associations in Port Coquitlam, BC, raised money for library books, slide projectors, radios, pianos, playground equipment, and PA systems.[4] The Home and School Association for Clarkson Public School in Peel County, Ontario, raised $410 in 1957–58 (roughly $3,600 in today's dollars), by organizing a band concert, a hobby show, and a field day booth, among other things. It used these funds to provide a donation to the band, organize a Christmas party, contribute to the district and province-wide home and school associations, and provide a Grade 8 graduation dinner and field day trophies.[5]

This type of fundraising continued into the 1980s. For example, the New Brunswick Gunningsville Home and School Association paid for window blinds for a school auditorium, water coolers for school portables, a springboard for the gym, and knee pads for floor hockey, and also provided a donation to the school library. Similarly, in 1986–87 parents at Scarborough's Knob Hill School raised $3,000 (almost $6,000 in today's dollars) for sweaters, four computers, one printer, computer software, library books, student class trip subsidies, student awards, and teacher retirement gifts, while at Norman Cook Junior Public School parents purchased a new Apple II computer, an item procured by means of a Christmas raffle, annual fun fair, and three hot dog days.[6]

Over the course of the year, in short, parents across the country raised funds for school activities and special events, for "extras" such as playgrounds, pianos, musical instruments, library books, field trips, and extracurricular activities, as well as for equipment to keep the school up to date such as slide projectors, radios, P.A. systems, and computers. Much of this type of activity continues today. Yet by the end of the 1980s, teachers began to find that pressure on schools, parents, and students to engage in significant and ongoing fundraising was intensifying. In 1989 the Ontario Public Schools Teachers' Federation issued a report stating that government funding shortfalls had resulted in students having to undertake major fundraising efforts. Bake sales and yard sales were no longer enough. As one journalist reported, "large-scale, big volume, door to door sales of citrus fruits, cheese, spices, Christmas ornaments and chocolate bars requiring considerable time on the part of students, teachers and parent volunteers" had become a regular feature of school life.[7]

The pressure to raise more funds led to large-scale events previously unimaginable. For example, in 1994 parents at three schools in the small community of Cochrane, near Calgary, banded together to hold what they dubbed a "Cow's Paradise Lotto." The winner would become the proud owner of "an instant ranch—116 acres of farmland, 40 head of cattle and a mobile home." Bruce Kendall, one of the organizers, reported the event to be a resounding success, raising $490,000 gross and $225,000 in profits (over $344,000 in today's dollars), an amount significantly more than could have been obtained through bake sales and selling chocolate bars. Parents needed that amount of cash as they had their eyes set on an ambitious goal: to equip the schools with computers.[8]

Although it was certainly one of the more eye-catching examples of a new form of fundraising, the Cochrane lottery was not unique. In 2002, Port Moody, BC, parent Lisa Bateman organized a silent auction to support Heritage Mountain Elementary School. The auction, held at a popular local restaurant, included "a DVD home theatre system, Canucks tickets and a flat-screen computer monitor" along with "dozens of gift certificates for spas and hair salons," and it raised $7,000. Whitney Public School, located in the high-income area of Rosedale, in Toronto, regularly organized a pasta dinner that brought in as much as $35,000 a year.[9]

Many of these large-scale fundraising activities continued to be parent-conceived and initiated, but home and school associations also began to draw on an emerging variety of commercial enterprises. Again, this was not a new approach. Fred Thompson Sales Ltd. in Toronto had placed ads in *Quest* magazine as early as the mid-1960s inviting parent-teacher associations and student councils to use their products to raise funds. They offered cans of McLean's Instant Chocolate and sugar-coated candies as two of the many items on offer.[10] Still, whereas these types of ads seem few and far between in the 1960s, thirty years later, principals were overwhelmed by companies pushing products for fundraising purposes. Rod Kostex, principal of Rio Terrace School in Edmonton, complained of the constant attempts, "Cold calls, phone calls, fax calls, selling quick returns and instant wealth ... a day doesn't go by when some fundraising organization doesn't send us some money-making idea." He was inundated by an array of products: "citrus fruit. Sausage. Chocolate. Spice sets. Christmas ornaments, wrapping paper. Light bulbs. Maple syrup, greeting cards, magazines, telephone calling cards." The list seemed endless.[11]

By the 1990s fundraising companies offered not only products but a full range of services. A mid-decade Calgary home and school association newsletter, for instance, advertised the services of Horizons West Marketing, which would provide products, sales assistance, and aid with paperwork. In return, clients received a percentage of the sales. The early years of the twenty-first century saw an expansion in this approach, made possible by technological leaps. In 2004 Fundstream Inc. of Montreal developed FundScrip, modelled after an American program developed in the early 1980s, enabling parents to buy gift certificates, with a percentage of the funds returned to the school. In 2006 a Montreal-based company that was already making a substantial profit south of the border began offering its services to Canadian schools. EFundraising.com, owned by Reader's Digest Association Inc., provided online technology enabling students to sell goods over the Internet rather than door-to-door. In 2010 Sarah and Darryl Davis created the Wealthy School Revolution, allowing parents to buy online products ranging from dry goods to school supplies and in bypassing retailers, pass some of the profits on to schools. By 2014 they reported that they worked with three hundred schools across the country.[12]

Fundraising companies became popular as fewer parents had time to devote to these activities and as fundraising ventures became more frequent and intense. In the 1990s and early 2000s not only did parent councils feel that they needed to continue to raise money for resources that had traditionally fallen under the "extras" category such as library books and music, athletic, and club programs, but they also increasingly found themselves doing so for items they believed should be considered basic to schooling. Home and school associations in earlier decades had also faced this quandary. In 1956 an article in *Canadian Home and Garden* asked, should parents "buy the school's typewriters, tape recorders, movie projectors, books, curtains for the auditorium?" One father replied forcefully, "Home and School isn't here to provide material support to the school system. . . . The cost of equipment should be spread over all the taxpayers, and the boards should assume this responsibility." Other parents agreed, but as one noted, "if the community waited for the government to do everything for them, nothing would ever be accomplished."[13]

Fifty years later the debate continued over what a parent support committee ought to provide. The advent of computers brought fundraising to the fore, hence the "Cow's Paradise Lotto." While a school might be able to raise the funds for one computer through hot dog sales, it certainly could not equip each classroom, let alone each student, in this manner. Moreover, the place of computers in schools increasingly moved from the sidelines to a central concern. Whereas in the 1980s and early 1990s a computer might be considered one more additional, though expensive, "extra," increasingly through the nineties and early years of the twenty-first century many parents and educators came to see computers as crucial to children's education. While more government funding would be allocated to computer equipment and technology more generally, it never seemed to be enough to keep up with demand or to ensure a school had technology that was up to date. As a result, home and school associations often ended up supplementing school shortfalls.

Moreover, some home and school associations found themselves raising funds for things outside what might be considered their original mandate. In 1996, Carlyle Elementary School in Montreal paid for a music teacher's salary for weekly lessons for each class and launched a fundraising campaign to secure the services of "a part-time teacher in math and computer science for gifted students."[14] Two years later Bob Zechel, chairperson of the parent advisory council at Grovenor Elementary School in Edmonton, Alberta, noted that among other things they had paid for a consultant to help children with anger management. In 2003 Heritage Mountain Elementary in Port Moody, BC, fundraised for everything from money to supplement literacy programs to an expensive earthquake preparedness container kit that the school was expected to have. The following year the parents' council at St. George School in Ottawa noted that they had had to organize a chocolate bar drive in order to provide teachers with language arts books.[15] And teacher unions and parent groups reported teachers paying increasing amounts out of their own pockets for classroom needs while parents were paying for what seemed to be basic resources such as paper, classroom supplies, textbooks, technology, and even academic programs.[16]

Of course, much of the fundraising in schools continues to the present day as in the past, with parents, teachers, and students running yard and rummage sales, food sales, art auctions, and bottle drives to supplement extracurricular activities, fill library shelves, or maintain playground equipment. Yet clear patterns emerged at the end of the twentieth century. Fundraising activities became more frequent and intense, with some very large-scale events and constant attempts to raise larger amounts of money. Commercial enterprises and marketing firms became more common as parents and teachers looked for ways to make these initiatives easier. And a growing number of parent councils and teacher unions felt that fundraisers were increasingly needed to provide what seemed like basics rather than "extras." As a result, home and school associations, school administrators, and school boards sought out new and creative ways to raise funds.

Corporate Grants, Casinos, and Charitable Foundations

While local businesses and corporations have long provided resources to schools, in the past twenty years the size of donations and the level of involvement have increased significantly. In particular, corporate grants and competitions have proliferated, offering schools one means by which they can access funds for a specific purpose. As noted in the introduction, in 2004 Home Depot donated $18,000 for improvements to the playground at Lynn Valley Elementary School in North Vancouver, money sought by the school's parents' group. Steve Coffin, whose child attended the school, was shocked by the marketing surrounding the event. He told the Vancouver *Province* that advertising accompanied the donation on two occasions. At the September meet-the-teacher night, some parents sported Home Depot aprons and handed out "rubber Home Depot hammers" to the children. On the actual day of the build, parent volunteers wore Home Depot shirts and hats while some students put on temporary Home Depot tattoos and sang a ditty about the corporation that one of the teachers had quickly written to enliven the proceedings. According to Coffin, this activity was accompanied by a large "orange Home Depot sign on school grounds." The build-day was organized by KaBOOM!, an American-based nonprofit organization that helps provide communities with playgrounds and that is itself supported by prominent corporations, such as Target and Snapple, focused on "cause-marketing."[17]

Other adults did not share Coffin's sense of alarm. One stated, "I most whole-heartedly disagree with the opinion of the parents who felt it was inappropriate to expose children to advertising in schools regarding Home Depot's funding of the Lynn Valley elementary playground. . . . What a kick in the teeth for Home Depot and for the various people involved in getting funding for such a necessary aspect of a child's life at school."[18] Another declared, "Home Depot is helping schools because our schools are in need of money. Would we rather that large, profitable corporations hold on to their profits with an iron fist, instead of helping in our communities where the need is greatest?"[19]

Home Depot's involvement with the North Vancouver school was not unique, though in other places the nature of its activities differed. Students and principals from several Regina schools partook in the grand opening of a local store. A group from École St. Angela Merici opened the event

Front and back of playground sign at Edith Cavell Elementary School, Vancouver, BC. Personal collection of the author.

by singing the national anthem. The principal of Rosemont Community School participated in a ribbon-cutting ceremony before receiving a $2,500 donation given, according to a company press release, "in keeping with the company's commitment to build better communities." Students from various schools then headed indoors to do crafts. Throughout the event many of the students and school administrators could be seen wearing Home Depot aprons.[20]

While Home Depot offers grants for which individual schools can apply, other companies prefer to develop competitions. Majesta and Tree Canada, for instance, promote the Majesta Trees of Knowledge Competition that provides the winning school with $20,000 to develop an outdoor classroom. Tree Canada was originally the National Community Tree Foundation, established in 1992 and funded by the Canadian Forest Service, to create public awareness around climate change, encourage tree replantation, and offer advice on urban forest diversification and management. When its funding was cut in 2007, it shifted to a corporate sponsorship model in partnership with a range of companies, including TDBank, Shell Canada, and Canada Post.[21] Ads for the contest ran in local newspapers. At Nashwaak Valley School in New Brunswick, a parent saw an ad for the competition and approached the school. Teachers and students worked together on an application outlining their ideal outdoor classroom. As one of ten finalists in 2014, the school then publicized their selection, urging everyone in the province to visit the Majesta website and vote online for their school.[22]

Majesta was hardly alone in offering these types of competitions. Staples developed its version in 2016. The Superpower your School Contest, a joint Earth Day Canada and Staples Canada endeavour, provided $25,000 in technology to winning schools for their green projects. Likewise, Samsung Canada has a "Solve for Tomorrow" challenge, established in 2016, in which schools compete for $20,000 worth of technology by developing a short video championing an idea about how to use STEM to improve the community.[23]

Another type of program is Indigo's Love of Reading Foundation. Since 2004, it has distributed monetary grants every year to a number of schools. The program began after Heather Reisman, the CEO of Indigo, visited Church Street Public School in downtown Toronto and found a bare library. As a result, she spearheaded a four-year pilot project that saw the school richly "equipped with books and related learning materials."[24] The experiment led to the creation of the Foundation. In 2005 almost two hundred schools applied, with ten chosen to receive a three-year commitment of $50,000 a year. The program requests that winning schools report back to the Foundation on how the money is spent and acknowledge the donation in some way. In one case, for example, the principal chose to mention the donation on the school website.

Although these programs differ quite significantly, they raise the same ethical questions. To a greater or lesser degree, they are based on a sense of corporate responsibility and the desire of corporate leaders, some of whom are parents, to help their communities. The Love of Reading Foundation is perhaps the most altruistic and least commercially intrusive within schools, while the Majesta competition is akin to advertising. Still, all the companies are drawing on their support of schools to portray themselves as socially responsible corporations. In the twenty-first century, marketeers have turned their attention to the uses of promoting good corporate social responsibility as a strategy to promote brand awareness and image and ultimately increase corporate value. In the context of schools, this sometimes results in children and their teachers becoming the advertisers, such as in the Home Depot and Majesta examples. Hidden behind the scenes is the fact that individual schools are placed in competition with one another in order to obtain corporate grants and that applications require significant effort and time from teachers and parent groups. Funds do not necessarily come solely from the company itself. The Indigo Love of Reading Foundation Literacy Fund Grants, for instance, draw on donations from Indigo's customers. "Every dollar donated by customers goes to high-needs elementary schools," the company notes, "and the schools we support receive a 30% discount on books."[25] In other words, funds come from taxpayers and the grants support the reinvestment of donated money back into the corporation.

In addition to applying for corporate grants or participating in corporate-sponsored competitions, parent groups have found other ways to secure funds. In the 1990s and first years of the twenty-first century, many Alberta schools became reliant on state-run casinos for their fundraising activities. Giving an ironic twist to a term coined by the Ralph Klein government, Margaret Wente dubbed this the "Alberta Advantage"—the ability of parent groups in that province to raise large sums through casino nights. Parents of Catholic schools in the Calgary area pulled in over $2 million in 2005–6, while those in Edmonton close to $3 million.[26] Such initiatives were not limited to Alberta. By the late 1990s schools in the Windsor, Ontario, area that were located near large casinos had also turned to bingo nights. Still, in Alberta, casino nights became particularly popular. In 2006 there were seventeen casinos in that province, each of which allotted some evenings to charitable events, for which the casinos received a return on the money raised.[27] For schools that had traditionally raked in $10,000 or $12,000 a year through numerous time-consuming events, from silent auctions to yard sales, one bingo night offered the opportunity to quickly obtain $3,000 to $5,000, while a casino night could bring in anywhere from $30,000 to $70,000.[28]

By the late 1990s, however, Catholic leaders began to denounce schools' reliance on casinos and bingos as a means to raise money. They voiced concerns, expressed as well by community activists and academic researchers, about the growing negative social effects caused by compulsive gambling and encouraged by provincial governments' increasing reliance on lotteries and regulated casinos for tax revenue. Despite a pastoral letter from bishops in Alberta condemning such activity for fundraising purposes, some Catholic school districts refused to follow clerical leadership. The issue became particularly heated in Calgary where that district continued to allow individual schools to decide whether to participate in casino fundraising. In turn, Calgary Bishop Fred Henry, declaring the decision "a failure in Catholic leadership," threatened to pull the Church designation for schools refusing to conform. In a letter to the school board, he forcefully maintained that "it is morally wrong for a Catholic institution to formally co-operate in an industry that exploits the weak and vulnerable."[29]

The arguments for using casinos for school fundraisers repeat those noted in previous chapters. Much like Tabachnick's defence of the Montreal English School Board's right to make local decisions when faced with the province's tightening of regulations regarding advertising, the chairwoman of the Calgary Catholic School Board District stated, "It is our moral and legal right to make policy decisions that govern the district's operations, including decisions affecting school-based fundraising." In addition to defending the jurisdiction of the school board, she went on to maintain that "a 'no gambling' policy would have a profoundly negative impact on our students, their families and school communities," as the revenue reduces school fees for low-income families and helps supplement the cost of school activities.[30] Taking up this "school needs" argument, one parent claimed:

> our school parent council uses casino money to fund literacy support books, computer labs, audio/video equipment, and the rebuilding of our aging playground. There simply are no other sources of funding that will bring in revenues even close to what a casino can earn. The areas we have chosen to fund are not frills or extras—they are the basic supports a modern school needs to function, but which are not provided for by the funding schools receive, through their boards, from the province. . . . Where will the funds to replace casino revenue come from?[31]

That revenue was also being used to supplement specialized activities, such as, for example, Bishop Grandin School's marching band program, which cost over $100,000 annually to run. Students paid $500 each and raised money for travel expenses, but that still left the program considerably short of funds.[32]

Despite such arguments, Bishop Henry was determined to halt the use of casinos. Asked if he was willing to risk parents pulling their children from Catholic schools, he remained defiant: "I'm prepared to see us become smaller rather than larger, providing we become more Catholic."[33] The school district eventually acceded, although it allowed schools a transition period to wean themselves off casino revenues. However, other districts beyond Henry's jurisdiction continued their use of such fundraisers. In 2014 Grande Prairie and District Catholic Schools instituted a ban effective in 2018–19 but offered an exemption for high schools demonstrating a need for significant infusions of cash. Parents also found ways around such bans, in some cases creating societies at arm's length from the school that raised funds using casinos and then donated these funds directly to the school.[34]

In their continued use of bingo and casino nights, parents and school trustees registered their ambivalence about the decrees against this form of fundraising made by Catholic leadership. While most parents and school administrators understood, and likely supported, that moral stance in principle, the perceived need for large fundraising efforts often made them less willing to uphold it in practice. The nature of a school-by-school or district-by-district decision resulted in discontent as some fundraising committees felt their hands were tied while others pursued this method of securing money. This was particularly true given that non-Catholic public schools continued to use gaming facilities for fundraising purposes.[35]

One response to declining access to casino money was the creation of foundations. In 2009 the Calgary Catholic School District did exactly this.[36] In doing so, it embraced a growing trend. Charitable foundations emerged in the late 1980s and through the next decade as a popular solution to fundraising shortfalls. In 1987, the Ottawa-Carleton Learning Foundation brought together five boards of education, over one hundred businesses, several postsecondary institutions, and a number of provincial government departments. The Foundation aimed to provide "vocational guidance and work experience" for students, to secure for teachers "information about industry" to enable them to better inform students about workforce preparation, and to orient "school programs to the skill requirements of employers."[37] In 1996 a former Calgary superintendent of education, along with several prominent business leaders, created the Calgary Educational Partnership Foundation, modelled on the Ottawa initiative, to support the "fundamental restructuring of education in Alberta" and create "powerful relationships between businesses and educators."[38] That Foundation justified its existence by emphasizing the need to maintain the district's current levels of service.[39] Similarly, the managing director of the West Island Educational Foundation, created in the same year to seek out donations to support English schools within Montreal's Lakeshore School Board, stated of its purposes, "It's a business in the most crass sense of the word."[40] A decade later charitable foundations existed across the country, with school boards often putting aside funds to establish such initiatives even as they cut resources in other areas.[41] Hence it is not surprising that the Calgary Catholic School District saw this type of institution as a possible solution to the loss of casino revenue.

While school districts forged ahead in creating charitable foundations, administrators at some schools also embraced the idea. One of the earliest examples appeared in the early 1990s at Sentinel High School in West Vancouver, initiated by its principal, Peter Lefaivre, who had written a paper as part of his MEd requirements at the University of British Columbia on school fundraising. In 1991 the district management committee of the West Vancouver School Board urged its board to seek out new ways of increasing revenue. Lefaivre, well placed to do so, developed an ambitious plan to raise $750,000 over three years with the help of a professional fundraiser.[42]

To start with, Lefaivre went straight to the executive of the school's parents' association for support. With permission from the superintendent, Doug Player, the association hired Allan Holender for six months at a salary of $32,000, to be paid by parents and cafeteria sales, to initiate the project. Player believed in the need for school districts to be more creative financially. In the late 1980s and early 1990s, he had helped West Vancouver Secondary School transform an exchange program into a moneymaking scheme, charging wealthy students from Asia a significant fee for attending the school, monies divided between the school and the district. He thus supported Lefaivre's initiative. Holender, who had worked in development offices at both the University of Alberta and UBC, created an organizational framework for the fundraising campaign, involving students, parents, grandparents, alumni, and community members. The plan included a Major Gifts Committee, chaired by a parent, that aimed to attract $150,000 each year from corporate and individual donors; a Business Booster Committee, led by the head of the West Vancouver Chamber of Commerce, which would attempt to raise $5,000 a year; and an alumni committee focused on securing $20,000 annually. Students would be expected to raise $5,000 a year and parents urged to develop a variety of supplementary campaigns. The aim was to upgrade labs and musical instruments, provide fine arts and drama supplies, and establish "an endowment fund for scholarships and a visiting teacher chair."[43]

Teachers at the school were divided over the proposed plan. Some appreciated it as they did not have to be directly involved and the initiative seemed to eliminate existing expectations that they participate in activities such as casino nights. Others worried about the possible outcomes. Of the thirteen subject departments, two refused to co-operate with the development officer, raising a variety of issues from lack of consultations and unanswered questions regarding dispersal of funds to general concerns about the contribution of the plan to inequities within the school system. The British Columbia Teachers' Federation (BCTF) equally opposed the initiative on that latter ground, fearing the development of severe inequities in facilities and resources between schools in more affluent neighbourhoods and those in poorer ones.[44]

The BCTF had little to worry about in this particular case as the plan ended in shambles. The principal left the school abruptly in October 1992 before the project was fully in place. An independent audit conducted the following year found that the school had only raised $34,000, mostly from international student fees. Still, the initiative was indicative of a general trend that worried teachers' unions. Despite the maelstrom resulting from Lefaivre's scheme, the superintendent continued to believe that it had merit if executed in a more focused manner. "The structure is still there," he maintained. "I still think it's an idea that can work."[45] Indeed, other schools did take this route, though in much more modest form. In the mid-1990s, for example, Westmount High School in Montreal created a "Technology Fund" in order to update the school's antiquated computer equipment.[46]

Charitable foundations, then, became one answer to covering funding shortfalls. However, while the use of prominent corporations and casinos to address school needs brought the issue of commercialism in schools directly into the public eye, the creation of foundations drew less attention. These are much more nebulous organizations, most commonly working alongside school districts but in ways that are not always clear to the public. Alison Taylor, a critic of the Calgary Educational Partnership Foundation, argues that these types of institutions allow local business leaders a means to "increase their influence over the school system and over provincial educational reform more generally."[47] They "promote themselves as 'apolitical' organizations where stakeholders can work toward common goals." In reality, their creation has meant

> that activities that were once managed by the Department of Education and were controlled to a greater extent by educators (such as

curriculum development, professional development of teachers, and skills development opportunities for students) are now managed also by broker institutions that arguably provide corporate sponsors with greater opportunities to influence outcomes.[48]

Their popularity has also contributed to yet another structural addition to the increasingly complicated institutional landscape making up provincial education systems.

Charitable foundations, like the use of casino nights or corporate grants, also reveal a number of inequities and ethical issues around fundraising. Teachers' unions and parents have long noted the problem of discrepancies between schools, with those best able to fundraise usually located in neighbourhoods where incomes are highest. People for Education reported that in Ontario in 2002 "the top 10 percent of fundraising elementary schools raised as much money as the bottom 60 percent put together."[49] While schools could generally count on $10,000 to $15,000 a year, some drew in considerably more. In 2005 Queen Mary Elementary School in Vancouver raised $50,000 while one Ontario high school brought in an astounding $250,000. Around the same time, Bessborough Drive Elementary and Middle School in Toronto, with just over four hundred students, raked in almost $300,000 in 2009 to improve their school grounds, including the addition of artificial turf.[50]

Some school communities recognized this inequity. In 1999 parents at Whitney Public School in Rosedale, Toronto, raised $50,000 and decided to use 10 percent of this to help an inner city school.[51] A decade later, parents at Briar Hill Elementary School in Calgary worked with a local charity, EducationMatters, "to launch the Schools Helping Schools Fund." The program aimed to "help ensure Calgary schools that find fundraising a challenge can access grants for some of the same educational enhancements offered in other communities."[52]

To some, however, attracting private sponsors clearly seemed a good method of reducing inequities. In reaction to the fundraising success of Bessborough Drive School, an editorial in the *Globe and Mail* proclaimed, "If a private sponsor could give poor children what affluent children already have, why not?"[53] Much like the arguments around school-business partnerships and corporate sponsorship, many saw the solution to inequities in external funding sources. This was often reinforced by senior politicians, as illustrated by Premier McGuinty's comment noted at the beginning of this chapter that Ottawa trustees approach Home Depot for playground equipment. And at times it was also emphasized by senior educational administrators. In response to the fact that Sentinel's plans would place the school in a stronger financial position than other BC schools, the district superintendent indicated that "his primary responsibility is not to ensure equity but to provide the best education possible for the students of West Vancouver."[54]

The search for new sources of money, then, resulted in some cases in pitting school against school and district against district. Parents' focus on their children, a community's focus on its local school, or a district's scramble to secure its own financial needs reinforced inward-looking solutions to specific issues rather than assessments of the system as a whole. New fundraising methods also allowed the development of organizations, with their own priorities and structures, to enter the educational landscape. Charitable foundations, established under the wings of school boards, were one example. Others would soon join them.

The Learning Partnership

In the early 1990s, Charlie Pielsticker, the owner of an insurance agency in Toronto, was volunteering as part of a reading program at an inner city school when he realized that there were a number of businesses involved in schools but no co-ordination of their activities. He wondered how much more they could offer if they united their efforts. In June 1992 he helped bring together about fifteen business executives and ten representatives of local school boards. Pielsticker, along with several other executives, flew to the United States, stopping off at the National Association of Partners in Education in Washington before heading to Louisville, Kentucky, where in 1991 prominent CEOs and an influential citizen lobby group had joined to form the Partnership for Kentucky School Reform. The following year Pielsticker registered the Metro Toronto Learning Partnership, later renamed the Learning Partnership, as a not-for-profit organization that could bring together business leaders and educators to encourage support for public education through targeted and niche programs not directly funded by government.[55] The first board members developed four goals: "increasing literacy, enhancing readiness for school, reducing school dropouts and encouraging science and technology careers particularly for young women."[56]

The organization hired Gordon Cressy, a former Toronto municipal politician with experience in the nonprofit sector, as president and CEO. Cressy, who was working as vice-president of institutional relations at the University of Toronto at the time, took a leave of absence, while the new program director, Lori Cranson, did so from the Scarborough school board where she served as program director for Scarborough Venture Centre. About twenty firms helped with the initial financing, providing approximately $5,000 each, while seventeen school boards in the greater Toronto area also contributed some funds. The Partnership quickly gained the support of prominent corporations including Imperial Oil, Bell Canada, many of Canada's largest banks, Xerox, Hewlett Packard, Eaton's, and the *Toronto Star*. By 1996 the Learning Partnership included Toronto area school boards, over eighty businesses, four community colleges, and three universities. Interviewed in 2002, Pielsticker stated, "All we're trying to do is help youngsters—if we can do that, we're all winners."[57]

The organization started with two programs, "Take Our Kids to Work," which encouraged a wide range of businesses to open their doors for a day in order to expose students to workplace opportunities, and an inventor/mentor program that allowed Grade 6 to 8 students a chance to work with a local business and develop new projects in relation to science and technology. It would also develop a program titled "Change Your Future," which aimed to help struggling visible minority and Aboriginal teenagers to graduate from high school, and another, "Creative Arts Learning Partnership," allowing teachers of Grades 4 to 6 to attend various ballet and theatre performances so as to better teach their students. By 2002 the Partnership boasted a budget of $3 million, secured not only from businesses but also from school boards and various other arms of the government. Until 2003, "Take Our Kids to Work" was the only program offered beyond Ontario. After that year the organization worked to expand its programs nationally.[58]

The Partnership now includes a variety of additional initiatives: "Entrepreneurial Adventure"; "I^3—Investigate! Invent! Innovate!" (I Cubed); "Welcome to Kindergarten"; and "Turning Points." Its flagship program, "Take Our Kids to Work," is offered in all provinces and territories, while "Welcome to Kindergarten," which provides parents with a bag containing tools such as books and magnetic fridge letters and numbers to encourage literacy and numeracy at home in order to prepare preschoolers for kindergarten, is offered in most provinces. "Turning Points" includes "national Essay Contests, Presentations and Anthology Publications" in which students are recognized for sharing "intimate turning points and values that guide their lives." The aim of "Entrepreneurial Adventure" is to develop "global perspectives, technology and 'business' skills through the process of transforming ideas into profitable ventures—the proceeds of which are given back to the community." According to the Learning Partnership, it creates relationships "with employers from diverse sectors as program mentors to illustrate real life business principles in transforming ideas into reality through Entrepreneurial Adventure Showcases." In "I Cubed" students identify a problem, develop a prototype to deliver a solution, and create a business and marketing plan to promote the invention, which is showcased at an Invention Convention.[59]

While the Learning Partnership offers a range of programs, some are very explicitly focused on the development of entrepreneurial spirit and business ideology with a focus on STEM. For example, "Entrepreneurial Adventure" and "I Cubed" seek to encourage exposure to, and interest in, STEM in the belief that "Canada's prosperous future lies in our ability to drive innovation and commercialization on the global stage." The programs are designed to "develop innovative thinking, collaborative spirit, problem solving and self-confidence." They also aim to unleash students' "entrepreneurial spirit" in the belief that "entrepreneurial thinking, creative problem solving and financial literacy are critical skills our students will need to succeed in today's complex work place." In addition, the Partnership intends these programs to encourage social responsibility.[60]

Corporate involvement in program development was key from the start. "I Cubed," for instance, was initially developed for Grade 7 and 8 students with $100,000 worth of support from Imperial Oil. Jim Levins, director of Imperial Oil's department of safety, health, and environment in Toronto, and a member of the board of directors of the Learning Partnership, and Fred Reichl, a retired former employee at Imperial, helped design the initiative.[61] This involvement by major corporations in creating programming adopted by schools led immediately to diverging opinions about the Partnership. In October 1994 the widely read magazine *Today's Parent* ran a long feature on a Partnership conference. The article highlighted the growing desire of business leaders to play a role in education and the voices of those opposing such endeavours. Speaking at the conference, Joan Green, director of education for the Toronto Board of Education, noted of school-business relationships, "It's not a merger,

"All We're Trying to Do Is Help Youngsters"   145

The Learning Partnership's "Welcome to Kindergarten" Kit, 2018, including bag, ball, scissors, glue stick, small bag of magnetic letters and numbers, and resource booklet of family activities to prepare for kindergarten, as well as crayons and several books (not shown). Photo: Jeff Crawford.

an acquisition or a takeover.... It's a partnership." She highlighted students' need to learn how to become life-long learners in order to respond to a constantly changing workplace, and schools' needs for community resources to prepare students for this reality. Asked by the magazine for his response to such ideas, David Noble, a historian concerned about the corporatization of universities, stated:

> the purpose of business is to get a return on their investment.... And what's their return in this case? Producing people to work within the corporate culture and grooming future consumers. The whole orientation of education becomes attuned to the interests of someone other than the people undergoing the education, and I think that's wrong.[62]

In contrast, Noble believed the purpose of education ought to be the development of "self-knowledge and a critical understanding of the world."

The reaction of the Ontario Secondary School Teachers' Federation (OSSTF) to the Learning Partnership was equally cool. Teacher activists complained that many of the corporations supporting the organization's aims were also those advocating privatization of services, cutting jobs, outsourcing work, and avoiding paying property taxes (revenue needed to sustain public schooling). Others criticized the ideological framing of some of the Partnership's activities. One teacher noted that the resource materials provided following workplace visits included no discussion of union activity or issues around unemployment or any critical discussion of the workplace. Instead, students were "asked to define words such as: 'downsizing,' 'restructuring,' 'adaptability,' 'flexibility,'" and to think creatively about new ways computers might be used in the site they visited.[63] In 1996, delegates to the Annual Meeting of the Provincial Assembly of the OSSTF voted overwhelmingly against supporting the Learning Partnership's "Take Our Kids to Work" day, favouring a program independent of that organization instead.

Despite OSSTF's reservations, the Learning Partnership continued to grow, building programs that corresponded to provincial curricula and could be easily integrated into the classroom. "Coding Quest," a recent addition to its repertoire, is a good example. Aimed at Grades 4 to 6, the program, in which students create a video game to learn basic coding skills, was piloted in spring 2016 and launched that fall. It was developed in collaboration with, among others, RBC Foundation, NB Power, the Ontario, PEI and New Brunswick governments, Manitoba Education and Advanced Learning, the Halifax International Airport Authority, Visa Canada, and the Delta and Richmond school districts in BC. According to the Learning Partnership, "teachers are assisted as they deliver our 25-class adjustable framework, through an in-service workshop and online resources via The Learning Partnership's eLearning Moodle." The program "focuses on STEM education, 21st century and computational thinking, while incorporating learning skills, science and technology, mathematics, language arts, visual arts and social studies," culminating "in a regional Arcade hosted by The Learning Partnership."[64] Because the Partnership tightly links its programs to curricula, schools can use these initiatives to meet some provincial mandates.[65]

When the Learning Partnership was established in the early 1990s, the general view circulating within business and government circles held that the education system and Canadians' learning skills needed to be improved in order to meet the demands of a globally competitive economy.[66] Indeed, "lifelong learning" became a mantra for the 1990s and beyond, a positive spin on the emerging new realities of part-time and contract work, as well as the constant movement between jobs. In keeping with this interpretation, the education system was tasked with the central role of developing twenty-first-century skills. Technological know-how was at the core of this rhetoric, though in practice it was more often on the edge of the curriculum. Despite the emphasis on the importance of coding, for instance, in many places, students' exposure to it remained limited. And the emphasis on technological skills often meant learning how to use PowerPoint, at the expense of the harder work of writing an essay.

The link between technology and entrepreneurship is now reinforced within the Maker Education movement, with departments of education promoting "makerspaces" within schools. Maker education promotes STEAM (science, technology, engineering, art, and mathematics), adding elements of art and design to the more technological emphasis of STEM. In New Brunswick, for example, the provincial government stated, "The goal in school is to make learning more interesting, fun and relevant for young people, allowing them to solve everyday challenges and reinforce curricular outcomes." In one school, this task included working on projects "involving robotics, stop-motion video using green screen technology, rapid prototyping with 3D printers, and coding electronics." In order to promote makerspaces the government provided $500,000 to Brilliant Labs, "a not-for-profit, hands-on technology and experiential learning platform that supports the integration of creativity, innovation, coding, and an entrepreneurial spirit within classrooms and educational curriculums."[67]

Proponents of Maker Education emphasize STEAM as a necessary component of education, in turn requiring significant funds from schools and thus the need for partnerships. Undergirding the movement is an ideology of entrepreneurship and competitive individualism that is celebrated in the school "marketplace." It is couched in a rhetoric of social responsibility, with an option included for students to use technology to create something of benefit to the community and for the "marketplace" to raise money for a local charity. In some cases, the Learning Partnership is directly linked to the Maker Education movement. For example, Bliss Carman Middle School hosted Fredericton's first ever School Maker Faire in May 2017. Billed as "a student-led entrepreneurship initiative facilitated by The Learning Partnership," it was organized by Grade 7 students who presented workshops on topics such as coding and 3D design, sold the products they had made, and in the process aimed to help create greater interest in the Maker Education movement. The Faire was put on during New Brunswick Innovation Week and supported by Brilliant

Labs as an event "to celebrate innovation in student entrepreneurship." The program is reinforced as a virtuous public enterprise by charging a small entrance and activity fee, donated to a local charity, in this case the Canadian Cancer Society.[68]

The method of introducing New Brunswick students to Maker Education and the activities of the Learning Partnership might seem far removed from the fundraising initiatives examined at the start of this chapter. Yet they are, in many respects, the outcome of forces that have been reshaping the educational landscape. Since the 1970s, schools have faced increasing demands for students to be technologically, and particularly computer, literate, but the meaning of that literacy is constantly changing, with some materials and methods becoming quickly obsolete. Schools are unable to keep up. Companies focused on technological change can more easily respond, creating inventive, adaptable programs aimed at the education sector. The turn since the 1990s to an emphasis on the need for school districts and education ministries to forge partnerships with community organizations and business created a niche in which private organizations supplement school technology programs. This is also made possible by government funding being directed toward private or nonprofit organizations rather than invested directly in the public school system. And the inability of regular fundraising efforts to meet school needs (both real and perceived) means that partnerships that offer innovative and exciting programming appear as a creative solution. The focus on students creating, inventing, and making glosses over the fact, however, that in many cases they are being taught to develop a sellable product. Thus technological innovation and experimentation are framed primarily within an ideology of entrepreneurship and competitive individualism.

Conclusion

In the face of changing educational needs, school districts and provincial ministries have attempted to think creatively about how to provide programs considered important for students' future success. At root, the provision of such programs requires money and leads to questions about how to fund new or specific initiatives and where the money should come from. Parents, educators, and students continue to fundraise to support and enrich their schools, as they have done for over a hundred years. In the past few decades, however, such activities have become more frequent, more intense, and increasingly used to help provide basic resources rather than just extra services. School boosters have turned to corporate grants and competitions, the use of casinos, and the creation of charitable foundations to gain access to more funds. With continuing funding shortfalls, some department of education civil servants, school administrators, educators, and trustees have also sought out and supported partnerships that can fill gaps in the system.

Much more work is needed to understand the impact of technological change on school funding and fundraising efforts. What seems clear, however, is that as the pressure to fundraise has increased, parents and school administrators have turned to new methods to increase revenue. The need to raise ever larger amounts is accompanied by a series of moral dilemmas: how does one weigh support for musical instruments or sports teams against the encouragement of gambling, an application for an outdoor playground against promoting a company that profits from cutting down trees, the encouragement of partnerships against the creation of inequities within the public school system, the use of business or corporate grants and donations against the presence of advertising and marketing practices within the school, the desire for creative programming against market-driven values and ideology? In light of the overwhelming pressure to secure funds, and perceived need for those funds, the social and moral implications of fundraising are sometimes overlooked or ignored. Yet how funds are raised, and why they are raised, are important issues that help set educational priorities.

Conclusion

> The *Globe* looks with equanimity, even approval, on corporate sponsorships within public schools.... I, however, am condemned for life to seeing the four corners of maps of Canada and the world marked by Neilson's chocolate bars as an early variant of this insidious practice.[1]
> —JOHN FISHER, *Globe and Mail*, April 17, 2009

JOHN FISHER wrote his letter to the *Globe and Mail* in response to an editorial that encouraged readers to embrace the benefits of corporate sponsorship in public schools "in return for naming rights." In this case, the Toronto District School Board was considering allowing Future Shop to donate $50,000 "to each of two Toronto high schools for computer labs." The schools would be located close to stores and boast a lab painted in the company's corporate colours and including its name. The newspaper's justification? That "public schools are a point of pride in Canada, but it would be foolish pride indeed that prevented school boards from accepting help for less affluent young people."[2] The *Globe*'s solution to financial inequities within the school system smacked not only of an elitism in which poorer children would be subject to increased levels of commercialism, but, as Fisher pointed out, it also ignored the long-term impact of school commercialism.

As his letter reminds us, commercialism aimed at children is hardly new. As early as the 1920s advertisers recognized the enticing possibilities of the school market. Companies and their marketing departments developed a wide range of teaching aids, handed out logo-laden textbook dust covers, and sponsored essay contests. They drew in students through school banks, the creation of extracurricular clubs, and funds for field trips. Commercialism appeared on school maps, in corporate-sponsored films, on school milk cartons at lunch, and in the myriad fundraising endeavours undertaken by parent-teacher associations. Educators, parents, and concerned citizens periodically raised their voices against such activities, particularly in the 1920s and 1930s and again in the 1970s, eras that saw the development of broad-based consumer movements. Still, educators continued to rely on these materials for a variety of reasons, including lack of good alternatives, the quality of some of the corporate resources, the attempt to keep students engaged, and pressure from senior education officials. Moreover, advertising agents crafted materials to fit very specifically within curricula. In the first three-quarters of the twentieth century, then, corporate advertisers and marketeers gained a foothold within schools.

Beginning in the 1980s, but particularly through the 1990s and early 2000s, marketing and advertising initiatives aimed at youth intensified, with the schoolhouse becoming a battleground for corporations seeking to gain an advantage over their competitors. This intensification coincided with the intersection of several phenomena. In the 1980s school administrators increasingly promoted school-business partnerships. This was part of a broader ideological movement that saw business practices as the solution to failing schools. That approach gained a foothold alongside a massive and ongoing technological revolution. Leaders of high-tech corporations pushed the idea, one that many quickly adopted, that the microcomputer could transform schooling and, in the process, reignite the flagging North American economy. The cost of providing and maintaining computers and the information network, however, was often beyond the means of schools, school boards, or even provincial governments. By the 1990s, school systems across the country faced a period of significant fiscal restraint. Many educators and parents came to see school-business partnerships as an alternative and beneficial means to provide for schools' needs. This openness to partnerships occurred at the very time that corporations were searching for new markets. Thus corporations and their advertising agents set their sights on a growing youth market, focusing particularly on schools—where children and teens spent most of their day.

Some forms of commercialism from earlier in the century remained: teaching aids, corporate-sponsored films, funding for field trips, development of school banks, donations of materials and money. But new approaches also appeared: fast food giants or banks supporting reading or fitness programs or large grocery chains promoting contests for school computers; attempts to gain a foothold for commercial television; and the advent of exclusivity contracts by soda companies. The scale of these initiatives increased dramatically. And an infrastructure developed to support this process with, for example, marketing experts brokering deals and the emergence of companies focused on school fundraising. Schools have been complicit in this process, selling space ranging from washroom stalls to school buses for advertising, allowing logos in gyms or corporate colours on walls, and making use of vending machines and fast food providers in cafeterias.

The intensification of commercialism in this period did not go unchecked. Starting in 1992 and continuing through the decade, YNN raised a furor among students, parents, teachers and their associations, and concerned citizens. Exclusivity agreements with soda companies, which began to appear after 1994, equally drew attention to the negative consequences of the growing presence of commercialism in schools. In the 1990s teachers' unions, parent associations, and educational watchdogs began calling for better definitions of school-business partnerships and guidelines for tracking this phenomenon. Teachers' unions also became more militant and parents more active, linking what they saw as the commercialism and privatization of schools to part of a broader attack on public education as provinces worked to create efficiencies within the school system. All of this occurred within the context of a growing anti-corporate and anti-globalization movement.

What those opposed to the increasing commercialism within schools often found was that the task of taking on powerful corporations was a difficult one amid a cultural context generally supportive of business involvement in schools. Resistance was most successful when it targeted television in the classroom, exclusivity clauses, or fast-food chains promoting fitness—specific issues that highlighted blatant commercialism and drew public condemnation. Where school boards remained in charge of guidelines, the level of commercialism differed depending on the character of the leadership and constituency of that district. Provincial ministries could provide a more uniform approach, something more common in Quebec than elsewhere. Resistance became less successful the more complicated the issue. Whereas a broad-based coalition could be created against exclusivity clauses or in support of reducing the availability of sugary drinks, opponents of commercialism had less success in eliminating vending machines completely, encouraging the use of tap water rather than bottled water, or promoting home-made lunches rather than the use of fast food companies for cafeteria programs.

Resistance to commercialism in schools was, however, far from unanimous. Many parents and educators saw partnerships and corporate sponsorships as beneficial. After all, some argued, schools needed money and corporations could help. Moreover, schools usually drew on the same businesses that families frequented on a regular basis. Students, supporters were keen to argue, were already exposed to a wide variety of advertising and familiar with the brands appearing in schools. Equally, parents, grandparents, and community members, many of whom worked at these corporations, simply wanted to help their local school. Tolerance for commercialism, then, was justified on a variety of grounds.

Still, there are a number of reasons why we should think twice about in-school commercialism. Schools are a manifestation of the public sphere. They are different from malls because "they are an expression of the public will, the product of a collective and conscious effort to mobilize public resources to promote human flourishing."[3] They provide an important space for the teaching and practice of democratic ideals, for thinking about issues of public interest, and for imparting societal values. This does not mean that they are fully democratic institutions or free from political or class interests. Parents often feel they have lost control over their children's education, while teachers argue the same thing about their workplace. Still, schooling remains part of a public conversation. Corporations' first obligation, on the other hand, is to their shareholders. Their promotion and protection of their brand can come into conflict with freedom of expression and critical thinking occurring within schools, particularly if this involves criticism of the corporation. Their bounty is ultimately tied to being seen as a good corporate citizen while their aim of increasing goodwill is undergirded by the need to increase profits.[4]

Social critics argue that corporate philanthropy or corporate social responsibility (CSR) has become central to doing business. "Corporate charity," the authors of one commentary note, "is no longer a garnish, an optional nicety, but instead sits at the center of the corporate plate, an integral element of a firm's core business strategy."[5] Marketeers readily acknowledge this. As Sonny Vaccaro, the founder of one of Nike's school equipment contribution programs, bluntly put it, "It's a marketing ploy." Referring to the "cool factor" of seventeen-year-old high school athletes, Vaccaro stated, "they drive product sales."[6] But more than this, CSR aims to garner credibility and trustworthiness, thereby promoting sales while deflecting attention from any potential negative practices or publicity. At the local level, this process works by turning a corporate sponsor or partner into a school-family member, making it difficult for individuals within the community to take a critical stance.[7] This is not to say that there are not altruistic executives or that the public does not benefit from corporate largesse. But public and private interests are not the same. The more that the education system draws on corporate funding and implements corporate business models, the less schools are able to provide space for teaching critical reflectivity and civic action.

Corporations are also constantly at work, both implicitly and explicitly, in "framing" their activities. Sociologists Scott Davies and Neil Guppy note that some industrial groups "provide good-quality teaching resources." However, they also warn that in the provision of educational materials, corporations impose "their particular slant on the world. . . . In one sense their curriculum resources are pure and simple altruism, but in another sense this is important public relations work for these organizations."[8] Beyond simply using corporate materials or resources as a means to present themselves as good citizens, corporations put forward a particular version of events, without a countering interpretation. Equally, as schools adopt commercial materials, business practices, and models, or integrate technology into curricula primarily through the lens of entrepreneurship, these ways of doing things become naturalized. This frame of reference, David Harvey argues, becomes the "way many of us interpret, live in, and understand the world," making it difficult to work outside, or act beyond, its bounds.[9]

By forging links to corporations, schools help bring the public will in line with private interests. Schools', teachers', and parents' acceptance of corporate material, viewpoints, or methods is an indirect endorsement. The school is a symbol of authority and brings legitimacy to all that occurs within its walls. As a result, the presence of corporate logos, names, brands, or products in schools helps to promote a vision of particular companies, and free-market ideology more broadly, as benevolent.[10]

But corporations do not operate on the same playing field as schools. School-business partnerships often involve an unequal relationship. For one thing, business holds a more advantageous position, able to offer a school more than that party can provide in return. As Trevor Norris argues, while these arrangements "imply a fair and equal relationship," in reality it is one of inequality as "one group is wealthy and seeking private gain while the other is desperate and needy." He also notes that while the relationships are presented as beneficent, they often contribute to the erosion of resources available to public schools. Donations, for example, can be "used as a tax write-off, further draining the public resources needed to support our schools in the first place." Partnerships also target particular schools at the expense of other ones. "Funding and resource decisions," Norris contends, "are made by corporations based on their own gains rather than democratically elected—and accountable—school officials."[11] These types of agreements exacerbate inequities within the system, with particular schools or school districts benefitting more than others. Thus, the theory that partnerships are simply a means by which businesses can help the local community and that schools can benefit from local skill sets is much more complicated in practice.

In addition to supporting corporate aims and market values, school commercialism also adversely affects student health. Juliet Schor has forcefully argued that commercialism promotes insidious practices of consumption that are antithetical to human flourishing. The current heightened period of consumerism, she notes, includes "an upscaling of lifestyle norms; the pervasiveness of conspicuous, status goods and of competition for acquiring them; and the growing disconnect between consumer desires and incomes." It has equally contributed to the erosion of, and reduction of support for, resources for public services, private savings, and free time. Personal and financial investment in consumer goods has been accompanied by a decline in "basic quality-of-life measures." As a result, "general increases in income and consumption" have not yielded "gains in well-being."[12]

The incorporation of advertising and marketing into schools reinforces corporate aims fuelling consumer desire and a culture based on material accumulation that often counters schools' emphases on intellectual creativity, personal development, and individual well-being. Much research suggests that the physical health of children contributes to their mental and intellectual health. This is one of the reasons that school curricula specifically teach nutrition and devote time to physical education. Yet the separation of the classroom from the hallway or the cafeteria ignores the reality of school as a learning environment in all of its dimensions. It ignores the fact that for better or worse some of the most significant and long-lasting lessons are learned once students step outside the classroom door. Fundraising using chocolate bars, candy, pizza, cookies, or soft drinks supports the industries built on those products and legitimizes this consumption at school and home, risking the health of children and future citizens.

This history of in-school commercialism provides an overview. It aims to pull together separate stories and understand how they fit together. Much more research is needed to fully comprehend the nature, process, and impact of commercialism in Canadian schools. While this book illuminates the national story, for example, it does less justice to the nuances at the provincial and local level. In focusing on particular case studies that caught the public eye, stories remain untold. Equally, the nature of the sources leaves hidden the myriad daily forms of resistance by parents, students, and teachers within their schools. Our understanding of in-school commercialism could benefit significantly from detailed case studies of many of the topics in this book at the local and provincial level and comparatively across provinces.

We also need more research into current forms of advertising and continuing types of sponsored classroom materials and incentive programs in schools. While this book offers a guide to the varied forms of commercialism up to the recent past, the current pace of technological innovation makes continued research into the topic imperative. The rapid evolution and expansion of a networked society will bring new opportunities for commercialism as well as unforeseen variations.[13] Tracking its changing form and nature will provide greater understanding of the growing impact of market forces within education systems.

Educators, parents, concerned citizens, and students themselves can continue to play an important role in raising awareness about the impact of the corporate presence in schools. So too can the media, without which much of this story could not have been told. However, raising such questions may become increasingly difficult with the pervasiveness of corporate culture and market ideology. Jane Kenway and Elizabeth Bullen persuasively argue that students "need to understand how consumer culture works with and against them, and when and how to oppose it, to comprehend what else is possible and how these possibilities may be made real."[14] One wonders if that perspective will gain the corporate support readily offered to programs encouraging the development of entrepreneurship.

At the heart of this study lie a number of questions: What purposes does schooling serve? What educational initiatives should be publicly funded? When should parents demand more from their governments? How can equity be maintained between schools, school districts, and across provinces? What types of citizens should schools help to create and how should they do so? What values should schools impart? These are difficult questions and there are no easy answers. Nor is the way forward always evident. But what is clear is that individuals and groups can effect change. That some solutions can't be worked out at the local level—government intervention is required to ensure all students have access to healthy, commercial-free spaces. And, most of all, that corporations, and corporate ideology, should not be allowed to direct the nature, content, and outcomes of our schools. Commercialism, as an expression of corporate interests, has the effect of turning children into a captivated, and captive, audience.

Acknowledgements

As with all books, this one has incurred a number of debts. The research for this project would not have been undertaken without the support of a Social Sciences and Humanities Research Council of Canada Standard Research Grant. I am also grateful for the institutional support provided by St. Thomas University, particularly from the members of the history department. I benefitted significantly from the research assistance of Funké Aladejebi, Natalie Cormier, Ashley Doiron, and Kelly Ferguson. John Pungente handed over a wealth of primary source material that contributed to the development of chapter 5. Ellen Rose provided comments on chapter 3 that helped improve my understanding of issues related to educational technology. Mike Dawson, R. D. Gidney, W. P. J. Millar, and two anonymous reviewers generously read the manuscript in its entirety. Cameron Duder provided helpful copyediting. At Between the Lines, Amanda Crocker, along with Renée Knapp, David Molenhuis and Jennifer Tiberio, ably guided the project through the publication process, responding to my many queries along the way.

Chapter 1 draws heavily on material that first appeared in Catherine Gidney and R.D. Gidney, "Branding the Classroom: Commercialism in Canadian Schools, 1920–1960," *Histoire sociale/Social History* 41, no. 82 (November 2008): 345–79. Parts of chapter 6 were previously published as "'Nutritional Wastelands': Vending Machines, Fast Food Outlets, and the Fight over Junk Food in Canadian Schools," *Canadian Bulletin of Medical History/Bulletin canadien d'histoire de la médecine* 32, no. 2 (2015): 391–409. It is reprinted with permission from University of Toronto Press (utpjournals.press), doi.org/10.3138/cbmh.32.2.391, © 2015 Canadian Society for the History of Medicine/Société canadienne d'histoire de la médecine, ISSN 0823-2105, printed in Canada/Imprimé au Canada. My thanks to R. D. Gidney and to these journals for allowing me to use this material.

This book had its origins in material brought to my attention by R. D. Gidney, resulting in a co-authored article that traced historical processes with contemporary implications. It gained a sense of immediacy as my children entered the school system, leading me to encounter many of the questions raised herein. I dedicate it to them, not only because they have lived with its fruition with grace, but because their lovely faces are a daily reminder that we can always do better.

Notes

INTRODUCTION

1 Cited in Maude Barlow and Heather-jane Robertson, *Class Warfare: The Assault on Canadian Public Education* (Toronto: Key Porter Books, 1994), 112.
2 Kim Bolan, *Vancouver Sun*, June 20, 1998, B5, cited in Naomi Klein, *No Logo: Taking Aim at the Brand Bullies* (Toronto: Knopf Canada, 2000), 94; Steve Coffin, "This Isn't Charity," *National Post*, December 22, 2004, A21; Allen Garr, "Ad Policy Fights Corporate Tide," *Vancouver Courier*, November 9, 2005, 10; Larry Kuehn, "Education Roundup," *Our Schools, Our Selves* 15, no. 2 (Winter 2006): 12.
3 Increased commercialization occurred at the same time as a turn toward privatization of educational services, from the creation of charter schools to privately built school buildings, to instituting a variety of user fees. While there is significant overlap in topics, the issue of privatization deserves separate attention. This book focuses specifically on the extensive phenomenon of in-school commercialism. For a useful definition of the latter in the American context, see Alex Molnar, *School Commercialism: From Democratic Ideal to Market Commodity* (New York: Routledge, 2005), 21–26.
4 Peter N. Stearns, *Consumerism in World History: The Global Transformation of Desire* (London: Routledge, 2001), ix; Gary S. Cross, *An All-Consuming Century: Why Commercialism Won in Modern America* (New York: Columbia University Press, 2000), viii, 1–2; Lizabeth Cohen, *A Consumers' Republic: The Politics of Mass Consumption in Postwar America* (New York: Alfred A. Knopf, 2003), 11; Graham Broad, *A Small Price to Pay: Consumer Culture on the Canadian Home Front, 1939–45* (Vancouver: UBC Press, 2013), 3.
5 Susan Linn, *Consuming Kids: The Hostile Takeover of Childhood* (New York: The New Press, 2004), 2. J. B. Schor found that as television viewing declines, so too do children's requests for toys. See *Born to Buy: The Commercialized Child and the New Consumer Culture* (New York: Scribner, 2004), 66–67.
6 Roy F. Fox, *Harvesting Minds: How TV Commercials Control Kids* (Westport, CT: Praeger, 1996), 146–50, 154.

7 Marion Nestle, *Food Politics: How the Food Industry Influences Nutrition and Health*, rev. ed. (Berkeley: University of California Press, 2007), 180–88.
8 Shirley R. Steinberg and Joe L. Kincheloe, "Introduction: No More Secrets—Kinderculture, Information Saturation, and the Postmodern Childhood," in *Kinderculture: The Corporate Construction of Childhood*, ed. Shirley R. Steinberg and Joe L. Kincheloe, 1–30 (Boulder, CO: Westview Press, 1998), 8.
9 Fox, *Harvesting Minds*, 13–19.
10 Schor, *Born to Buy*, 167.
11 Steinberg and Kincheloe, "Introduction," *Kinderculture*, 8; Schor, *Born to Buy*, 169; Alex Molnar, Faith Boninger, Michael D. Harris, Ken M. Libby, and Joseph Fogarty, "Promoting Consumption at School. Health Threats Associated with Schoolhouse Commercialism. The Fifteenth Annual Report on Schoolhouse Commercializing Trends: 2011–2012," 3, nepc.colorado.edu; Alex Molnar and Faith Boninger, *Sold Out: How Marketing in School Threatens Children's Well-Being and Undermines Their Education* (Lanham, MD: Rowman & Littlefield, 2015), chapter 3.
12 Steinberg and Kincheloe, "Introduction," *Kinderculture*, 8. In 2005, for example, the Ontario Medical Association proclaimed childhood obesity to be an epidemic, warning of a likely decline in lifespan for current and future generations. See also Caroline Alphonso, "Class Warfare: The Clash of the Cafs," *Globe and Mail*, October 8, 2005, A12; "Healthy Weights for Healthy Kids: Report of the Standing Committee on Health," House of Commons (Canada), March 2007, 1, cited in Aileen Leo, "Are Schools Making the Grade? School Nutrition Policies across Canada" (Ottawa: Centre for Science in the Public Interest, October 2007), 1, cspinet.org; Kim D. Raine et al., "Restricting Marketing to Children: Consensus on Policy Interventions to Address Obesity," *Journal of Public Health Policy* 34, no. 2 (2013): 244. Recent research indicates that the simple act of watching soda drink commercials results in increased soda consumption. See Marion Nestle, *Soda Politics: Taking on Big Soda (and Winning)* (New York: Oxford University Press, 2015), 135.
13 Schor, *Born to Buy*, 173.

1: THE "DISCRIMINATING AND ALERT TEACHER"?

1 This chapter draws heavily on Catherine Gidney and R. D. Gidney, "Branding the Classroom: Commercialism in Canadian Schools, 1920–1960," *Histoire sociale/Social History* 41, no. 82 (November 2008): 345–79. My thanks to R. D. Gidney for permission to make extensive use of this article. Copp Clark published several versions of the map of Canada, updating the chocolate bars on display. For a slightly different version of the map, and for more extensive references, see page 372 of that article. For classroom numbers, see M. E. LaZerte, *School Finance in Canada* (Edmonton: Hamley Press, 1955), 13–15.
2 Bettina Liverant, "Canada's Consumer Election (1935)," in *Consuming Modernity: Gendered Behaviour and Consumerism before the Baby Boom*, ed. Cheryl Krasnick Warsh and Dan Malleck, 11–33 (Vancouver: UBC Press, 2013), 12.

3 Liverant, "Canada's Consumer Election (1935)," 14.
4 Graham Broad, *A Small Price to Pay: Consumer Culture on the Canadian Home Front, 1939–45* (Vancouver: UBC Press), 12. For the expansion of tourism through the 1930s and 1940s, see Michael Dawson, *Selling British Columbia: Tourism and Consumer Culture, 1890–1970* (Vancouver: UBC Press, 2004).
5 Lizabeth Cohen, *A Consumers' Republic: The Politics of Mass Consumption in Postwar America* (New York: Alfred A. Knopf, 2003), 11, 403; Doug Owram, *Born at the Right Time: A History of the Baby Boom Generation* (Toronto: University of Toronto Press, 1996), 93–99.
6 Lisa Jacobson, *Raising Consumers: Children and the American Mass Market in the Early Twentieth Century* (New York: Columbia University Press, 2004), 30–31; Daniel Thomas Cook, *The Commodification of Childhood: The Children's Clothing Industry and the Rise of the Child Consumer* (Durham, NC: Duke University Press, 2004), 2, 8; Steven Mintz, *Huck's Raft: A History of American Childhood* (Cambridge, MA: Harvard University Press, 2006), 215. For the growing importance of advertising in shaping North American culture, see also Jackson Lears, *Fables of Abundance: A Cultural History of Advertising in America* (New York: Basic Books, 1994); Susan Strasser, *Satisfaction Guaranteed: The Making of the American Mass Market* (New York: Pantheon, 1989); Roland Marchand, *Advertising the American Dream: Making Way for Modernity, 1920–1940* (Berkeley: University of California Press, 1985).
7 Peter N. Stearns, *Consumerism in World History: The Global Transformation of Desire* (London: Routledge, 2001), 48–49; Jacobson, *Raising Consumers*, 57; Cynthia Comacchio, *The Dominion of Youth: Adolescence and the Making of Modern Canada, 1920 to 1950* (Waterloo, ON: Wilfrid Laurier University Press, 2006), chapter 6.
8 Stearns, *Childhood in World History*, 72–74.
9 In 1911, 42 percent of fifteen-year-olds attended school. By 1951 that figure had risen to 76 percent. See R. D. Gidney and W. P. J. Millar, "Creating the Schooled Society" (unpublished manuscript), 5.
10 Comacchio, *The Dominion of Youth*, 100; Owram, *Born at the Right Time*, chapter 5.
11 Kelly Schrum, *Some Wore Bobby Sox: The Emergence of Teenage Girls' Culture, 1920–1945* (New York: Palgrave, 2004), 5, 14, 42; Cook, *The Commodification of Childhood*, 9; Donica Belisle, *Retail Nation: Department Stores and the Making of Modern Canada* (Vancouver: UBC Press, 2011), chapter 1; Katharine Rollwagen, "Eaton's Goes to School: Youth Councils and the Commodification of the Teenaged Consumer at Canada's Largest Department Store, 1940–1960," *Histoire sociale/Social History* 47, no. 95 (November 2014): 683–703.
12 The next several paragraphs draw heavily on Gidney and Gidney, "Branding the Classroom." For the US, see Strasser, *Satisfaction Guaranteed*, 164–65, 180; Sheila Harty, *Hucksters in the Classroom: A Review of Industry Propaganda in Schools* (Washington, DC: Centre for Study of Responsive Law, 1979), 102. By the end of the 1950s one in five American corporations provided free teaching aids to schools. See Elizabeth A. Fones-Wolf, *Selling Free Enterprise: The Business Assault on Labor and Liberalism, 1945–60* (Urbana: University of Illinois Press, 1994), 204.

13 "Their Future Smiles Need Help Now," *A.T.A. Magazine* 30, no. 2 (October 1949), 36–37. For a corresponding classroom initiative by Lifebuoy, see Gidney and Gidney, "Branding the Classroom," 346–47.

14 Chava Willig Levy, "Metropolitan Life Insurance and the American Educator: Partners in Leadership," in *American Business and the Public School: Case Studies of Corporate Involvement in Public Education*, ed. Marsha Levine and Roberta Trachtman, 29–43 (New York: Teachers College Press, 1988), 30–31.

15 "Ontario," *The School*, elementary edition 28, no. 3 (November 1939): 264.

16 Rollwagen, "Eaton's Goes to School," 610.

17 Belisle, *Retail Nation*, 124.

18 Rollwagen, "Eaton's Goes to School," 684.

19 Rollwagen, "Eaton's Goes to School," 693.

20 Dan McEwen, "Lesson with Logos: The Debate over Corporate Sponsorships," *Education Canada* 42, no. 3 (Fall 2002): 44–46; Martine Turenne, "L'école sauce PUB," *L'actualité* (Montreal), September 15, 1999, 37. For the continuation of this type of commercialism into the present in the United States, see Deron Boyles, "Uncovering the Coverings: The Use of Corporate Supplied Textbook Covers to Further Uncritical Consumerism," in *The Corporate Assault on Youth: Commercialism, Exploitation, and the End of Innocence*, ed. Deron Boyles, 174–86 (New York: Peter Lang, 2008).

21 See for example, *Norvoc* (Northern Vocational School) and *Oakwook Oracle* (Oakwook Collegiate Institute), Toronto District School Board Archives and Museum. In both cases ads dwindled in the 1980s, though in the case of the *Oracle*, they reappeared in the 1990s.

22 "Notes and News," *The School* 23, no. 7 (March 1935): 627; "Cominco Hosts Teachers," *BC Teacher* 35, no. 6 (March 1956): 291; "Teaching Turnabout" *ATA Magazine* (April 1949): 21, 24; "Shell Merit Fellowships," *Educational Review* 71, no. 3 (January–February 1957): 31–33.

23 Ontario Department of Education Circular, "The Penny Bank in the Schools," *The School* 4, no. 7 (December 1916): 612–13. See also Jacobson, *Raising Consumers*, 6, 57.

24 Mlle. Andréa Lanteigne, Ecole Supérieure, Caraquet, "Les Caisses Scolaires Complements Necessaires dans la Formation de la Jeunesse," *Educational Review* 62, no. 2 (December 1947): 44–45.

25 "Bringing Banking into the Schools," *Globe and Mail*, January 14, 1970, 5. CIBC established its fifth such branch in 1970.

26 "Children's Prizes Attract Attention in Ontario Schools," *Globe*, September 2, 1933, 11. "Teachers Invited to Spur Interest in Their Classes," *Globe*, September 1, 1934, 8. "Success of School Contest in 1934 Encourages The Globe to Increase Number of Handsome Shields," *Globe*, August 23, 1935, 18.

27 Dawson, *Selling British Columbia*, 205.

28 Gidney and Gidney, "Branding the Classroom," 376.

29 "More Young People Switch to Sample Brand," *Globe and Mail*, October 19, 1977, B5.

30 Judith Stamps, "Consumer Education and the Philosophy of Competitive Individualism in British Columbia," *BC Studies* 83 (Autumn 1989): 77. For the influence of Junior Achievement more generally, see Mayssoun Sukarieh and Stuart Tannock, "Putting School Commercialism in Context: A Global History of Junior Achievement Worldwide," *Journal of Education Policy* 24, no. 6 (November 2009): 769–86. On consumer education, see also Joel Spring, *Educating the Consumer-Citizen: A History of the Marriage of Schools, Advertising, and Media* (Mahwab, NJ: Erlbaum, 2003), 186–87.

31 Margaret Mironowicz, "McDonald's School Program: Filling, But Nutritious?" *Globe and Mail*, May 29, 1978, 5.

32 Gidney and Gidney, "Branding the Classroom," 367–69.

33 "Business in the Schools," *The School* 23, no. 5 (January 1935): 430–31.

34 B. C. C. Evoy, "Yours . . . for the ASKING," *ATA Magazine* 27, no. 2 (November 1946): 20.

35 Supervisor of Schools to C. E. Payne, Dept. of Trade and Commerce, Ottawa, September 24, 1937, box 4, file 32, Correspondence with Dominion Government, 79.334, Provincial Archives of Alberta (PAA).

36 For example, the Dominion government's Department of the Interior routinely provided Canadian schools with its monthly bulletin, "Natural Resources, Canada." See Deputy Minister, Dept. of the Interior, to Deputy Minister of Education, Alberta, October 31, 1930, box 4, file 29: Correspondence with Dominion Government, 1930-1951, 79.334, PAA.

37 "Some Interesting School Helps," *Educational Review* 52, no. 2 (October 1937): 24; "Canadian Schools at War," *Educational Review* 58, no. 2 (December 1943): 8; "Radio—School Broadcasts," *Educational Review* 57, no. 1 (October 1942): 11.

38 "Valuable Information and Where to Obtain It," *Educational Review* 66, no. 3 (February 1952): 22. In 1953 the Canadian Teachers' Federation published a "Bibliography of Free Teaching Aids Available in Canada" that included, among other nonprofit and commercial services, a thirty-two-page pamphlet of "Program Aids from Business and Industry" produced by the Canadian Manufacturers' Association. See Canadian Teachers' Federation, *Information Bulletin 53-1*, June 1953. In that same year, the National Education Association published a handbook for teachers entitled *Using Free Materials in the Classroom* "that told American teachers how to obtain and use free corporate materials." See Harty, *Hucksters in the Classroom*, 100.

39 For the WCTU materials see *Manitoba School Journal* 5, no. 4 (December 1942): 20.

40 Christabelle Laura Sethna, "The Facts of Life: The Sex Instruction of Ontario Public School Children, 1900–1950" (PhD diss., University of Toronto, 1995), 300. Research in the United States indicates that Kimberly-Clark was very effective in reaching young girls through schools, youth groups such as Girl Scouts, and individual mothers well into the 1960s. See Joan Jacobs Brumberg, *The Body Project: An Intimate History of American Girls* (New York: Random House, 1997), 47, 227n29. In the US the film was used well into the 1960s. See Sharra L. Vostral,

"Advice to Adolescents: Menstrual Health and Menstrual Education Films, 1946–1982," in *Gender, Health, and Popular Culture: Historical Perspectives*, ed. Cheryl Krasnick Warsh, 47–64 (Waterloo, ON: Wilfrid Laurier Press, 2011), 55.

41 Chief Superintendent of Schools to Canadian Education Association, May 26, 1948, box 11–12, 79.334, PAA. See also the cautious endorsement of oil company materials, in Chief Superintendent of Schools to Canadian Education Association, box 10, CEA Files, 1946, Deputy Minister [Alberta] to Dr. C. E. Phillips.

42 Annual Report of the Department of Education of the Province of Saskatchewan, 1948–49, "Provincial Film Library," 34. This was common practice in other provinces as well. See *Manitoba School Journal* 12, no. 3 (November 1950): 1, and 23, no. 1 (September 1961): 6; "Shell Presents! Free for Classroom use . . . ," *ATA Magazine* (November 1954): 3; Alberta, Department of Education, *Annual Report for 1950*, Report, Curriculum Branch, 52.

43 Mary M. Douglas, "Geography in the Secondary School," *The School* 24, no. 7 (March 1936): 591–93.

44 See *ATA Magazine* (October 1941): 61–63. One geography teacher, advocating the usefulness of such material, claimed he had accumulated two hundred booklets, "which are in constant use and have proved invaluable." *The School* 23, 5 (January 1935): 430.

45 James A. Turner, "Social Studies on a Screen," *The School*, elementary edition, 30, no. 5 (January 1942): 435–37.

46 Mironowicz, "McDonald's School Program: Filling, But Nutritious?," 5.

47 Jacobson, *Raising Consumers*, 44.

48 "Have You a Laggard Holding Back the Class," *Western School Journal* 18, no. 8 (October 1923): 721.

49 Rollwagen, "Eaton's Goes to School," 695–98.

50 Harty, *Hucksters in the Classroom*, 99–100. See also Alex Molnar, *School Commercialism: From Democratic Ideal to Market Commodity* (New York: Routledge, 2005), 7–8.

51 Kyle Asquith, "Protecting the 'Guinea Pig Children': Resisting Children's Food Advertising in the 1930s," in *Shopping for Change: Consumer Activism and the Possibilities of Purchasing Power*, ed. Louis Hyman and Joseph Tohill, 85–96 (Toronto: Between the Lines, 2017), 88–89.

52 Packard, *The Hidden Persuaders* (New York: David McKay, 1957), 158, quoted in Jason C. Blokhuis, "Channel One: When Private Interests and the Public Interest Collide," *American Educational Research Journal* 45, no. 2 (June 2008): 347.

53 Cited in Harty, *Hucksters in the Classroom*, 101. The Canadian educational press relayed this report to its constituency: "Choosing Free Material," *B.C. Teacher* 35, no. 1 (September–October 1955): 38.

54 Cohen, *A Consumers' Republic*, 347–63.

55 Harty, *Hucksters in the Classroom*, 109.

56 New Brunswick, *Annual Report 1924–25*, liii.

57 John Popkin, "The Exploitation of Schemes in School," *Western School Journal* 24, no. 6 (June 1929): 232.

58 H. E. Balfour, "Send for Free Literature," *ATA Magazine* (October 1936): 23.
59 Deputy Minister to Dr. C. E. Phillips, Edmonton, November 27 1945, box 10, CNEA files, 1945, 79.334, PAA.
60 See *BC Teacher* 52, no. 2 (November 1972): 44, and 52, no. 4 (January 1973): 104.
61 School District No. 43 (Coquitlam), District Office, Coquitlam District School Board Records, Minutes, January 20, 1948, 3, and February 6, 1948, 2.
62 Rollwagen, "Eaton's Goes to School," 694.

2: "EDUCATION IS TOO IMPORTANT TO BE LEFT TO THE EDUCATORS"

1 "Companies 'Adopt' Schools," *Toronto Star*, February 10, 1987, A6.
2 Partnership programs could be found as early as 1983 in the Vancouver School Board, 1984 in the East York Board of Education, and around 1985 in the North York Board of Education and Calgary Board of Education. While partnerships included relationships with universities and community groups, this chapter focuses primarily on those with business. On the development of school-business partnerships, see Sally Martin, "Schools Love Being 'Adopted,'" *Toronto Star*, October 29, 1987, A27; Angela Mangiacasale, "School Work with a Twist," *Ottawa Citizen*, November 26, 1990, B1; Cathryn Motherwell, "Business Links Gain Priority," *Globe and Mail*, April 23, 1991, B24; Chris Dawson, "Tomorrow's Classroom: What Does the Future Hold?" *Calgary Herald*, February 13, 1994, B1; Lisa Dempster and Paul Marck, "Business Goes to School: Enterprise, Part 4 of 9," *Edmonton Journal*, March 14, 1995, A6; Andrew Duffy, "Companies Go to School," *Toronto Star*, June 11, 1995, F4; Francine Dube, "Corporate Classrooms; Are We Letting the Moneylenders Loose in Our Temples of Learning?" *Ottawa Citizen*, November 18, 1995, B1; Jennifer Lewington, "Grappling with An Ethical Question," *Globe and Mail*, March 27, 1997, C1.
3 Jerry Paquette, *Publicly Supported Education in Post-Modern Canada: An Imploding Universe?* (Toronto: Our Schools/Our Selves Education Foundation, 1994), 163. Spending per pupil, in 1986 dollars, rose from $3,159 in 1973–74 to $5,163 in 1982–83. See Paquette, 167, Tables 3–8.
4 Kenneth Norrie, Douglas Owram, and J. C. Herbert Emery, *A History of the Canadian Economy*, 4th ed. (Scarborough, ON: Nelson, 2008), 92–97, 262–63, 387; Doug Owram, *Born at the Right Time: A History of the Baby Boom Generation* (Toronto: University of Toronto Press, 1996), 111–15; R. D. Gidney, *From Hope to Harris: The Reshaping of Ontario's Schools* (Toronto: University of Toronto Press, 1999), 57.
5 Norrie et al., *A History of the Canadian Economy*, 401–6, 416, 424–26; Janice MacKinnon, *Minding the Public Purse: The Fiscal Crisis, Political Trade-offs, and Canada's Future* (Montreal and Kingston: McGill-Queen's University Press, 2003), x, 4–11, 60; Terry Wotherspoon, "Educational Reorganization and Retrenchment," in *Hitting the Books: The Politics of Educational Retrenchment*, ed. Terry Wotherspoon, 15–34 (Toronto: Garamond Press, 1991), 19–20.

6 François Gendron, "Funding Public School Systems: A 25-Year Review," in *Education Finance: Current Canadian Issues*, ed. Y. L. Jack Lam, 9–24 (Calgary: Detselig Enterprises, 1998), 11–24, 17–18; Scott Davies and Neil Guppy, *The Schooled Society: An Introduction to the Sociology of Education*, 2nd ed. (Don Mills, ON: Oxford University Press, 2010), 84–85, 102–3; Gidney, *Hope to Harris*, especially chapters 4, 8, 11.

7 R. D. Gidney and Wyn Millar, "Creating the Schooled Society" (unpublished manuscript), chapter 2: Finance, Table 4. My thanks to the authors for generously providing access to this manuscript. See also Jon Young and Benjamin Levin, *Understanding Canadian Schools: An Introduction to Educational Administration*, 3rd ed. (Scarborough, ON: Nelson, 2002), 160; Gendron, "Funding Public School Systems," 19; Ben Levin, *Governing Education* (Toronto: University of Toronto Press, 2005), 120; Gidney, *Hope to Harris*, 170.

8 Young and Levin, *Understanding Canadian Schools*, 161; J. Young, B. Levin, and D. Wallin, *Understanding Canadian Schools: An Introduction to Educational Administration*, 5th ed., chapter 5, home.cc.umanitoba.ca. Though the statistics differ, Manzer also illuminates the declining priority of education. See Ronald Manzer, *Public Schools and Political Ideas: Canadian Educational Policy in Historical Perspective* (Toronto: University of Toronto Press, 1994), 208.

9 Gidney and Millar, "Creating the Schooled Society," Chapter 2, Table 4. In some provinces, expenditure per pupil rose slightly while in others it declined marginally, resulting in a stagnant picture at the national level. See Young and Levin, *Understanding Canadian Schools*, 162. For an excellent summary of the complexity of comparing the funding of schools over time, see Young et al., *Understanding Canadian Schools*, 5th ed., chapter 5. Even where funding increased in some provinces, it did not necessarily match actual costs. In Ontario, for example, funding did not cover real costs in three areas: school operations and maintenance, salaries of non-teaching staff, and transportation. See People for Education, "Annual Report on Ontario's Schools 2007," 33. Moreover, support for some non-classroom positions declined. For example, in 2017 only 52 percent of elementary schools had a part- or full-time teacher-librarian, down from 80 percent in 1998. See People for Education, *Competing Priorities* (Annual Report on Ontario's Publicly Funded Schools 2017) (Toronto: People for Education, 2017), "Libraries," 1, www.peopleforeducation.ca.

10 Manzer notes that while annual increases in expenditures per pupil continued to rise, there was a reduction in these increases from 9.7 percent in the late 1960s to 2 percent or less by the late 1980s. See *Public Schools and Political Ideas*, 208–9. See also Gidney and Millar, "Creating the Schooled Society," 9.

11 Stephen B. Lawton, "Current Issues in the Public Finance of Elementary and Secondary Schools in Canada," in *Canadian Public Education Systems: Issues and Prospects*, ed. Y. L. Jack Lam, 31–45 (Calgary: Detselig, 1990), 33–34. See also Terry Wotherspoon, *The Sociology of Education in Canada: Critical Perspectives*, 2nd ed. (Don Mills, ON: Oxford University Press, 2004), 79. Beginning in the 1940s, and increasingly over the next three or four decades, school funding shifted from local property taxes to primarily or exclusively provincial funding. See Gidney and Millar, "Creating the Schooled Society," chapter 2.

12 Gidney and Millar, "Creating the Schooled Society," 10. On the crisis of the 1990s see MacKinnon, *Minding the Public Purse*.

13 Levin, *Governing Education*, 127.

14 Robert Mansell, "Fiscal Restructuring in Alberta: An Overview," in *A Government Reinvented: A Study of Alberta's Deficit Elimination Program*, ed. Christopher J. Bruce, Ronald D. Kneebone, and Kenneth J. McKenzie, 16–72 (Toronto: Oxford University Press, 1997), 57–58; Dean Neu, "Re-Investment Fables: Educational Finances in Alberta," in *Contested Classrooms: Education, Globalization, and Democracy in Alberta*, ed. Trevor W. Harrison and Jerrold L. Kachur, 75–83 (Alberta: University of Alberta Press and Parkland Institute, 1999), 78–79; Frank Peters, "Deep and Brutal: Funding Cuts to Education in Alberta," in Harrison and Kachur, *Contested Classrooms*, 85–97, 91.

15 Gidney, *Hope to Harris*, 241–42. In the early 1990s school trustees who had been complaining that a 6 to 8 percent grant increase was insufficient now found themselves with a 1 percent increase when previously agreed upon contracts with teachers promised increases of up to 5 percent. See Gidney, *Hope to Harris*, 192.

16 Gidney, *Hope to Harris*, 267. For Alberta, see Alanna Mitchell, "Raising Cash and Raising Eyebrows," *Globe and Mail*, May 12, 1998, A2.

17 Young and Levin, *Understanding Canadian Schools*, 162; Gidney and Millar, "Creating the Schooled Society," 11–14; sk.cupe.ca/files/2013/04/P3-School-Fact-Sheet.pdf.

18 In 1992–93 expenditure per pupil was $6,898, an amount that decreased to $6,645 in 1995–96 and then rose to an estimated $6,881 in 1998–99. See Dawn Walton, "Alberta Schools Fill in Funding Blanks," *Globe and Mail*, January 10, 2001, A9. On Huron County, see Jennifer Lewington, "School Board Learns to Make Do," *Globe and Mail*, December 12, 1996, A12.

19 Neu, "Re-investment Fables," 77, 80.

20 Walton, "Alberta Schools Fill in Funding Blanks."

21 Victor Soucek and Raj Pannu, "Globalizing Education in Alberta: Teachers' Work and the Options to Fight Back," in *Teacher Activism in the 1990s*, ed. Susan Robertson and Harry Smaller, 35–69 (Toronto: Lorimer, 1996), 52–53.

22 For a clear summary of these developments, see Phillip McCann, "From Christian Humanism to Neoliberalism—A Decade of Transition, 1985–1995," in *Education Reform: From Rhetoric to Reality*, ed. Gerald Galway and David Dibbon, 85–93 (London: Althouse Press, 2012), 85–87. See also David Harvey, *A Brief History of Neoliberalism* (Oxford: Oxford University Press, 2005), 2, 13, 29, 160; Manuel Castells, *The Rise of the Network Society*, 2nd ed. (Oxford: Blackwell, 2000), 18, 502–3; Larry Cuban, *Oversold and Underused: Computers in the Classroom* (Cambridge, MA: Harvard University Press, 2001), 8, 13.

23 P. Michael Timpane, "Afterword," in *American Business and the Public School*, ed. Marsha Levine and Roberta Trachtman, 228–30 (New York: Teachers College Press, 1988), 228. For the intensification and spread of business and industry values in education elsewhere, see for example, Jane Kenway, C. Bigum, L. Fitzclarence, and J. Collier, "Marketing Education in the 1990s: An Introductory Essay,"

Australian Universities' Review: Special Issue on Educational Marketing 32, no. 2 (1993): 2–6.

24 National Commission on Excellence in Education, *A Nation at Risk: The Imperative for Educational Reform* (Washington, DC: Government Printing Office, 1983), 5, in Cuban, *Oversold and Underused*, 4.

25 Cuban, *Oversold and Underused*, 7. See also William J. Reese, *America's Public Schools: From the Common School to 'No Child Left Behind'* (Baltimore: Johns Hopkins University Press, 2005), 8; Alex Molnar, *School Commercialism: From Democratic Ideal to Market Commodity* (New York: Routledge, 2005), 10–12.

26 Reese, *America's Public Schools*, 323. See also pp. 307, 324.

27 Timpane, "Afterword," in Levine and Trachtman, *American Business and the Public School*, 228.

28 Levine and Trachtman, *American Business and the Public School*, ix.

29 Levine and Trachtman, *American Business and the Public School*, ix. Metropolitan Life Insurance helped print and distribute *Investing in Our Children*. See Chava Willig Levy, "Metropolitan Life Insurance and the American Educator: Partners in Leadership," in Levine and Trachtman, *American Business and the Public School*, 36.

30 G. J. M. Abbarno, "Huckstering in the Classroom: Limits to Corporate Social Responsibility," *Journal of Business Ethics* 32, no. 2 (July 2001): 181.

31 Timpane, "Afterword," in Levine and Trachtman, *American Business and the Public School*, 228. Business involvement in education formed part of a larger corporate turn beginning in the mid-1980s with philanthropic activities aimed at youth. See Mayssoun Sukarieh and Stuart Tannock, *Youth Rising? The Politics of Youth in the Global Economy* (New York: Routledge, 2015), 13–14.

32 Adam Davidson-Harden and Suzanne Majhanovich, "Privatisation of Education in Canada: A Survey of Trends," *International Review of Education* 50, no. 3–4 (July 2004): 272, 275; Lawton, "Current Issues in the Public Finance of Elementary and Secondary Schools in Canada," 33; Jerrold L. Kachur and Trevor W. Harrison, "Introduction: Public Education, Globalization, and Democracy: Whither Alberta?," in Harrison and Kachur, *Contested Classrooms*, xvi–xvii, xx–xxi. See also Keith Walker and Brent Kay, "Chaperonic Reflections on the Relations Between Business and Education Sectors," in Lam, *Education Finance*, 115–19; Emery J. Hyslop-Margison, "The Market Economy Discourse on Education: Interpretation, Impact and Resistance," *Alberta Journal of Educational Research* 46, no. 3 (Fall 2000): 203–13.

33 For a lucid account of this side of the crisis, see Jennifer Lewington and Graham Orpwood, *Overdue Assignment: Taking Responsibility for Canada's Schools* (Toronto: Wiley & Sons, 1993). See also Alison Taylor, *The Politics of Educational Reform in Alberta* (Toronto: University of Toronto Press, 2001), 3.

34 Davidson-Harden and Majhanovich, "Privatisation of Education in Canada," 272, 275; Lawton, "Current Issues in the Public Finance of Elementary and Secondary Schools in Canada," 33; Kachur and Harrison, "Introduction," xvi–xvii, xx–xxi; Taylor, *The Politics of Education Reform in Alberta*; Walker and Kay, "Chaperonic Reflections," 115–19; Manzer, *Public Schools and Political Ideas*, 212, 236–37; McCann, "From Christian Humanism to Neoliberalism," 90; Gidney, *Hope to Harris*, 173.

35 Graham Orpwood, "A New Approach to What Goes On in the Classroom," *Globe and Mail*, November 24, 1987, A7.
36 Orpwood, "A New Approach to What Goes On in the Classroom."
37 Bertrand Marcotte, "Canada's Schools Failing the Grade," *Montreal Gazette*, May 5, 1993, cited in Maude Barlow and Heather-jane Robertson, *Class Warfare: The Assault on Canadian Public Education* (Toronto: Key Porter Books, 1994), 15.
38 Lewington and Orpwood, *Overdue Assignment*, 3.
39 Tom R. Williams and Holly Millinoff, *Canada's Schools: Report Card for the 1990s* (Toronto: CEA, 1990), cited in Tom McConaughy, "Canadians Speak Out on Education," *The Phi Delta Kappan* 72, no. 6 (February 1991): 83. For other polls see Gidney, *Hope to Harris*, 171–72.
40 For more on the discontinuity between public perception of schools and the rhetoric of school failure by those promoting educational reform, see Wotherspoon, *The Sociology of Education in Canada*, 161–64.
41 Walker and Kay, "Chaperonic Reflections," 115; Taylor, *The Politics of Educational Reform in Alberta*, 26–30.
42 Tony Carusi, "Introduction," in *The Corporate Assault on Youth: Commercialism, Exploitation, and the End of Innocence*, ed. Deron Boyles, ix–xv (New York: Peter Lang, 2008), xii.
43 Janice Newson and Howard Buchbinder, *The University Means Business: Universities, Corporations and Academic Work* (Toronto: Garamond Press, 1988), 59.
44 Newson and Buchbinder, *The University Means Business*, 8. For ties between universities and the business community prior to the 1980s see Paul Axelrod, *Scholars and Dollars: Politics, Economics, and the Universities of Ontario, 1945–1980* (Toronto: University of Toronto Press, 1982).
45 To give just a sample of the variety, these included, but were certainly not limited to, the following: Canadian Chamber of Commerce, *Focus 2000: Report on the Task Force on Education and Training*, August 1989; First National Conference on Business-Education Partnerships, Conference Board of Canada, *Reaching for Success: Business and Education Working Together*, July 1990; Human Resource Development Committee, National Advisory Board on Science and Technology, *Learning to Win: Education, Training and National Prosperity*, April 1991; Business Council of Canada, *Canada at the Crossroads: The Reality of a New Competitive Environment* (The Porter Report), October 1991; Minister of Supply and Services, *Learning Well . . . Living Well: The Prosperity Initiative*, 1991; Science Council of Canada, *Reaching for Tomorrow: Science and Technology Policy in Canada*, 1991; Economic Council of Canada, *A Lot to Learn: Education and Training in Canada*, 1992; Information Technology Association of Canada, *A Knowledge-Based Canada: The New National Dream*, 1992. Numerous similar reports appeared at the provincial level. See, for example, Wotherspoon, *The Sociology of Education in Canada*, 159; Manzer, *Public Schools and Political Ideas*, 211; Gendron, "Funding Public School Systems," 11, 24.
46 Minister of Supply and Services, *Learning Well . . . Living Well*, v.
47 Economic Council of Canada, *A Lot to Learn*, 5, 9, 51–57; Minister of Supply and Services, *Learning Well . . . Living Well*, vii–ix. See also Wotherspoon, *The Sociology of Education in Canada*, 159.

48 Minister of Supply and Services, *Learning Well ... Living Well*, viii–ix.
49 Economic Council of Canada, *A Lot to Learn*, 25.
50 See "Education-Business Partnerships," www.conferenceboard.ca, accessed October 2, 2015. On the Conference Board of Canada's role in promoting educational reform, see Taylor, *The Politics of Educational Reform in Alberta*, chapter 3.
51 Lewington, "Grappling with An Ethical Question."
52 Conference Board of Canada, *100 Best Business-Education Partnerships: 1997 Idea-Book*, 6, www.conferenceboard.ca, accessed October 2, 2015.
53 Erika Shaker, "Classrooms and Other Commodities," *Teacher* 11, no. 4 (January/February 1999): 8.
54 Barlow and Robertson, *Class Warfare*, 161.
55 Jennifer Lewington, "Provinces Take Their Own Steps toward Links," *Globe and Mail*, March 27, 1997, C12.
56 Bernie Froese-Germain, Colleen Hawkey, Alec Larose, Patricia McAdie, and Erika Shaker, *Commercialism in Canadian Schools: Who's Calling the Shots?* (Ottawa: CCPA, 2006), 19, policyalternatives.ca; Davidson-Harden and Majhanovich, "Privatization of Education in Canada," 263–87; Molnar, *School Commercialism*, chapter 2; Susan Linn, *Consuming Kids: The Hostile Takeover of Childhood* (New York: The New Press, 2004), chapter 5; Deron Boyles, *American Education and Corporations: The Free Market Goes to School* (New York: Garland, 1998).
57 Barlow and Robertson, *Class Warfare*, 15.
58 Louise Crosby, "Adopt-a-School Plan Receiving High Marks" *Ottawa Citizen*, March 2, 1987, A15.
59 Michael Grange, "Publisher Nurtures Growing Relationship," *Globe and Mail*, March 27, 1997, C2.
60 Duffy, "Companies Go to School."
61 Crosby, "Adopt-a-School Plan Receiving High Marks."
62 Mangiacasale, "School Work with a Twist."; "How the Corporate World Is Entering the Classroom," *Today's Parent*, October 1994, 67–73; Duffy, "Companies Go to School." Increased commercialism in schools and privatization of educational services are key issues as schools and school boards attempt to maintain or introduce vocational programming. See Robert E. White, *How Corporate Business Practices Are Transforming Education: Case Studies of Five Canadian Secondary Schools* (Queenston, ON: Edwin Mellen Press, 2010), 141; Dave Waddell, "Skilled Trades Trending," *Windsor Star*, February 4, 2015, A2.
63 Conference Board of Canada, *100 Best Business-Education Partnerships: 1997 Idea-Book*, 47.
64 Conference Board of Canada, *100 Best Business-Education Partnerships: 1997 Idea-Book*, 6, 30.
65 Coquitlam School District, BC, *Partners in Education*, cited in Barlow and Robertson, *Class Warfare*, 78. See also Dawson, "Tomorrow's Classroom."
66 Dube, "Corporate Classrooms."
67 Catherine Porter, "Business Ties to Schools 'Only the Beginning,'" *Vancouver Sun*, November 26, 1998, A1. For more on this type of case, see White, *How Corporate Business Practices are Transforming Education*, chapter 5.

68 Dempster and Marck, "Business Goes to School."
69 Wendy Warburton, "Corporate Intrusions in the Classroom," *Ottawa Citizen*, January 29, 1994, C3.
70 Linda Rainsberry, "Building Our Own Beach: Embracing Partnerships to Maximize Student Learning," *Education Canada* 41, no. 3 (Fall 2001): 16.
71 Dempster and Marck, "Business Goes to School."
72 Warburton, "Corporate Intrusions in the Classroom."
73 Resolution 92-1, Saskatchewan Federation of Home and School Associations, 54th Annual Meeting and Convention, April 3–4, 1992, file Saskatchewan 1992, MG 28 I 451, vol. 16, Library and Archives Canada.
74 Cited in Larry Kuehn, "Selling Education" *Teacher* 8, no. 3 (November/December 1995), 3.
75 For the ATA see Karen Unland, "Teachers Don't Want Sales Pitches in Schools," *Edmonton Journal*, May 21, 2000, A6. See also Lewington, "Provinces Take Their Own Steps toward Links"; Walker and Kay, "Chaperonic Reflections," 113–28.
76 Erika Shaker and Bernie Froese-Germain, "Beyond the Bake Sale: Exposing Schoolhouse Commercialism," *Our Schools, Our Selves* 15, no. 4 (Summer 2006), 89. Italics added.
77 In conjunction with the kits, B.C. Hydro offered energy education seminars. The ad for the kit in the teachers' magazine was accompanied by an article by David R. Stronck, affiliated with the University of Victoria, that summarized a paper presentation he had given at one such seminar sponsored by Hydro and attended by thirty-five educators from the province. See Stronck, "Education Now for Energy in the Future," *B.C. Teacher* 60, 5 (May/June 1981): 174–77.
78 Lewington, "Grappling with An Ethical Question."
79 Conference Board of Canada, "Ethical Guidelines for Education-Business Partnerships," conferenceboard.ca, accessed October 2, 2015.
80 Linda Eyre, "'No Strings Attached?' Corporate Involvement in Curriculum," *Canadian Journal of Education* 27, no. 1 (2002): 63.
81 Eyre, "No Strings Attached?" 66. For the quotation, see page 72. For a good critique of corporate funded curriculum materials on bitumen mining and the Alberta tar sands, see Andres Hodgkins, "Petrol's Paid Pipers," *Our Schools, Our Selves* 20, no. 2 (Winter 2011), 53–65, and Stuart Tannock, "'Not Mining is Not An Option!' Corporate Lessons from the Mining Matters Curriculum," *Our Schools, Our Selves* 18, no. 4 (Summer 2009), 107–14. On the incorporation of Junior Achievement materials into classrooms in the US and elsewhere, see Mayssoun Sukarieh and Stuart Tannock, "Putting School Commercialism in Context: A Global History of Junior Achievement Worldwide," *Journal of Education Policy* 24, no. 6 (November 2009): 769–86.
82 Dube, "Corporate Classrooms."
83 Dawson, "Tomorrow's Classroom." See also Barlow and Robertson, *Class Warfare*, 79.
84 Crosby, "Adopt-a-School Plan Receiving High Marks." See also Barlow and Robertson, *Class Warfare*, 79.
85 "How the Corporate World Is Entering the Classroom."

3: TAPPING THE EDUCATIONAL MARKET

1 Melanie Franner, "Three Rs of Education: RAM, ROM and Retry," *Globe and Mail*, March 24, 1994, C7. In the US the ratio of computers to students was 1:125 in 1981, 1:18 in 1991, and 1:5 in 2000. See Larry Cuban, *Oversold and Underused: Computers in the Classroom* (Cambridge, MA: Harvard University Press, 2001), 17.
2 "Case Study: State-of-the-Art Oakville School Has It All," *Globe and Mail*, December 9, 1994, C6. See also Steven Chase, "Burnaby South 'Cool' School," *Globe and Mail*, August 6, 1992, C5. For the massive investment in Burnaby South see also Maude Barlow and Heather-jane Robertson, *Class Warfare: The Assault on Canadian Public Education* (Toronto: Key Porter Books, 1994), 148–51. This was part of an international trend. See Neil Selwyn, *Education in a Digital World: Global Perspectives on Technology and Education* (New York: Routledge, 2013), 53–54.
3 Alison Taylor, "Visioning Education in the Information Economy," in *Tech High: Globalization and the Future of Canadian Education*, ed. Marita Moll, 15–31 (Ottawa: Canadian Centre for Policy Alternatives and Fernwood Publishing, 1997), 26.
4 Chase, "Burnaby South 'Cool' School."
5 Selwyn, *Education in a Digital World*, 58.
6 Quoted in Larry Cuban, *Teachers and Machines: The Classroom Use of Technology Since 1920* (New York: Teachers College Press, 1986), 9.
7 Cuban, *Teachers and Machines*, 12. See also page 10.
8 *Annual Report – Department of Education, 1945*, Ontario, No. 11 Elementary Education, "School Radio Broadcasts," 13; Department of Education, Alberta, *Annual Report, 1956*, "Audio-Visual Equipment," 22–23; *Manitoba Annual Report of the Department of Education, 1955–56*, 51. See also New Brunswick, *Annual Report*, 1953–54, "Chief Superintendent's Report," 18.
9 R. A. Morton, "Educational Television," *Canadian Education* 14, no. 2 (March 1959): 36–37. By the mid-1960s almost 30 percent of Nova Scotia students were exposed to regular educational television programming. There, the Department of Education, the Nova Scotia Association of Urban and Municipal School Boards, the Canadian Broadcasting Corporation, the Nova Scotia Teachers' Union and the Board of Governors of Dalhousie University allocated resources for developing programs in science and mathematics that could then be televised at set times. See Department of Education [NS], *Annual Report*, 1962–63, H. M. Nason, "Elementary and Secondary Education," 22–23; Department of Education [NS], *Annual Report*, 1963–64, "Educational Television, 28–29; Department of Education [NS], *Annual Report*, 1964–65, "Educational Television," 28–29. For similar developments in Saskatchewan, see Barrie Zwicker, "The Most Up-to-Date High School," *Globe Magazine*, January 7, 1967, cited in Douglas Lawr and Robert Gidney, *Educating Canadians: A Documentary History of Public Education*, 2nd ed. (Toronto: Van Nostrand Reinhold, 1973), 259.
10 David Buckingham, *Beyond Technology: Children's Learning in the Age of Digital Culture* (Cambridge, UK: Polity, 2007), vii.
11 Cited in Buckingham, *Beyond Technology*, iv.

12 Ellen Rose, *Hyper Texts: The Language and Culture of Educational Computing* (London, ON: Althouse Press, 2000), 69–77.
13 Cuban, *Teachers and Machines*, 16.
14 Karen Howlett, "Micro Makers Pursuing Sales to Schools," *Globe and Mail*, August 23, 1985, B11; Ivor F. Goodson and J. Marshall Mangan, "Computer Studies as Symbolic and Ideological Action: The Geneology of the ICON," in *Subject Knowledge: Readings for the Study of School Subjects*, ed. Ivor F. Goodson with Christopher J. Anstead and J. Marshal Mangan, 122–36 (London: Falmer Press, 1998), 125; Renate Lerch, "Micro Makers Line Up to Tap Education Market," *Financial Post*, June 15, 1987, C3.
15 Brian Milner, "Educational Market for New Technology Still Untapped," *Globe and Mail*, February 28, 1983, B18.
16 Milner, "Educational Market for New Technology Still Untapped." See also Lerch, "Micro Makers Line Up to Tap Education Market."
17 Franner, "Three Rs of Education: RAM, ROM and Retry."
18 Karen Howlett, "Upgraded Education Microcomputer Being Launched by Apple Canada," *Globe and Mail*, September 16, 1986, B6.
19 *Globe and Mail*, 1985, 7, cited in R. D. White, "Education and Work in the Technological Age," in *The Political Economy of Canadian Schooling*, ed. Terry Wotherspoon, 99–116 (Toronto: Methuen, 1987), 113n2.
20 Milner, "Educational Market for New Technology Still Untapped"; Renate Lerch, "Micros Make Mark in Canadian Schools," *Financial Post*, September 7, 1985, C3; Lawrence Surtees, "Icon's Delivery Delays Irk Schools," *Globe and Mail*, January 11, 1985, B13. Ontario was not the only province attempting to bolster Canadian industry through its education plan. Two years after the Ontario announcement, Quebec Premier René Lévesque revealed his government's plan to subsidize the purchase of the Max 20E, a computer developed by Comterm-Mantra, a partnership between investors in Quebec and France that was 56 percent Quebec owned. Politicians believed it would encourage trade with France and "allow research and development of software in Quebec." See Margot Gibb-Clark, "Quebec May Delay School Computer Purchase," *Globe and Mail*, March 7, 1984, 8.
21 Goodson and Mangan, "Computer Studies as Symbolic and Ideological Action," 124–27. They note: "The specifications set high standards and high ideals for the use of computers in Ontario schools. Included were such things as high resolution colour graphics and sound synthesis capabilities, which were little more than possibilities at the time of writing, but which the authors felt might be important in the future. They also specified a local area network (LAN) type of architecture. Curiously, they did not specify either a large amount of internal memory (at first models had as little as 64K RAM), nor very high speed communications capabilities. This combination of features had the effect of making the specified computer unique—so unique that no existing machine could fill the bill—but also rather slow and limited in its operation" (127).
22 The machine was manufactured by Microtel Ltd. of Burnaby, BC, at its plant in Brockville, Ontario. The Ontario government provided a subsidy for other brands but at a lower rate than for ICON purchases. See Jonathan Chevreau, "Ontario

Announces Its Plans for An Educational Computer," *Globe and Mail*, March 25, 1983, B13; Geoffrey York, "Ontario Computer Set for Schools," *Globe and Mail*, March 25, 1983, 5; Surtees, "Icon's Delivery Delays Irk Schools"; Sandy Fife, "Educators See Need for Sharing Computer Resources," *Globe and Mail*, March 1, 1985, R3; Lerch, "Micros Make Mark in Canadian Schools."

23 Fife, "Educators See Need for Sharing Computer Resources."

24 Jonathan Chevreau, "Educational Computers Evoke Nagging Doubts," *Globe and Mail*, February 24, 1984, R3. Chevreau noted that the standard model ICON cost $1,800 ($450 after the application of the government grant) and the advanced model cost $3,750 ($938 with the grant). See Chevreau, "Ontario Announces Its Plans For an Educational Computer."

25 The Alberta Department of Education took this direction when it selected Apple machines. Milner, "Educational Market for New Technology Still Untapped."

26 Karen Howlett, "IBM Knocking on Schoolroom Door to Tap a Growth Market," *Globe and Mail*, October 6, 1986, B4.

27 Chris Hall, "Ontario Auditor Tells Schools to Sign Off 'Ideal' Computers," *Ottawa Citizen*, December 1, 1988, A3; "Ontario Schools Opened to More Computer Makers," *Globe and Mail*, July 28, 1988, B8.

28 Franner, "Three Rs of Education." See also Scott Feschuk, "The Embarrassment of Dinosaurs," *Globe and Mail*, November 25 1993, C3.

29 Amber Nasrulla, "Fundraising Plans Take All Forms," *Globe and Mail*, August 17, 1995, D9.

30 Florence Loyie, "Riverdale Has the Byte Stuff," *Edmonton Journal*, February 8, 1995, B3.

31 See Franner, "Three Rs of Education."

32 "Students Tapping In to World," *Ottawa Citizen*, October 19, 1993, B8; Chris Cobb, "Cyberschool; Canada Leads the World with An On-Line Educational Network Called SchoolNet," *Ottawa Citizen*, November 26, 1995, A1; Gordon Powers, "Managing How They Did It: One Company's Challenge," *Globe and Mail*, November 21, 1996, B16.

33 Marita Moll, "Canadian Classrooms on the Information Highway: Making the Connections," in Moll, *Tech High*, 33–64, 36; Brent Wilson, "Schoolnet," *C.A.P. Journal* 6, no. 1 (Spring 1996): 7–8; Cobb, "Cyberschool"; Marlene Orton, "Patching into the Web: Schools Discover World on Net," *Ottawa Citizen*, October 6, 1998, G19.

34 David Beattie and David McCallum, "Electronic Scholarly Publishing Initiatives at Industry Canada," *The Serials Librarian* 33, no. 3/4, 224, doi:10.1300/J124v33n03_02. See also Moll, "Canadian Classrooms on the Information Highway," 34.

35 Taylor, "Visioning Education in the Information Economy," 18.

36 The *Statement* was developed by ITAC's "Education Committee," the chair of which was also the ITAC representative on the national advisory board of School-Net as well as the chair of the SchoolNet communications subcommittee. For the quotation, see Information Technology Association of Canada/Canadian

Advanced Technology Association (ITAC/CATA), *Stepping Stones: A Summary of Powering Up North America: Realizing the Information Infrastructure for a Knowledge-Based Continent* (Toronto, 1994), cited in Moll, "Canadian Classrooms on the Information Highway," 51.

37 Bruce Sheppard, Wilbert Boone, and Ken Stevens, "Information Technology, Innovation and Success in a Small Rural School" (paper presented at the EDUCAUSE Annual Conference, Memorial University, 1999), 2, 4, eric.ed.gov. See also Susan Noakes, "Computers Give Students New Learning Opportunities," *Financial Post*, July 9, 1994, S17.

38 Robert Sheppard, "Boards in Remoter Places Can't Afford SchoolNet," *Victoria Times Colonist*, February 15, 1995.

39 Heather-jane Robertson, *No More Teachers, No More Books: The Commercialization of Canada's Schools* (Toronto: McClelland & Stewart, 1998), 167–69; Bev Wake, "Computers versus Classrooms," *Ottawa Citizen*, September 8, 2000, F3.

40 Shannon Kari, "Gates Launches Internet Initiative for Canadian Schools," *Ottawa Citizen*, October 16, 1998, E3; "AOL Gives $1M to SchoolNet," *St. John's Telegram*, January 19, 2001, 1; Conference Board of Canada, *Canada's SchoolNet Grass-Roots Program: Case Studies* 2000/2001 (Ottawa: Industry Canada, 2001), prior to page 1.

41 Jennifer Lewington, "What Are Schools Wired To?" *Globe and Mail*, June 26, 1997, C1.

42 "Laptop Computers a Little Pricey Now," *Fredericton Daily Gleaner*, September 8, 2001, Section: Opinion.

43 For the quotation, see Elizabeth Mehren, "Computer Plan Clicks with Maine Students," *Saint John Telegraph-Journal*, November 26, 2002, Section: Life. Maine was not the only state creating such programs. Michigan developed one in 2002–3 with the help of Hewlett Packard, and Texas in 2004 with the help of Dell and Apple. These programs are often called one-to-one computing or ubiquitous computing. See Abell Foundation, "One-to-One Computing in Public Schools: Lessons from 'Laptops for All' Programs," 2008, 3–4, 5–9, eric.ed.gov.

44 In 1999, RCS Netherwood, a New Brunswick private school, instituted mandatory laptops for Grades 10 to 12 and Lester B. Pearson School Board piloted a laptop program for Grade 4 students at two schools. See John Chilibeck, "First Laptop Class Set to Graduate," *Saint John Telegraph-Journal*, June 18, 1999; Karen Seidman, "Laptops or Textbooks? Pilot Program to Introduce Computers to Grade 4 Students Raises Ire of Teachers' Union," *Montreal Gazette*, May 12, 1999, A3.

45 "Grits Criticize School Laptops," *Times and Transcript* (Moncton), March 9, 2005.

46 Rose, *Hyper Texts*, 128, 136–37.

47 David Akin, "Schools Overcoming the Digital Divide," *National Post*, August 5, 2000, E3. The problem of school budgets eaten up by the cost of computer maintenance and software purchases was a common one. See, for example, Jean-Claude Couture, "Teacher's Work: Living in the Culture of Insufficiency," in Moll, *Tech High*, 153–54.

48 Penny Milton, "A Review of New Brunswick's Dedicated Notebook Research Project. One-to-One Computing—A Compelling School-Change Intervention" (Toronto: Canadian Education Association, 2008), 2, cea-ace.ca. The pilot phase saw 1.1 million invested in the program. Thereafter, the Lord government reportedly earmarked $20 million for laptops to just under three thousand middle-school students. See Milton, 3, and, Daniel McHardie, "Tories Pledge More Student Laptops," *Times and Transcript* (Moncton), September 6, 2006, A1.
49 "Grits criticize school laptops"; Daniel McHardie, "Computer Giants Fund School Laptop Program," *Times & Transcript* (Moncton), October 1, 2004, Section: Money; Milton, "A Review of New Brunswick's Dedicated Notebook Research Project," 2.
50 Milton, "A Review of New Brunswick's Dedicated Notebook Research Project," 2; Michael Fox, Jim Greenlaw, and M. A. MacPherson, *The New Brunswick Dedicated Notebook Research Project: Final Report*, New Brunswick Department of Education, November 2006, 24, www2.gnb.ca.
51 Jennifer Dunville, "Laptop Program in Limbo," *Saint John Telegraph-Journal*, June 11, 2007; "Provincial Government Should Give Every Student a Laptop," *Saint John Telegraph-Journal*, August 18, 2007, A1.
52 Janet Steffenhagen, "District Wakes Up from Laptop Dream," *Vancouver Sun*, May 26, 2008, B7. For the US see Bryan Goodwin, "Research Says . . . One-to-One Laptop Programs Are No Silver Bullet," *Educational Leadership* 68, no. 5 (February 2011): 78.
53 Milton, "A Review of New Brunswick's Dedicated Notebook Research Project," 4.
54 Daniel McHardie, "School Laptop Program Exceeds Expectations," *Times and Transcript* (Moncton), April 4, 2006, A4.
55 Milton, "A Review of New Brunswick's Dedicated Notebook Research Project," 1.
56 Lauren Earle, "Laptops in Schools: Are Students Really Learning More?" *Saint John Telegraph-Journal*, July 3, 2006, A1/A8.
57 Abell Foundation, "One-to-One Computing in Public Schools," 17. See also Goodwin, "Research Says," 78–79.
58 Goodwin, "Research Says," 79. On the problematic nature of some of the research see also Todd Oppenheimer, *The Flickering Mind: Saving Education from the False Promise of Technology* (New York: Random House, 2004), xix, 391. Although a number of studies have shown that simply saturating the classroom with technology does not affect teaching, others have argued that with proper support the use of computer technology can help re-shape teaching practices to allow for student-centred classrooms. See Judith Haymore Sandholtz, Cathy Ringstaff, and David C. Dwyer, *Teaching with Technology: Creating Student-Centered Classrooms* (New York: Teachers College Press, 1997).
59 Goodson and Mangan, "Computer Studies as Symbolic and Ideological Action," 129; Ellen Rose, *User Error: Resisting Computer Culture* (Toronto: Between the Lines, 2003), 31–32, 154.
60 Cited in Orton, "Patching Into the Web."
61 Cuban, *Oversold and Underused*, 192. Italics in original.

62 Chris Bigum, "Computers and the Curriculum: The Australian Experience," *Journal of Curriculum Studies* 22 (1990), 64, cited in Goodson and Mangan, "Computer Studies as Symbolic and Ideological Action," 131.
63 Barlow and Robertson, *Class Warfare*, 146–48. For the US, see Cuban, *Oversold and Underused*, 193; Oppenheimer, *The Flickering Mind*, xvi.
64 Brad Evenson, "You Can Lead Students to Computers But It Won't Make Them Think," *Saint John Telegraph-Journal*, July 19, 1998. Section: News.
65 Buckingham, *Beyond Technology*, 7. See also 6, 54. See also Stephen Petrina, "Getting a Purchase on 'The School of Tomorrow' and Its Constituent Commodities: Histories and Historiographies of Technologies," *History of Education Quarterly* 42, no. 1 (March 2002): 77.
66 Feschuk, "The Embarrassment of Dinosaurs."
67 Buckingham, *Beyond Technology*, 11.

4: "IT'S SO PERVASIVE, IT'S LIKE KLEENEX"

1 YTV Tween Report, 2005, cited in Bernie Froese-Germain, Colleen Hawkey, Alec Larose, Patricia McAdie, and Erika Shaker, *Commercialism in Canadian Schools: Who's Calling the Shots?* (Ottawa: Canadian Centre for Policy Alternatives [CCPA], 2006), 4, www.policyalternatives.ca. Other spending estimates are considerably higher, with one 1999 report indicating that nine- to nineteen-year-olds had spent $13.5 billion the previous year. See Andrew Clark, Shanda Deziel, Susan McClelland, and Susan Oh, "How Teens Got the Power: Generation Y Has the Cash, the Cool—and a Consumer Culture," *Macleans*, March 22, 1999, 42.
2 Juliet Schor, *Born to Buy: The Commercialized Child and the New Consumer Culture* (New York: Scribner, 2004), 11–16; Susan Linn, *Consuming Kids: The Hostile Takeover of Childhood* (New York: The New Press, 2004), 2–5.
3 Dana Flavelle, "Boards Turn to Advertisements for Revenue," *Toronto Star*, October 31, 1996, A3.
4 Martine Turenne, "L'école sauce PUB," *L'actualité*, September 15, 1999, 32.
5 Graham Thomson, "Give Them An 'E' for Effort," *Edmonton Journal*, May 31, 1998, A1; Tom Spears, "Painting It Green," *Ottawa Citizen*, February 20, 1992, A1.
6 Stuart Tannock, "'Not Mining is Not an Option!' Corporate Lessons from the Mining Matters Curriculum," *Our Schools/Our Selves* 18, no. 4 (Summer 2009): 107.
7 David Crary, "Critics Pan Pizza Hut Literacy Program," *Fredericton Daily Gleaner*, March 5, 2007, C5.
8 George Oake, "See Dick. See Jane. Get Big Mac." *Toronto Star*, September 23, 1990, B1. For corporate-sponsored material that encourages the consumption of fast food, see also Deron Boyles, "Would You Like Values with That? Chick-fil-A and Character Education," in *The Corporate Assault on Youth: Commercialism, Exploitation, and the End of Innocence*, ed. Deron Boyles, 108–25 (New York: Peter

Lang, 2008), 117, and Joel Spring, *Educating the Consumer-Citizen: A History of the Marriage of Schools, Advertising, and Media* (Mahwab, NJ: Erlbaum, 2003), 201–6.

9 "Corporations Make Allies of Schools," *Toronto Star*, October 11, 1988, W5.

10 Amal Ahmed Albaz, "York Region Public Schools Ban Free Books Over Corporate Logo," *Toronto Star*, November 11, 2015, www.thestar.com.

11 Elizabeth Payne, "Every Month of Every School Year, Millions of Canadian Elementary Schoolchildren Bring Home Brightly Coloured Flyers," *Canwest News Service/Ottawa Citizen*, October 20, 2003. Scholastic Corporation was founded in the US in 1920, with a Canadian division incorporated in 1957. It now employs around eight hundred Canadians in part-time or full-time positions. "About Us," www.scholastic.ca.

12 Mark MacKinnon, "A Penny Saved Is a Future Customer Earned," *Edmonton Journal*, April 20, 1998, A1.

13 For the quotations see respectively, Duncan Thorne, "Students Get Credit at New School Bank," *Edmonton Journal*, June 12, 1995, B3, and Brooke Larsen, "Kids Bank at School Credit Union," *Surrey Now*, April 30, 2005, 13. Slightly different programs also appeared. At Second Street Community School in Burnaby, for example, VanCity donated ten dollars to the school for each student who opened an account. See Erin Hitchcock, "Lesson at Youth Credit Union," *Burnaby Now*, May 31, 2006, 13.

14 David Howell, "Education Inc.," *Edmonton Journal*, June 25, 2006, A1.

15 Michele Simon, *Appetite for Profit: How the Food Industry Undermines Our Health and How To Fight Back* (New York: Nation Books, 2006), 34–35. Coke and Pepsi developed similar fitness programs in the US. See Simon, 38–39.

16 Darah Hansen, "Ronald McDonald Fronts 2010 Olympic Fitness Pitch," *Vancouver Sun*, June 5, 2006, A1. The presentation occurred in at least ninety schools in BC while over eleven schools (with close to one thousand students) in Saskatchewan and over two hundred schools in Ontario, Quebec, and Atlantic Canada signed on for the fitness challenge. See Jack Knox, "Unease over Corporate Role in Schools," *Victoria Times Colonist*, December 6, 2005, A3; "Six Schools Complete Fitness Challenge," *Saskatoon Sun*, July 9, 2006, 24; Caroline Alphonso, "Taking the Brand to the Classroom," *Globe and Mail*, April 30, 2005, A13.

17 Howell, "Education Inc."

18 Eve Lazarus, "Cafeteria Blues," *Marketing Magazine*, January 19, 2004, 11; Julie Saccone, "Kellogg Takes Step in New Direction," *Saskatoon StarPhoenix*, June 4, 2005, A3. Active Healthy Kids Canada produced a yearly report card on children's physical activity. In 2006, one of its sponsors was Kellogg Canada. See Internet Archive Wayback Machine, October 12, 2006: www.activehealthykids.ca:80.

19 Denise Helm, "Athletes Help Start School Project," *Victoria Times Colonist*, October 7, 1994.

20 Michael Staples, "New Program Tackles Bullying in Schools," *Fredericton Daily Gleaner*, November 17, 2000.

21 Rhonda Whittaker, "Thumbs Up for Ads in School?" *Times and Transcript*, August 13, 2002.

22 Sarah Schmidt, "The Field Trip Goes Retail," *National Post*, June 13, 2003, A3. For more on Field Trip Factory, see Alex Molnar, *School Commercialism: From*

Democratic Ideal to Market Commodity (New York: Routledge, 2005), 34–35, and Trevor Norris, *Consuming Schools: Commercialism and the End of Politics* (Toronto: University of Toronto Press, 2011), 43–45.

23 Barbara Turnbull, "Real Food Trips Turn Grocery Store into a Classroom," *Toronto Star*, December 9, 2013, www.thestar.com; Ann Ruppenstein, "An Out-of-Classroom Experience," May 11, 2014, mytowncrier.ca.

24 Alexandra Lopez-Pacheco, "Business Fills Funding Void in Public Schools," *National Post*, August 16, 2002, SR1; Deborah Nobes, "Attention, Wal-Mart Students," *Saint John Telegraph-Journal*, November 1, 1999; Hilary Paige Smith, "Wal-Mart, Customers Forge Generous Relationship," *Saint John Telegraph-Journal*, June 26, 2009, C8. In another case a local Wal-Mart supported the Devon Middle School band in Fredericton, New Brunswick, which thanked the store by playing there on a Saturday afternoon. See Erin McCracken, "Song of Thanks to Store," *Fredericton Daily Gleaner*, April 17, 2000.

25 In 1995, both the Hamilton School District and the Wellington County Board of Education put advertising on buses. A year later the York Region Board of Education and York Region Roman Catholic Separate School Board, as well as the Calgary Board of Education, approved advertisements on the inside and outside of school buses. Foothills School Division, just south of Calgary, reportedly received $15,000 for placing ads on the rear of roughly forty of its buses. See Ian Dutton, "School Bus Billboards Not in Sight," *Victoria Times Colonist*, May 23, 1995; Ross Longbottom, "Signs of the Times," *Ottawa Citizen*, June 21, 1995, C3; Marina Strauss, "School Buses to Get Advertising Boards," *Globe and Mail*, October 30, 1996, B1; Andy Marshall, "Trustees Studying Ways to Raise Cash," *Calgary Herald*, March 24, 1995, B7.

26 In 1997, the Peel Board of Education approved screen-saver ads that included corporations such as McDonald's and Wrigley's. They received approximately $500,000 from the deal. The following year Calgary public school board trustees approved a similar pilot project. The school board estimated it would gain roughly $35,000 from the venture. See Foster Smith, "Out of the Classroom," *National Post*, August 5, 2000, E2; Monte Stewart, "Students to Get Ads on School Computers," *Calgary Herald*, September 9, 1998, A1.

27 Scott Simpson, "Corporate Sponsorship Stirs Debate for School Board," *Vancouver Sun*, December 1, 1999, B1.

28 Olive Elliott, "Look Beyond YNN's Commercials," AHSCA (Alberta Home and School Councils' Association) Newsletter, vol. 1 (December 1992), MG 28 I 451, vol. 16, Library and Archives Canada; Kendra Gaede, "Kids Learning by Collecting Labels," *Leader-Post*, May 4, 2000, A3; Elizabeth Thompson, "Kellogg's Cancels Student Contest to Design Float," *Gazette* (Montreal), January 21, 2000, A5. The program ceased in 2017 due, according to the company, to declining interest. See Lani Harac, "An End for Campbell's Labels for Education Program," *PTOToday*, February 8, 2016, www.ptotoday.com.

29 The survey received a 23 percent return rate, with 75 percent of responses from elementary schools and 17 percent from secondary schools. See Froese-Germain et al., *Commercialism in Canadian Schools*, 7–8, 10, 30.

30 British Columbia Teachers' Federation (BCTF), "Highlights of BCTF Survey: Corporate Involvement in Schools," *Issues in Education* (Spring 2000), bctf.ca.
31 Albaz, "York Region Public Schools Ban Free Books Over Corporate Logo."
32 MacKinnon, "A Penny Saved Is a Future Customer Earned."
33 Schmidt, "The Field Trip Goes Retail."
34 Marshall, "Trustees Studying Ways to Raise Cash."
35 Caroline Alphonso, "What's in Store for Classes of the Future?" *Globe and Mail*, April 14, 2009, A9.
36 Lazarus, "Cafeteria Blues."
37 Denise Helm, "Athletes Help Start School Project."
38 John Bermingham, "Stores 'Adopt' a School Each," *The Province* (Vancouver), October 27, 1999, A17. See also Lopez-Pacheco, "Business Fills Funding Void in Public Schools."
39 Jennifer Gray-Grant, "Vancouver School Board Rejects Computer Offer," *Vancouver Sun*, January 21, 1992, B3.
40 "Six Schools Complete Fitness Challenge."
41 Andy Marshall, "Shaw Helps Teach How to Turn It Off," *Calgary Herald*, March 25, 1998, B4.
42 Flavelle, "Boards Turn to Advertisements for Revenue."
43 "Could Scrolling Ads in the Hallways Be Next?" *Saskatoon StarPhoenix*, February 6, 2001, B6.
44 Schmidt, "The Field Trip Goes Retail."
45 Strauss, "School Buses to Get Advertising Boards."
46 Lazarus, "Cafeteria Blues."
47 Catherine Porter, "Business Ties to Schools 'Only the Beginning,'" *Vancouver Sun*, November 26, 1998, A1.
48 Thomson, "Give Them An 'E' for Effort."
49 Thorne, "Students Get Credit at New School Bank." For similar comments made by marketing firms and corporate representatives in the US, see Jef I. Richards, Ellen A. Wartella, Cynthia Morton, and Lisa Thompson, "The Growing Commercialization of Schools: Issues and Practices," *Annals*, AAPSS 557 (May 1998): 157.
50 Spears, "Painting It Green." For other detailed critiques of corporate material, but in the American context, see, for example, Robin Truth Goodman and Kenneth J. Saltman's chapter on Amoco in *Strange Love: Or How We Learn to Stop Worrying and Love the Market* (Lanham, MD: Rowman & Littlefield, 2002), the 1995 Consumers Union report, *Captive Kids: Commercial Pressures on Kids at School* (Yonkers, NY: Consumers Union Education Services, 1995), chapter 2, and Henry A. Giroux, *Stealing Innocence: Youth, Corporate Power, and the Politics of Culture* (New York: St. Martin's Press, 2000), chapter 3.
51 Elliott, "Look Beyond YNN's Commercials."
52 Naomi Klein, *No Logo: Taking Aim at the Brand Bullies* (Toronto: Knopf Canada, 2000), 329.

53 Klein, *No Logo*, 327–29.
54 Klein, *No Logo*, 335.
55 Naomi Klein, "Campus Brand Deals Can Backfire," *Toronto Star*, June 25, 1998, A25. United Students Against Sweatshops was established in the US in 1998, though activism against university contracts with companies such as Nike that used sweatshop labour had begun several years earlier on a number of campuses. See Liza Featherstone, "Students Against Sweatshops: A History," in *Sweatshop USA: The American Sweatshop in Historical and Global Perspective*, ed. Daniel E. Bender and Richard A. Greewald, 247–64 (New York: Routledge, 2003), 250.
56 In 2001 UBC revealed its deal with Coke. In 1999 Université du Québec à Montréal cancelled their contract and Université Laval halted plans to enter into an exclusivity deal. See Kerry Segrave, *Vending Machines: An American Social History* (Jefferson, NC: McFarland, 2002), 220.
57 Klein, *No Logo*, 410, and Craig Kielburger with Kevin Major, *Free the Children: A Young Man Fights Against Child Labor and Proves that Children Can Change the World* (New York: HarperCollins, 1998). For the protest at Terry Fox Secondary School, see Simpson, "Corporate Sponsorship Stirs Debate for School Board"; Jerome Bouvier and Ted Kuntz, "Terry Fox Stands For Integrity Not Exploitation," *Teacher* 12, no. 4 (January/February 2000): 9.
58 See, for example, Janice Newson and Howard Buchbinder, *The University Means Business: Universities, Corporations and Academic Work* (Toronto: Garamond Press, 1988); Neil Tudiver, *Universities for Sale: Resisting Corporate Control over Canadian Higher Education* (Toronto: Lorimer, 1999); Jim Turk, ed. *The Corporate Campus: Commercialization and the Dangers to Canada's Colleges and Universities* (Toronto: Lorimer, 2000); James L. Turk, *Universities at Risk: How Politics, Special Interests and Corporatization Threaten Academic Integrity* (Toronto: Lorimer, 2008); Adrienne S. Chan and Donald Fisher, eds., *The Exchange University: Corporatization of Academic Culture* (Vancouver: UBC Press, 2008); Jamie Brownlee, *Academia, Inc.: How Corporatization is Transforming Canadian Universities* (Halifax: Fernwood, 2015); Claire Polster and Janice Newson, *A Penny for Your Thoughts: How Corporatization Devalues Teaching, Research, and Public Service in Canada's Universities* (Ottawa: Our Schools/Our Selves and the Canadian Centre for Policy Alternatives, 2015). There is a much larger literature in the United States. For entry into the debate, see, for example, Derek Bok, *Universities in the Marketplace: The Commercialization of Higher Education* (Princeton: Princeton University Press, 2003).
59 Molnar, *School Commercialism*, 20–21; Alex Molnar, *Giving Kids the Business: The Commercialization of America's Schools* (Boulder, CO: Westview, 1996); Goodman and Saltman, *Strange Love*. For patterns elsewhere, see, for example, Jane Kenway and D. Epstein, "Introduction: The Marketization of School Education: Feminist Studies and Perspectives," *Discourse* 17, no. 3 (1996): 301–14.
60 "Commercialization in Our Schools—Trends in Commercialization," www.osstf.on.ca; BCTF, "Highlights of BCTF Survey"; Erika Shaker and Bernie Froese-Germain, "Beyond the Bake Sale: Exploring Schoolhouse Commercialism," *Our Schools, Our Selves* 15, no. 4 (Summer 2006): 75; Froese-Germain et al., *Commercialism in Canadian Schools*, 7.

61 Shaker and Froese-Germain, "Beyond the Bake Sale."
62 D. J. Flower and J. L. Booi, "Challenging Restructuring: The Alberta Teachers' Association," in *Contested Classrooms: Education, Globalization, and Democracy in Alberta*, ed. Trevor W. Harrison and Jerrold L. Kachur, 123–35 (Edmonton: University of Alberta Press and Parkland Institute, 1999), 129; Victor Soucek and Raj Pannu, "Globalizing Education in Alberta: Teachers' Work and the Options to Fight Back," in *Teacher Activism in the 1990s*, ed. Susan Robertson and Harry Smaller, 35–69 (Toronto: Lorimer, 1996), 55–56, 60.
63 For example, in October 1993 over two thousand students, parents, and teachers in Calgary protested the government's proposed cuts. In October 1997 over twenty thousand Alberta teachers descended on the Alberta legislature to show their frustration with what they perceived as over a decade of attacks on schools. See Flower and Booi, "Challenging Restructuring," 123–24, 127; Karen Unland, "Teachers Don't Want Sales Pitches in Schools," *Edmonton Journal*, May 21, 2000, A6.
64 *Public Education: Not for Sale. Proceedings of a Public Education Conference Sponsored by the Coalition for Public Education* and "Public Education Conferences," www.bctf.ca. The BCTF, particularly through the work of Larry Kuehn, became a prominent voice against commercialization and privatization of education. See, for example, Kuehn, "What's Wrong with Commercialization of Public Education?" *Teacher* 15, no. 4 (2003): 1.
65 Virginia Galt, "School Fund-Raising Raises Hackles," *Globe and Mail*, March 29, 1996, A1, A12.
66 Michael D. Reid, "Branding New Trend in Schools," *Daily News*, November 23, 2007, C7.
67 "Pizza Hut Pulls Out," *Montreal Gazette*, June 1, 2001, A4; "Campbell's Drops Its Label Program," *Montreal Gazette*, A5. Shaker and Froese-Germain, "Beyond the Bake Sale," 89. In 1980 Quebec enacted the first regulations to limit commercial advertising aimed at children under thirteen. In 1991 Sweden banned advertising on television and radio aimed at that age group while Norway did so a year later. Ireland has banned fast food and candy commercials on television. See Simon, *Appetite for Profit*, 265–66. On the limits of the Quebec Consumer Protection Act, see Kim D. Raine et al., "Restricting Marketing to Children: Consensus on Policy Interventions to Address Obesity," *Journal of Public Health Policy* 34, no. 2 (2013): 243.
68 Chris Morris, "Ronald McDonald Gets Boot from N.B. Classrooms," *Saint John Telegraph-Journal*, November 21, 2006, A2.
69 Jennifer Lewington, "Carefully Watching for Minefields," *Globe and Mail*, March 27, 1997, C12.
70 Peter Owens, "Put the Brakes on Corporate Intrusion," *B.C. Teacher*, 12, no. 3 (Nov/December 1999): 5.
71 Duncan Thorne, "Schools Official Screens Out Computer Screen Ads," *Edmonton Journal*, September 10, 1998, B2.
72 Howell, "Education Inc."
73 In some years the books still made it into children's hands. In 2013 and 2014, for example, they were sent to public libraries and given away from there. See Albaz, "York Region Public Schools Ban Free Books Over Corporate Logo."

74 Christina Kowalewski, "Vanoc Has No Business Targeting School Children," *Vancouver Sun*, June 7, 2006, A16.

5: YOUTH NEWS NETWORK OR "YOU'RE NUTS TO SAY NO"

1 David Brand, "Why YNN Sucks," *Adbusters* 31 (August/September 2000), 21. See also Erika Shaker, "In the Corporate Interest: The YNN Experience in Canadian Schools" (Ottawa: CCPA, 2000), 27–29, policyalternatives.ca.
2 Erika Shaker, "Youth News Network and the Commercial Carpet-Bombing of the Classroom," *Education, Limited* 5 (October 1999), 1, ccpanews.ca; Mike Boone, "Youth News Network: An Educational Tool or Just a Marketing Pitch," *Montreal Gazette*, May 15, 1990, C9; Ann Carroll, "Classrooms Shouldn't Be Newsrooms, Baldwin Cartier Says," *Montreal Gazette*, December 12, 1991, G7; Susan Ruttan, "Schools Pondering News/Ads Package," *Calgary Herald*, August 28, 1992, A1.
3 Andrew Nikiforuk, "Zapped," *National Post Business Magazine*, May 1, 2001.
4 Alex Molnar, *School Commercialism: From Democratic Ideal to Market Commodity* (New York: Routledge, 2005), 18, 92; Susan Linn, *Consuming Kids: The Hostile Takeover of Childhood* (New York: The New Press, 2004), 82; Juliet Schor, *Born to Buy: The Commercialized Child and the New Consumer Culture* (New York: Scribner, 2004), 86–88; Shaker, "Youth News Network and the Commercial Carpet-Bombing of the Classroom," 5; Anne Marie Barry, "Advertising and Channel One: Controversial Partnership of Business and Education," in *Watching Channel One: The Convergence of Students, Technology, and Private Business*, ed. Ann De Vaney, 102–36 (Albany: State University of New York Press, 1994), 102; Jason C. Blokhuis, "Channel One: When Private Interests and the Public Interest Collide," *American Educational Research Journal* 45, no. 2 (June 2008): 344; Nikiforuk, "Zapped."
5 Frances Bula, "TV Ads Have No Place in High School," *Montreal Gazette*, October 28, 1991, A4.
6 YNN Promotional Video, 1992, in possession of author. See also Boone, "Youth News Network: An Educational Tool or Just a Marketing Pitch."
7 Jim Farrell, "Gov't Flunked Youth TV Plan Last Spring," *Edmonton Journal*, August 29, 1992, B3; Lynn Moore, "Promoters of TV News Plan for Schools," *Montreal Gazette*, October 7, 1992, A4.
8 Carroll, "Classrooms Shouldn't Be Newsrooms"; Farrell, "Gov't Flunked Youth TV Plan Last Spring"; Florence Loyle, "No Decision Yet on Allowing Youth TV into Classes," *Edmonton Journal*, October 3, 1992, B4; Pat Bell, "Education Ministry against TV News Plan," *Ottawa Citizen*, January 10, 1993, A6.
9 Bula, "TV Ads Have No Place in High School"; Carroll, "Classrooms Shouldn't Be Newsrooms"; Lynn Moore, "Protestant Boards Heard Ads-in-Class Pitch," *Montreal Gazette*, January 4, 1993, A3; Lynn Moore, "PSBGM Committee Rejects News-with-Advertising Proposal," *Montreal Gazette*, March 29, 1993, A3; "PSBGM Gives Thumbs Down to YNN Plan," *Montreal Gazette*, April 1, 1993, A4.

10 Jim Farrell, "Broadcast Plan Gets Sympathy," *Edmonton Journal*, September 3, 1992, B2; Allen Panzeri, "Youth News Program Makes Province Uneasy," *Edmonton Journal*, September 18, 1992, A7.
11 Ruttan, "Schools Pondering News/Ads Package."
12 Florence Loyle, "Parents Oppose TVs in Classroom," *Edmonton Journal*, October 1, 1992, B1.
13 Paul Marck, "Montreal Faced Same Debates over TV in the Schoolroom," *Edmonton Journal*, October 10, 1992, B1.
14 Florence Loyle, "Schools End Talks with Youth Network," *Edmonton Journal*, November 12, 1992, B3.
15 Ontario Federation of Home and School Associations Memo Packet, "OFHSA Alert, Beware of YNN," file Ontario 1992 (2/2), vol. 17, MG 28I451, Library and Archives Canada.
16 Bertrand Marotte, "Classroom Ads: Business Venture Worries Teachers," *Ottawa Citizen*, August 28, 1992, C1.
17 Ted Schmidt, "Trojan Horse Arrives at Meadowvale High," *Catholic New Times*, March 1999, Pat Johansen, "OFHSA Opposes Introduction of YNN in Ontario Schools," March 1, 1999 (Media Release), and "CAMEO Efforts Related to YNN," www.jcp.proscenia.net/CAMEO/ynn.
18 Tom Arnold, "Trustees Say Yes To Youth Network," *Edmonton Journal*, September 16, 1992, B1.
19 Susan Ruttan, "Board Gives Nod to Commercial TV," *Calgary Herald*, September 23, 1992, B3.
20 Marotte, "Classroom Ads: Business Venture Worries Teachers."
21 Bell, "Education Ministry against TV News Plan."
22 Steven Fouchard and Julian Celms, "YNN Offers More Pluses than Negatives," *Ottawa Citizen*, January 22, 1993, B6.
23 Diane Francis, "Youth News Network Takes On the Luddites," *Financial Post*, September 15, 1992, 13.
24 Susan Rattan, "School TV Plans Delayed," *Calgary Herald*, November 26, 1992, B4; Susan Ruttan, "YNN Courting Alberta as Base," *Calgary Herald*, March 17, 1993, B3.
25 Heather-jane Robertson, *No More Teachers, No More Books: The Commercialization of Canada's Schools* (Toronto: McClelland & Stewart, 1998), 213; Shaker, "In the Corporate Interest," 2–4.
26 Louise Surette, "Group Warns against Ads in Classrooms," *Ottawa Citizen*, February 12, 1999, A5; Katrina Onstad, "'Free' Computers Come with Strings," *National Post*, February 22, 1999, D4.
27 Parker Barss Donham, "Reselling Access to Our Children," *Halifax Daily News*, February 28, 1999, www.jcp.proscenia.net/CAMEO/ynn.
28 Chris M. Worsnop, "Screening Images. He's Back!!" www.jcp.proscenia.net/CAMEO/ynn.
29 Onstad, "'Free' Computers Come with Strings"; "Groups Opposed to YNN—as of March 31, 2000," www.jcp.proscenia.net/CAMEO/ynn. Erika Shaker, director

of the Education Project at the Canadian Centre for Policy Alternatives, produced the first full-scale critical reports on YNN's activities. See Shaker, "Youth News Network and the Commercial Carpet-Bombing of the Classroom" and "In the Corporate Interest," July 2000. See also Robert E. White, *How Corporate Business Practices are Transforming Education: Case Studies of Five Canadian Secondary Schools* (Queenston, ON: Edwin Mellen Press, 2010), chapter 8.

30 "Manitoba Boards to Decide If They Want Classroom TV," *St. John's Telegram*, April 22, 1999, 10; Lori Culbert, "NDP Vows to Kick Ads out of Manitoba Classrooms," *National Post*, September 1, 1999, A11. While eight Manitoba schools signed up, only one actually received the equipment and programming: Kildonan-East Collegiate in Winnipeg. The school showed the programming outside instructional time, between second and third periods. See Nick Martin, "Youth News Network Slow to Hit Classrooms," *Winnipeg Free Press*, February 9, 2000, www.jcp.proscenia.net/CAMEO/ynn.

31 Les McLean, "Metamorphosis of YNN: An Evaluation of the Pilot Program of the Youth News Network" (Toronto: Governing Council of the University of Toronto, 2000), 1, 5.

32 "Saskatchewan Minister Says No to YNN," *CPWire*, February 19, 2000, www.jcp.proscenia.net/CAMEO/ynn. While the Saskatchewan provincial government initially left the decision to local school boards, the education minister later requested that school divisions not sign contracts. See, "Decision on Classroom," *Saskatoon Star Phoenix*, July 20, 1999, A3; Kevin O'Connor, "Youth News Network is Not Welcome Here," *Regina Leader-Post*, February 21, 2000, A1.

33 McLean, "Metamorphosis of YNN," 1, 5, 10–11; Nikiforuk, "Zapped." Changing the school schedule was a tactic employed by some American schools in the early 1990s in order to bypass state opposition to Channel One. See Robert Muffoletto, "Drawing the Line: Questions of Ethics, Power and Symbols in State Policy and the Whittle Concept," in De Vaney, *Watching Channel One*, 189–207, 203.

34 Paul Favaro, Elana Gray, and Rochelle Zorzi, "Youth News Network (YNN) Evaluation Report," Peel District School Board, June 2000, 5.

35 YNN episodes, February 2000, in possession of author.

36 McLean, "Metamorphosis of YNN," 21–22.

37 For this example, along with others, see Shaker, "In the Corporate Interest," 23.

38 See the following articles by Karen Seidman in the *Montreal Gazette*: "YNN Gets Go-Ahead in Three Schools," June 15, 1999, A3; "Legault Looks at Legality of YNN," June 22, 1999, A5; "Volume Rises in Debate over YNN," June 29, 1999, A9; "YNN Blackout Angers School Board," July 10, 1999, A3; "Youth Network Tries Again," September 14, 1999, A4.

39 Karen Seidman, "Board Chief Sees Double Standard," *Montreal Gazette*, October 27, 1999, A9. See also Seidman, "High Schools Tune Out YNN," *Montreal Gazette*, February 15, 2000, A3.

40 Margaret Wente, "Margaret Wente on High-School Kids for Sale," *Globe and Mail*, June 24, 1999, www.jcp.proscenia.net/CAMEO/ynn.

41 Shaker, "Youth News Network and the Commercial Carpet-Bombing of the Classroom," 13, and "In the Corporate Interest," 28–34.

42 Favaro et al., "Youth News Network (YNN) Evaluation Report," iv.
43 James MacKinnon, "First In, First Out," *Adbusters* 31 (August/September 2000), 20.
44 Instructional Programs/Curriculum Committee, "Update on Youth News Network Project at Meadowvale Secondary School," February 16, 1999, 119–20, Minutes of the Peel District School Board, Peel Art Gallery, Museum and Archives.
45 Cited in Shaker, "In the Corporate Interest," 31.
46 Rob O'Flanagan, "YNN Gets Rough Ride at Meeting," *Sudbury Star*, February 21, 2000, www.jcp.proscenia.net/CAMEO/ynn; Erika Shaker, "Notes from the YNN Presentation to the Sudbury Community," www.jcp.proscenia.net/CAMEO/ynn; "YNN Update: Rainbow Board of Education Backs Off, Not Down," *Update* 27, 8 (January 11, 2000): 4; Brian Babineau, "Nays to YNN in Lively," *Update* 27, 12 (7 March 2000): 3.
47 Ted Schmidt, "Trojan Horse Arrives at Meadowvale High"; Maureen A. Darling, letter to editor, "Bad Behaviour Marked Meeting to Discuss YNN," *Toronto Star*, March 26, 1999.
48 Michelle Landsberg, "Let's Signal 'No' to TV Network in Schools," *Toronto Star* March 14, 1999, www.jcp.proscenia.net/CAMEO/ynn. For a response defending Pedwell, condemning the disruption of the meeting, and accusing Landsberg of inaccurate reporting, see Maureen A. Darling, letter to editor, "Bad Behaviour Marked Meeting to Discuss YNN."
49 MacKinnon, "First In, First Out"; See also Shaker, "In the Corporate Interest," 37–38, and Sarah Elton, "Parental Discretion is Advised," *This Magazine* 35, 1 (July/August 2001): 18–23.
50 Cited in MacKinnon, "First In, First Out," 20.
51 Favaro et al., "Youth News Network (YNN) Evaluation Report," ii, 29, 37; Nikiforuk, "Zapped."
52 Nancy Nelson Knupfer and Peter Hayes, "The Effects of the Channel One Broadcast on Students' Knowledge of Current Events," in De Vaney, *Watching Channel One*, 42–60, 58; Roy F. Fox, *Harvesting Minds: How TV Commercials Control Kids* (Westport, CT: Praeger, 1996), 11–12.
53 Fox, *Harvesting Minds*, 2. See also 127, 148.
54 Molnar, *School Commercialism*, 18, 92; Linn, *Consuming Kids*, 82; Schor, *Born to Buy*, 86–88.
55 Ann De Vaney, "Introduction," in De Vaney, *Watching Channel One*, 2.
56 CTF, "Canadians Say No to Advertising in Schools" (Press release), www.ctf-fce.ca.
57 Favaro et al., "Youth News Network (YNN) Evaluation Report," v.
58 Favaro et al., "Youth News Network (YNN) Evaluation Report," ii.
59 Favaro et al., "Youth News Network (YNN) Evaluation Report," iii.
60 McLean, "Metamorphosis of YNN," 26. See also 24.
61 Nikiforuk, "Zapped"; Shaker, "In the Corporate Interest," 2. For the US, see Blokhuis, "Channel One," 355–56.

62 McLean, "Metamorphosis of YNN," 34–35.
63 Susan Ruttan, "Teenagers Able to Tune Out TV Commercials," *Calgary Herald*, September 20, 1992, A5.

6: BUILDING BRAND LOYALTY

1 Janet Steffenhagen, "Fast Food Back on School Menu," *Vancouver Sun*, November 3, 2003, A1.
2 See, for example, "One Hot Dish," *Canadian Teacher* 38, no. 3 (October 9, 1933): 197, 268; Letter to the editor, "I'm Marigold, Too," *Canadian Teacher* 38, no. 4 (28 October 1933): 329.
3 See for example, T. L. Sullivan, "Use of Rural School Buildings and Equipment," in *Addresses and Proceedings of the Canadian Conference on Education, 1958*, ed. George G. Croskery and Gerald Nason (Ottawa: Mutual Press, 1958), 137. Scarborough High School had a cafeteria as of the mid-1920s as many of its students lived far from the school. More commonly, cafeterias became part of the school landscape in the 1950s as administrators built new suburban schools for the expanding baby boom or as part of school consolidation. When Burnaby Central High School opened in 1958, 90 percent of students stayed for lunch. Still, many schools did not have cafeterias in the late 1950s and early 1960s, as was the case in Alberta. See R. H. King, "The High School Cafeteria," *The School* 14, no. 9 (May 1926): 859; J. S. Burton, "One Solution to the School Lunch Program," *BC Teacher* 42, no. 2 (November 1962): 116; "School Lunch Programs," Alberta Department of Education, *Annual Report*, 1961, 25. See also "School Cafeterias," in *Report of the Royal Commission on Education and Youth*, Province of Newfoundland and Labrador, 1968, 80–81.
4 Monda Rosenberg, "School Trims Its Menu," *Toronto Star*, October 20, 1976, E1.
5 See, for example, Linda Engel, President, Norman Cook School Association Annual Report, June 1987, in *Scarborough Home and School Council Bulletin*, File: Ontario 1987, vol. 16, MG 28 I 451, Library and Archives Canada (LAC).
6 This dating is based on anecdotal evidence. In the United States, in 1968, only 750 out of 25,000 schools had vending machines. Those numbers increased significantly after 1970 with an amendment to the National School Lunch Act (1945) that for the first time allowed food service companies to participate in lunch programs. See Kerry Segrave, *Vending Machines: An American Social History* (Jefferson, NC: McFarland, 2002), 181–83. For the reference to the 1980s in Canada see Janet Steffenhagen, "School Sets a Healthy–Meal Table," *Vancouver Sun*, November 6, 2003, A3.
7 "Chocolate Drink Ban Hinted in City Schools," *Globe and Mail*, March 8, 1949, 5; "Ban on Drink Eased," *Globe and Mail*, June 19, 1953, 5; "Committee Again Asks Ban on Chocolate Drink," *Globe and Mail*, September 22, 1953, 5; TDSB Museum and Archives, Minutes of the Toronto Board of Education, "Consideration of Reports," September 24, 1953, 101. Concern about sugar levels in chocolate milk remains an issue. Saskatoon area schools banned the drink in 2015 and New

Brunswick did so temporarily in 2018. See "Chocolate Milk Bans Backfire: Study," *Saskatoon Sunday Phoenix*, January 18, 2015, C3; "New Brunswick Parties Spar Over Chocolate Milk Ban," *Globe and Mail*, August 31, 2018.

8 Anne Wanstall, "School Lunch of Chips, Gravy Worries Adults," *Globe and Mail*, October 27, 1972, 65; "Junk Foods in Schools Bothers B.C. Nutritionist," *Globe and Mail*, May 21, 1973, 16; "US Consumer Group Goes After Junk Foods in schools," *Globe and Mail*, September 22, 1975, 12.

9 Stephanie Cameron, "Montreal Schools Flourish in No-Junk-Food Program," *Toronto Star*, March 22, 1978, C2; Jim White, "Health Costs Force New Eating Habits," *Toronto Star*, May 7, 1980, C1; "York Students Send Junk Food Back to the Kitchen," *Toronto Star*, April 17, 1980, A23.

10 Brian Vallée, "Junk Food Ban Looms in Metro Schools," *Toronto Star*, February 22, 1978, A4. See also White, "Health Costs Force New Eating Habits."

11 "School Food Has to be Junk or Nobody Will Eat, Board Told," *Toronto Star*, June 29, 1977, B1; For the history of this development, see Lana Povitz, "'It Used to Be about the Kids': Nutrition Reform and the Montreal Protestant School Board," *Canadian Historical Review* 92, no. 2 (June 2011): 330.

12 Kathleen Rex, "Apple-a-Day Attitude Worth Money," *Globe and Mail*, May 30, 1981, 17.

13 Gillian MacKay, "VS Gets Peel School Cafeteria Job," *Globe and Mail*, August 25, 1978, B3.

14 Report: "Reports, Resolutions, Notice of Motion for Annual General Meeting, June 1980," 23, 41-3, File: "Local Association Reports," box 32, CHSF R 1612, LAC.

15 For example, Naoibh O'Connor wrote in 2004 that although the Vancouver School Board "has had a food policy on the books since the early 1980s that, among other things, calls for the phasing out of sweetened, carbonated beverages from vending machines, it's never been fully implemented due to schools' need to generate revenue and desire to offer students choice." See "Kits Replaces Coke with Local Company," *Vancouver Courier*, January 28, 2004, 15.

16 Naomi Klein, "Only Pepsi to Be Sold in Schools," *Globe and Mail*, January 15, 1994, A6, A15. In the US, exclusivity or pouring rights deals spread rapidly, from 46 school districts in 16 states in 1998 to 140 school districts in 26 states a year later. By 2005, 50 percent of American elementary schools and 80 percent of high schools had signed exclusivity contracts with soft drink companies. See Segrave, *Vending Machines*, 218–19; Marion Nestle, *Soda Politics: Taking on Big Soda (and Winning)* (New York: Oxford University Press, 2015), 160; Alex Molnar, *School Commercialism: From Democratic Ideal to Market Commodity* (New York: Routledge, 2005), chapter 3.

17 Across the country "27 per cent of all schools had an exclusive marketing arrangement with soft drink giants Coke or Pepsi," with the highest rate in the Prairies, at 40 percent, and the lowest in Quebec, at 5 percent. See Bernie Froese-Germain, Colleen Hawkey, Alex Larose, Patricia McAdie, and Erika Shaker, *Commercialism in the Schools: Who's Calling the Shots?* (Ottawa: CCPA, 2006), 8, policyalternatives.ca.

18 Catherine Porter, "Single Firm Dominates as Institutions Make Deals to Sell

Products," *Vancouver Sun*, December 15, 1998, B3; Sterling News Service, "Soft Drink Deal Questioned," *Vancouver Sun*, September 8, 1999, B1. For the role of marketing firms in securing contracts with corporations in the US, see Eric Scholsser, *Fast-Food Nation: The Dark Side of the All-American Meal* (New York: Perennial, 2002), 51–53.

19 Sean Cook and Stephen Petrina, "Changing Tastes: Coca-Cola, Water and the Commercialization of Higher Education," *Workplace: A Journal for Academic Labor* 7, no. 1 (November 2005): 101.

20 Sarah Schmidt, "Teen Forces Cola Giants to Reveal School Deals," *Ottawa Citizen*, November 12, 2003, D1.

21 Shannon Hagerman, "Schools Guzzle Coke," *Fredericton Daily Gleaner*, February 2, 2000.

22 Editorial, "Selling Pop and Ethics," *London Free Press*, reprinted in *Toronto Star*, January 30, 1994, E2.

23 In 1976 Benton High School in Arkansas enlisted a McDonald's franchise to run its hot-lunch program in order to eliminate its cafeteria's deficit. See "McDonald's Takes Over Cafeteria," *Globe and Mail*, October 7, 1976, F12. Benton may have been an exception in using a fast food operator in the 1970s, but by the mid-1990s the federal government had changed the rules for schools involved in the National School Lunch Program, allowing a variety of fast food chains to open in schools. Some fast food companies, recognizing that the school market was not, in fact, particularly profitable, offered their franchisees monetary incentives to enter that market, with a long-term view of creating brand loyalty. See Susan Levine, *School Lunch Politics: The Surprising History of America's Favorite Welfare Program* (Princeton: Princeton University Press, 2008), 168–69, 182–83. By 2000, "about 30 percent of the public high schools in the United States offered branded fast food." See Schlosser, *Fast-Food Nation*, 56.

24 Most schools did not introduce such kiosks. Martingrove Collegiate Institute had a Tim Hortons for about three years. West Humber Collegiate Institute had a Tim Hortons and Pizza Pizza outlet for about one year. In 1998 the Etobicoke Board of Education was incorporated into the newly formed Toronto District School Board.

25 Bruce Constantineau, "Fast Food Outlets Going Off Beaten Track," *Vancouver Sun*, June 6, 1998, E1.

26 Peter Clough, "School-Lunch Breakthrough," *The Province*, September 24, 1999, A4. A BCTF survey undertaken in Spring 2000 noted that about 9 percent of food services were operated by fast food franchises. See "Highlights of BCTF Survey: Corporate Involvement in Schools," bctf.ca.

27 Cited in S. Leith, "A Lesson for Coke: Atlanta-Based CEO Takes On Critics, Defends Soft-Drink Sales in Schools," *Atlanta Journal-Constitution*, April 6, 2003, in Leo, "Are Schools Making the Grade?," 4n18.

28 Margaret Wente, "Things Go Better with Coke," *Globe and Mail*, November 27, 2003, A23.

29 Janet Steffenhagen, "Schools Earning Bonuses for Pushing Pop," *Canwest News Service*, November 4, 2003; Robyn Chambers, "Pop Culture," Chilliwack

Times, January 9, 2004, 1; Sterling News Service, "Soft Drink Deal Questioned," *Vancouver Sun*, September 8, 1999, B1; Roseann Danese, "Generation X-Cess," *Windsor Star*, September 4, 2003, A12; Byron Churchill, "Schools Face Possible Cuts to Programs," *Vancouver Sun*, May 3, 2000, B1.

30 Wente, "Things Go Better with Coke"; Shawn Jeffords, "Student Uncaps Details of School Soft-Drink Pacts," *National Post*, November 25, 2003, A7. In Quebec, the Commission scolaire des Découvreurs signed an agreement with Coca-Cola in 1999 that would bring in $500,000 over five years. See Martine Turenne, "L'école sauce PUB," *L'Actualité*, September 15, 1999, 32.

31 Jennifer Lewington, "Pepsi Deal Ignites Corporate Debate," *Globe and Mail*, March 27, 1997, C5; Jock Ferguson, "Dishing It Out So Teens Will Take It," *Globe and Mail*, April 7, 1994, A1; Scott Simpson, "Pizzas, Subs Keep Kids on Campus at Terry Fox," *Vancouver Sun*, June 7, 2000, A1.

32 Andrew Duffy, "Trustees Reaffirm Pepsi Deal," *Toronto Star*, January 28, 1994, A1; Churchill, "Schools Face Possible Cuts to Programs"; Barbara Aarsteinsen, "Students Protest 'Corporate Invasion,'" *Globe and Mail*, January 27, 1994, A7. Researchers have found this to be the case elsewhere. In the US, contracts with soft drink corporations are estimated to have brought in just under $2 per elementary school student and just over $4 for each high school student. See Nestle, *Soda Politics*, 160. In 1996–97, Colorado Springs District 11 sold advertising space on school grounds and in school buses that amounted to $4.35 per student. See Jane Kenway and Elizabeth Bullen, *Consuming Children: Education, Entertainment, Advertising* (Buckingham: Open University Press, 2001), 109. See also Alex Molnar and Faith Boninger, *Sold Out: How Marketing in School Threatens Children's Well-Being and Undermines Their Education* (Lanham, MD: Rowman & Littlefield, 2015), Kindle ed., 6, and Brian O. Brent and Stephen Lunden, "Much Ado about Very Little: The Benefits and Costs of School-Based Commercial Activities," *Leadership and Policy in Schools* 8, no. 3 (July 2009): 321, doi: 10.1080/15700760802488619.

33 Quoted in Mia Stainsby, "Cola Wars Worry Students, Parents," *Vancouver Sun*, November 20, 2000, B1. See also Wente, "Things Go Better with Coke."

34 Cited in Barlow and Robertson, *Class Warfare*, 163.

35 Duffy, "Trustees Reaffirm Pepsi Deal."

36 Steffenhagen, "Fast Food Back on School Menu"; Chambers, "Pop Culture."

37 Scott Simpson, "Port Coquitlam Students Can Order Variety of Foods," *Vancouver Sun*, September 29, 1999, B1.

38 Ferguson, "Dishing It Out So Teens Will Take It.

39 Klein, "Only Pepsi to Be Sold in Schools"; Ferguson, "Dishing It Out So Teens Will Take It; Scott Simpson, "PoCo's Terry Fox Has School Food from Sushi to Subs," *Vancouver Sun*, September 29, 1999, B1; Clough, "School-Lunch Breakthrough"; Simpson, "Pizzas, Subs Keep Kids on Campus at Terry Fox." In a study of high schools in one Ontario district, Anthony Winson discovered that most schools were within walking distance of a fast food outlet. See "School Food Environments and the Obesity Issue: Content, Structural Determinants, and Agency in Canadian High Schools," *Agriculture and Human Values* 25 (2008): 507.

40 Minutes of the Etobicoke Board of Education, 527-6 (c), September 23, 1992, TDSB Museum and Archives; Duffy, "Trustees Reaffirm Pepsi Deal"; Jody Paterson, "Schools Should Get More from Cola Wars," *Victoria Times Colonist*, November 11, 1998, A3.
41 Andrew Duffy, "Pepsi Deal 'Dangerous' in Schools, Students Say," *Globe and Mail*, January 19, 1994, A12; Clough, "School-Lunch Breakthrough."
42 BCTF, "Highlights of BCTF Survey"; Froese-Germain et al., *Commercialism in Canadian Schools*; Janet Steffenhagen, "Minister Seeking Early Ban on Junk Food in Schools," *Vancouver Sun*, November 23, 2005, A3.
43 Aarsteinsen, "Students Protest 'Corporate Invasion'"; Duffy, "Trustees Reaffirm Pepsi Deal." The Toronto Association of Student Councils requested a greater role in the decision-making process regarding such deals and that either some of the monies go directly to student councils or that students be involved in the allocation of funds rather than this being left to the discretion of individual school administrators. See Report No. 1 of the Student Affairs Committee, January 18, 1994, in Minutes of the Toronto Board of Education, February 24, 1994, 126–29, TDSB Archives and Museum. See also Caroline Alphonso, "School Board Urged to Stop the Pop," *Globe and Mail*, June 23, 2000, A11, and "Bid to Block Pepsi Deal with Schools Fizzles," *Globe and Mail*, June 24, 2004, A13.
44 Earle Gale, "Students Alarmed by School District's Deal with Coke," *Vancouver Sun*, January 13, 1999.
45 Darren Bernhardt, "Soft Drink Deals Draw Public Scorn," *Saskatoon StarPhoenix*, May 30, 2001, A5.
46 Darren Bernhardt, "Students Demand School Share Juicy Details of Deal," *Saskatoon StarPhoenix*, May 11, 2001, A12.
47 Schmidt, "Teen Forces Cola Giants to Reveal School Deals." See also "Coke's the One, Peel Board Decides," *Globe and Mail*, February 23, 2000, A17.
48 Jeffords, "Student Uncaps Details of School Soft-Drink Pacts"; Stainsby, "Cola Wars Worry Students, Parents." This has certainly been the case in the US. See Nestle, *Food Politics*, 202–6.
49 Schlosser, *Fast-Food Nation*, 55. See also Molnar and Boninger, *Sold Out*, 23–27.
50 Stainsby, "Cola Wars Worry Students, Parents."
51 Peter Simeon, letter to the editor, *Globe and Mail*, April 20, 1994, A21.
52 "Kids Plea for Cheap, Good Food," *Regina Leader-Post*, October 21, 2006, H10.
53 Mary MacKay, "School Changes from Fries to Healthier Options," *Fredericton Daily Gleaner*, October 30, 2007, C6.
54 For Canada see Anthony Winson, "Spatial Colonization of Food Environments by Pseudo-food Companies: Precursors of a Health Crisis," in *Critical Perspectives in Food Studies*, ed. Mustafa Koç, Jennifer Sumner, and Anthony Winson, 186–207 (Don Mills, ON: Oxford University Press, 2012), 199. For the US, see Keith Morgan and Roberto Sonnino, *The School Food Revolution: Public Food and the Challenge of Sustainable Development* (London: Earthscan, 2008), 58–62.
55 Adam Bowie, "Nutritional Lunches Are Critical Part of Educational Process, Says School Survey," *Fredericton Daily Gleaner*, August 27, 2011, A4.

56 J. Eric Oliver, *Fat Politics: The Real Story behind America's Obesity Epidemic* (New York: Oxford University Press, 2006), 9. On snacking see also Janet Poppendieck, *Free For All: Fixing School Food in America* (Berkeley: University of California Press, 2010), 13.

57 For this point, see Steffenhagen, "Fast Food Back on School Menu."

58 Graham Thomson, "Cola Wars in the Classroom," *Edmonton Journal*, February 12, 1998, A1.

59 For this argument see, for example, "Healthy Weights for Healthy Kids," cited in Leo, "Are Schools Making the Grade?," 2. Dr. David Kessler, the former head of the U.S. Food and Drug Administration, notes that there is increasing evidence "that foods high in sugar, fat and salt are altering the biological circuitry of our brains" leading to an addiction to, and overeating of, those foods and resulting in many individuals in significant weight gain or obesity. See David A. Kessler, *The End of Overeating: Taking Control of the Insatiable American Appetite* (New York: Macmillan, 2009), 60.

60 Winson, "School Food Environments and the Obesity Issue," 507.

61 Anne Jarvis, "Food for Thought," *Windsor Star*, September 27, 2008, A6.

62 Laura Landon, "Grease is the Word in High Schools," *Ottawa Citizen*, August 2, 2000, C3.

63 Sherri Zickefoose, "Pulling the Plug on Pop Machines," *Calgary Herald*, September 5, 2002, S17.

64 Jodie Sinnema, "Recipe for Success," *Edmonton Journal*, January 11, 2004, A6.

65 David Howell and Mide Sadava, "McKernan School Has Been Pop-Free for a Year," *Edmonton Journal*, October 23, 2004, A2.

66 Caroline Alphonso, "Class Warfare: The Clash of the Cafs," *Globe and Mail*, October 8, 2005, A12; Erin Phelan, "The Fink Effect," *Best Health* (September 2012), www.besthealthmag.ca.

67 Anna Olson, "Happy Kids. Happy Parents," *National Post*, March 19, 2008, AL4.

68 Amy Reid, "Catering to Schools' Culinary Needs," *Surrey Now*, April 7, 2009, 17; Layne Christensen, "The Battle of the Childhood Bulge," *North Shore News*, October 9, 2005, 3.

69 Clare Ogilvie, "Healthy Foods a Hard Sell," *The Province* (Vancouver), June 4, 2008, A3.

70 Levine, *School Lunch Politics*, 189. For similar activities by the Education Department in New York City, see Alissa Quartz, *Branded: The Buying and Selling of Teenagers* (New York: Basic Books, 2003), 225–26. For the difficulties in achieving this legislation see Simon, *Appetite for Profit*, 224–28.

71 Editorial, "Ban Soft Drinks in Schools," *Montreal Gazette*, August 30, 2004, A14; Caroline Alphonso, "Will Canada Nix Nuggets and Fries?" *Globe and Mail*, September 29, 2005, A1. On the development of this legislation see Morgan and Sonnino, *The School Food Revolution*, 93–95.

72 Cited in Aileen Leo, "Are Schools Making the Grade? School Nutrition Policies Across Canada" (Ottawa: Centre for Science in the Public Interest, 2007), 10,

cspinet.org. See also Winson, "School Food Environments and the Obesity Issue," 502.

73 Steffenhagen, "Minister Seeking Early Ban on Junk Food in Schools"; Marian Scott, "Learning to Eat Well," *Montreal Gazette*, October 10, 2005, D1. Similarly, the 2006 report of BC's Select Standing Committee on Health, formed to investigate strategies to reduce childhood obesity and physical inactivity, recommended, among other things, that the government speed up the elimination of junk food in schools. See "A Strategy for Combatting Childhood Obesity and Physical Activity in British Columbia Report," November 29, 2006, www.leg.bc.

74 Nova Scotia developed a policy to eliminate nutritionally poor foods and beverages in 2006, to be implemented in the subsequent three years. New Brunswick created a policy, effective in 2005, while BC's 2005 policy would not be fully implemented until 2010. In 2004 Ontario developed a memorandum, replaced by the School Food and Beverage Policy in 2010, implemented by all school boards by 2011. See Winson, "School Food Environments and the Obesity Issue," 502; Leo, "Are Schools Making the Grade?" 11; "Healthy Schools Strategy," Section 3.03, *2013 Annual Report*, Office of the Auditor General of Ontario, 107.

75 "Quebec Schools to Keep Junk Food," *CanWest News*, March 30, 2006, 1; "Quebec to Ban Junk Food from Schools," *Canadian Press*, September 14, 2007. Montreal already had policies banning vending machines in elementary and high schools as well as foods such as poutine in school cafeterias. See Allison Lampart, "School Board Pulls Plug on Exclusive Contract," *Montreal Gazette*, July 8, 2005, A13.

76 Michael F. Jacobson, "How Soft Drinks Are Harming Americans' Health" (Washington: Center for Science in the Public Interest, 2005), cspinet.org.

77 For a strong critique of the shortfalls of the Alliance and of the effectiveness of industry self-regulation, see Nestle, *Soda Politics*, 162, 333.

78 Agence France-Presse, "Soft-Drink Makers Join Childhood-Obesity Fight," *The Province* (Vancouver), August 19, 2005, A40.

79 Refreshments Canada's guidelines included the elimination of carbonated beverages from vending machines in elementary and middle schools. Critics argued that this policy ignored the continued sale of diet sodas, high-fructose fruit juices, and sports drinks. Nor did it cover high schools, where most of the vending machines were actually located. See David Heyman, "Soft Drink Makers Agree to Cap Access in Schools," *Victoria Times Colonist*, January 6, 2004, A1; Cathy Lord, "School Pop Ban Seen As a Watered-Down Solution," *Edmonton Journal*, January 7, 2004, B1; Editorial, "Pop Decision Effects Limited," *Regina Leader-Post*, January 8, 2004, B11.

80 Such developments were not altruistic. Kellogg announced plans at least partially in reaction to a threat by the Campaign for a Commercial-Free Childhood and the Center for Science in the Public Interest to sue Kellogg and Nickelodeon. See Nichola Groom, "Kraft to Cut Back on Snack Advertising," *Globe and Mail*, January 13, 2005, B12; "Snack Food Makers Sell Healthier Treats," *Times and Transcript*, June 23, 2007, E2. Corporations such as Kellogg and Kraft also joined the Alliance for American Advertising, created in 2005, to fight legislation limiting their right to advertise to children and which questions the role of advertising in encouraging obesity. See Schor, *Born to Buy*, 217.

81 Emily Fredrix, "Pepsi to Stop Selling Sugary Drinks," *Saint John Telegraph-Journal*, March 17, 2010, B5. Despite encouraging bottlers to stop selling to schools, Coca-Cola did not offer any incentives to them to do so. Coke is part-owner of some of its bottling companies while others are independent. See "Coke Having Tough Time with School Beverage Policy," *Globe and Mail*, July 6, 2001, M2 [reprint from *Wall St. Journal*, n.d.].

82 Kevin Bissett, "As a Growing Number of Canadian Schools Move to Ban the Sale of Junk Food," *Canadian Press NewsWire*, November 19, 2005; Joel O'Kane, "School Nutrition Policy," *Fredericton Daily Gleaner*, December 7, 2005, A6.

83 Editorial, "Pizza off the Table," *Fredericton Daily Gleaner*, October 10, 2007, B7. For similar comments by parents, see Jarvis, "Food for Thought."

84 Jarvis, "Food for Thought."

85 Bissett, "As a Growing Number of Canadian Schools Move to Ban the Sale of Junk Food"

86 Cassidy Olivier, "Teen Junk-Food Dealers Give Cash," *The Province* (Vancouver), September 24, 2008, A11.

87 Don Lajoie, "Province Bans Junk Food in Schools," *Windsor Star*, January 21, 2010, A1; Anne Jarvis, "Teaching Good Food Habits," *Windsor Star*, February 1, 2010, A3.

88 Leo, "Executive Summary," in "Are Schools Making the Grade," 2; "Lamrock Won't Hire 'Food Cop,'" *Fredericton Daily Gleaner*, October 9, 2007, A4. Eight years later a significant number of school menus still did not meet provincial guidelines. See Chris Morris, "School Menus in Province Get Failing Grades," *Fredericton Daily Gleaner*, January 27, 2015, B1.

89 As of 2013 nutrition policies existed in British Columbia, Ontario, New Brunswick, Nova Scotia and Newfoundland. See Michelle M. Vine and Susan J. Elliott, "Exploring the School Nutrition Policy Environment in Canada Using the ANGELO Framework," *Health Promotion Practice*, August 28, 2013, 2, doi: 10.1177/1524839913498087.

90 Tara Chislett, "Province, Student Clash over Food," *Fredericton Daily Gleaner*, September 16, 2013, A4; Gleneagle Secondary School, After Grad 2013, Flyer.

91 Simon, *Appetite for Profit*, 222.

92 Simon, *Appetite for Profit*, 223. Similarly, the American Beverage Association consistently organized hard-hitting campaigns against state bills aimed at improving school nutrition. See Simon, 13–19. Coca-Cola has also fought environmental initiatives such as bottle deposit laws both in the US and internationally. See Nestle, *Soda Politics*, 290. For the effects of lobbying efforts see also Poppendieck, *Free For All*, 231–32, and Joel Bakan, *Childhood Under Siege: How Big Business Targets Children* (New York: Free Press, 2011), 55.

93 Rosenberg, "School Trims Its Menu"; "School Food Has to Be Junk Or Nobody Will Eat, Board Told." See also "Decisions of the Whole Re. 1971 Budget, Adopted by Board, March 18 1971," Toronto Board of Education Minutes, 201, TDSB Museum and Archives.

94 Office of the Auditor General of Ontario, *Annual Report*, "Healthy Schools Strategy," Section 3-03, 2013, 105–6; Kristin Rushowy, "Some School Cafs Earn $35 a

Day," *Toronto Star*, June 16, 2012, G1; Editorial, "They Failed Lunch," *Globe and Mail*, December 12, 2013, A20. Researchers have found that there are a number of barriers to the success of the policies including the cost of healthy food, the proximity of fast food outlets, and the commitment of stakeholders, all of which point to the need to strengthen existing policies. Moreover, there has been no funding attached to the implementation of food and beverage policies. See Michelle M. Vine and Susan J. Elliott, "Examining Local-Level Factors Shaping School Nutrition Policy Implementation in Ontario, Canada," *Public Health Nutrition*, September 19, 2013, 7–8, doi: 10.1017/S1368980013002516, and Vine and Elliott, "Exploring the School Nutrition Policy Environment in Canada," 2.

95 Craig Offman, "Overhaul Needed to Stop Cafeteria Exodus," *Globe and Mail*, December 14, 2013, A15. Similarly, in New Brunswick, Chartwells stopped service to some schools in Anglophone West School District in December 2015 citing financial reasons. This occurred at the same time the district was proposing tightening its nutritional guidelines. See Tara Chislett, "New Standards May Have Led to Cafeteria Closures Says District," *Fredericton Daily Gleaner*, December 18, 2015, A1.

96 Christiana Wiens, "'Healthy Food Means Budget Cuts,'" *Comox Valley Echo*, October 13, 2009, 1; Ogilvie, "Healthy Foods a Hard Sell."

97 David Howell, "Fit Food versus Fast Food" *Edmonton Journal*, October 11, 2005, B1.

98 See, for example, Megan L. Mullally et al., "A Province-Wide School Nutrition Policy and Food Consumption in Elementary School Children in Prince Edward Island," *Canadian Public Health Association* 101, no. 1 (2010): 40–43; C. E. Driessen et al., "Effect of Changes to the School Food Environment on Eating Behaviours and/or Body Weight in Children: A Systematic Review," *Obesity Reviews* 15 (December 2014), 968–82, doi:10.1111/obr.12224; Philip S. J. Leonard, "Do School Junk Food Bans Improve Student Health? Evidence from Canada," *Canadian Public Policy* (June 2017), doi: 10.3138/cpp.2016-090.

99 Carly Weeks, "How to Fight Obesity? Ban Food and Drink Ads Targeted at Teens, Experts Say," *Globe and Mail*, March 22, 2013; Froese-Germain et al., *Commercialism in Canadian Schools*, 7–8, 17–18.

100 Conversation with Kathleen Thompson, June 2013.

101 Shaker and Froese-Germaine, "Beyond the Bake Sale," 90.

102 The Slush Puppies rated as moderate in nutritional value and thus could be served twice a week. See Emma Davie, "Slush Puppies in Schools Hit with Health Concerns," *Fredericton Daily Gleaner*, November 5, 2016, A1; Linda Ugrin and Jillian Higgs, "Common Sense Needed for Healthier Food Choices," *Fredericton Daily Gleaner*, November 19, 2016, A7; Editorial, "Keep Junk Drinks Out of Schools," *Fredericton Daily Gleaner*, November 9, 2016, A8. In the US 35.5 percent of "school districts offer fast-food-branded fare." See Marcus B. Weaver-Hightower, "Why Education Researchers Should Take School Food Seriously," *Educational Researcher* 40, no. 1 (2011), 18, doi:10.3102/0012189X10397043.

103 Jacques Poitras, "Burger King's Role in School Lunch Program Defended," October 29, 2015, www.cbc.ca.

7: "ALL WE'RE TRYING TO DO IS HELP YOUNGSTERS"

1 Chris Glover, "A Slippery Slope? The Escalation of Public-Private Partnerships in Ontario's Public Education," *Our Schools, Our Selves* 16, no. 1 (Fall 2006): 49.
2 Province of Nova Scotia, *Annual Report of the Superintendent of Education for Nova Scotia, 1934–35*, "School Improvement," 80.
3 *Annual Report of the Superintendent of Education for Nova Scotia, 1938–39*, xxxii–xxxiii.
4 Coquitlam District School Board [hereafter CDSB], Board of School District No. 43 Minutes, May 11, 1948, 3; December 14, 1948, 3; July 28, 1948, 1; July 12, 1949, 70; July 8, 1952, 259.
5 Clarkson Home and School Association, Financial Statement, September 1957 to June 1958, Peel Art Gallery, Museum and Archives.
6 "Reports, Resolutions, Notice of Motion for Annual General Meeting, June 1980," NB Home and School Federation, 41–43, box 32, file "Local Association Reports," CHSF R 1612, Library and Archives Canada (LAC); Knob Hill and Norman Cook Annual Reports, Scarborough Home and School Council Bulletin, June 1987, file Ontario 1987, vol. 17, MG 28 I 451, LAC.
7 Kim Zarzour, "Cuts in Grants Said Forcing Pupils into Fundraising," *Toronto Star*, January 13, 1987, A7.
8 Virginia Galt, "Schools Take Unusual Course for Cash," *Globe and Mail*, June 28, 1996, A8.
9 Simone Blais, "School Fundraising Joins the Big Leagues as Needs Increase," *Coquitlam Now*, November 22, 2003; Sarah Hampson, "Uptown School Reaches Out and Shares Fundraising Spoils," *Globe and Mail*, April 23, 1999, A11.
10 "You Can Raise $50.00 to $5,000," *Quest* 4, no. 1 (September–October 1966), 29, and 4, no. 2 (December 1966), 35.
11 Margaret Wente, "Things Go Better with Roulette," *Globe and Mail*, December 14, 1999, A21.
12 Horizons West Marketing Ad, Calgary Council of Home and School Associations Newsletter, November/December 1994, 7, file Alberta 1994, vol. 16, MG 28 I 451, LAC; Aloma Jardine, "Schools Seek New Fundraising Methods," *Times and Transcript*, May 8, 2006, A1; Allison Lampert, "Schools Plug Into Internet to Raise Cash," *Canwest News Service*, June 1, 2006; Dianne Buckner, "Companies Pitch New Fundraising Schemes to Cash-Strapped Schools," February 17, 2014, www.cbc.ca.
13 Jocelyn Dingman, "Money! Money! Money!" *Canadian Home and Gardens*, n.d., reprinted in *Canadian Home and School* 15, no. 3 (February 1956): 13.
14 Susan Semenak, "Schools Rely on Fundraising to Pay for Extras," *Montreal Gazette*, September 16, 1996, A1.
15 Tom Arnold, "Parent Fundraisers Pump $119M into Albert Schools," *Calgary Herald*, September 15, 1998, A1; Blais, "School Fundraising Joins the Big Leagues as Needs Increase"; Shauna Rempel, "Schools Stop Serving Junk Food, But Still Profit From It," *CapitalNews online*, October 22, 2004, temagami.carleton.ca. This remained true over a decade later. In 2017 People for Education reported: "48% of

elementary schools and 10% of secondary schools fundraise for learning resources (e.g. computers, classroom supplies, etc. . . .)." See People for Education, *Competing Priorities (Annual Report on Ontario's Publicly Funded Schools 2017)*, (Toronto, ON: People for Education, 2017), 33, www.peopleforeducation.ca.

16 Annie Kidder, "Fundraising and Corporate Donations in Schools: The Beginning of a Two-Tier Public Education System," *Education Canada* 42, no. 3 (Fall 2002): 42–43, 47; Catherine Porter, "Business Ties to Schools 'Only the Beginning,'" *Vancouver Sun*, November 26, 1998, A1; Abigail Esteireiro, "Back to School Shopping: Teachers Pay More Than Ever for Supplies," August 23, 2016, www.huffingtonpost.ca.

17 Jane Seyd, "Home Depot Crosses School Line," *North Shore News*, November 10, 2004, 1; Steve Coffin, "This Isn't Charity," *National Post*, December 22, 2004, A21; Elaine O'Connor, "Corporations Go to School," *The Province* (Vancouver), November 22, 2004, A15. See also Marion Nestle, Soda Politics: *Taking On Big Soda (and Winning)* (New York: Oxford University Press, 2015), 241.

18 Lawrence Brand, letter to editor, "Home Depot School Support Unselfish," *North Shore News*, November 17, 2004, 6.

19 Barb Wilkie, "Companies Helping Communities," *The Province* (Vancouver), November 23, 2004, A17.

20 Barb Pacholik, "School-Business Partnerships," *Regina Leader-Post*, April 17, 2006, B5.

21 treecanada.ca/en/about-us/history/.

22 See, for example, *Fredericton Daily Gleaner*, January 17, 2012, A1. See also Tara Chislett, "School Looking For Votes to Win Outdoor Classroom," *Fredericton Daily Gleaner*, April 8, 2014, A4.

23 Tara Chislett, "Two New Brunswick Schools Dig Up Big Bucks for High-Tech Gear and Green Projects," *Fredericton Daily Gleaner*, April 25, 2016, A8; Robert Williams, "Making Makers: Fredericton School Qualifies for National Samsung Contest," *Fredericton Daily Gleaner*, May 20, 2017, A4.

24 Heather Reisman, "Building Success from Books," *CanWest News Service*, October 6, 2005. See also Caroline Alphonso, "Taking the Brand to the Classroom," *Globe and Mail*, April 30, 2005, A13; Maria Kubacki, "New Funding Helps School Libraries Get the Word Out," *Ottawa Citizen*, June 25, 2005, E1. This is an incredibly successful foundation. By 2017 it was providing funds to thirty schools in need. See "Literacy Fund," www.loveofreading.org.

25 See "Donate," www.loveofreading.org.

26 In Calgary parent groups at fifty-nine of ninety-seven possible Catholic schools used this form of fundraising. See, "Bishop Slams School Board," *Edmonton Journal*, June 23, 2006, B6. See also David Howell, "Catholic Board May Abandon Casino Fundraising," *Edmonton Journal*, October 3, 2006, B6; Wente, "Things Go Better with Roulette."

27 Joe Woodard, "'I'm Asking Them to Confront a Moral Evil,'" *Calgary Herald*, June 27, 2006, B1.

28 Virginia Galt, "Chocolate Soldiers Fight for Funds," *Globe and Mail*, October 21, 1997, A10; Wente, "Things Go Better with Roulette"; Rick Pedersen, "Catholic

School District Bans Casinos, Bingos," *Edmonton Journal*, November 12, 2003, B1.
29 "Bishop Slams School Board." See also Suzanne Morton, *At Odds: Gambling and Canadians, 1919–1969* (Toronto: University of Toronto Press, 2003), 4, 198–201.
30 "Bishop Slams School Board."
31 Nancy MacDonald, "Casino Cash is Crucial," *Edmonton Journal*, October 9, 2006, A19.
32 Sarah McGinnis, "Schools' Gambling Ban Raises Cash-Flow Fears," *Calgary Herald*, September 29, 2009, A1.
33 Woodard, "'I'm Asking Them to Confront a Moral Evil.'"
34 Alexa Huffman, "Catholic School District Reviews Casino Funding Policy," *Grande Prairie Daily Herald-Tribune*, October 16, 2014.
35 Schools that use casinos tend to be located in urban centres, particularly Calgary and Edmonton. See Support Our Students Alberta Foundation, "Levelling the Playing Field: A Comprehensive Resource Audit of Alberta Schools," 2017, 18–21, www.supportourstudents.ca.
36 McGinnis, "Schools' Gambling Ban Raises Cash-Flow Fears."
37 Economic Council of Canada, *A Lot to Learn: Education and Training in Canada* (1992), 25. By 2007 "at least 12 Ontario school boards" had charitable foundations to help "fund everything from breakfast programs to the assessment of special education students." See People for Education, "Annual Report on Ontario's Schools 2007," 4.
38 Government of Alberta, "Erratum to Private Schools Funding Discussion Paper," *Funding Private Schools in Alberta: Part I: Setting the Stage for Discussions: Private Schools Funding Task Force*, 1997, 12, quoted in Alison Taylor, "From Boardroom to Classroom: School Reformers in Alberta," in *Contested Classrooms: Education, Globalization, and Democracy in Alberta*, ed. Trevor W. Harrison and Jerrold L. Kachur, 99–106 (Edmonton: University of Alberta Press and Parkland Institute, 1999), 103.
39 Andy Marshall, "Trustees Studying Ways to Raise Cash," *Calgary Herald*, March 24, 1995, B7.
40 The Foundation "raises about $50,000 a year for the board's 15 schools." See Semenak, "Schools Rely on Fundraising to Pay for Extras."
41 Sarah Schmidt, "At Cash-Strapped School Boards, There Is at Least One Department That Is Still Growing: The Fundraising Wing," *Canwest News Service*, January 26, 2004.
42 Robert Williamson, "Fund Raising Enters New Semester," *Globe and Mail*, April 21, 1992, B1; Terry Gould, "High School Confidential," *Saturday Night*, September 1993, Canadian Business and Current Affairs Database; Rosalind Kellett, "One Public School Goes Corporate Route to Fund Raising," *Teacher* 4, no. 5 (June 1992): 18.
43 Williamson, "Fund Raising Enters New Semester." See also Kellett, "One Public School Goes Corporate Route to Fund Raising"; Gould, "High School Confidential."

44 Kellett, "One Public School Goes Corporate Route to Fund Raising"; Keith Fraser, "School's Private Fund Plan Rapped," *The Province* (Vancouver), February 11, 1992, A12.
45 Susan Balcom, "School Fund-Raising a Learning Experience," *Vancouver Sun*, September 14, 1993, B1. For the details of the scandal surrounding Lefaivre's departure, see Gould, "High School Confidential."
46 The school raised almost $7,000 in this way. See Semenak, "Schools Rely on Fundraising to Pay for Extras."
47 Taylor, "From Boardroom to Classroom," 104.
48 Taylor, "From Boardroom to Classroom," 105.
49 Kidder, "Fundraising and Corporate Donations in Schools," 42.
50 Caroline Alphonso, "Schools Rely On 4th 'r': Raising Cash for Basics," *Globe and Mail*, July 15, 2005, A6; Editorial, "Sponsors for Schools," *Globe and Mail*, April 15, 2009, A18.
51 Hampson, "Uptown School Reaches Out and Shares Fundraising Spoils," *Globe and Mail*, April 23, 1999, A11.
52 Sarah McGinnis, "Parents Group Launches Fund to Help Calgary Schools in Need," *Calgary Herald*, January 19, 2009, A9.
53 "Sponsors for Schools."
54 Paraphrased by Kellett in "One Public School Goes Corporate Route to Fund Raising."
55 Mark Nichols, "Education Adventure," *Imperial Oil Review* (Spring 2002), 11, 13. See also Robert F. Sexton, *Mobilizing Citizens for Better Schools* (New York: Teachers College, 2004), 93–94. For a critique of corporate-funded not-for-profit educational work, see Mayssoun Sukarieh and Stuart Tannock, "Putting School Commercialism in Context: A Global History of Junior Achievement Worldwide," *Journal of Education Policy* 24, no. 6 (November 2009): 769–86.
56 Sue-Ann Levy, "Their Business . . . Is Education," *Toronto Star*, March 26, 1994, 13. The CEO of Imperial Oil at the time, Robert Peterson, was a key player in developing the "goals and operating principles" of the organization. See Nichols, "Education Adventure," 11.
57 Nichols, "Education Adventure," 13. See also Levy, "Their Business . . . Is Education"; John Deverell, "Business Asked to Help Take 65,000 Kids to Work in Learning Partnership," *Toronto Star*, June 28, 1994; Lynne Ainsworth, "Class Conflict," *Financial Post*, May 11, 1996, 44.
58 Nichols, "Education Adventure," 8. See also Levy, "Their Business . . . Is Education."
59 "Student Programs at a Glance," www.thelearningpartnership.ca, accessed July 30, 2017.
60 "Student Programs," www.thelearningpartnership.ca, accessed July 30, 2017.
61 A number of retired former Imperial employees volunteered with the Partnership. See Nichols, "Education Adventure," 13.
62 "How the Corporate World Is Entering the Classroom," *Today's Parent*, October 1994, 67–73.

63 Camille Natale and Doug Joliffe, "Educational Restructuring: Toronto Teachers Respond and Resist," in *Teacher Activism in the 1990s*, ed. Susan Robertson and Harry Smaller, 71–88 (Toronto: Lorimer, 1996), 77–78. Natale, "Educational Restructuring," 78. See also pages 77-81.
64 "Coding Quest," www.thelearningpartnership.ca, accessed July 30, 2017.
65 Ben Bengtson, "Young Coders Show Digital Skills," *North Shore News*, June 11, 2017, A4.
66 Ministry of Supply and Services, *Learning Well . . . Living Well: The Prosperity Initiative* (1991), v.
67 By 2017 New Brunswick had these types of spaces in fifty of its schools. See Government of New Brunswick, "Makerspace Helps Make Learning Fun at Bathurst's Superior Middle School," *Focus on Education*, 15, insert in *Fredericton Daily Gleaner*, c. July 2017.
68 Bliss Carman Middle School, School Maker Faire flyer, 2017, in possession of author.

CONCLUSION

1 John Fisher, letter to editor, "Chocolate Boundaries," *Globe and Mail*, April 17, 2009, A14.
2 Editorial, "Sponsors for Schools," *Globe and Mail*, April 15, 2009, A18.
3 Jason C. Blokhuis, "Channel One: When Private Interests and Public Interest Collide," *American Educational Research Journal* 45, no. 2 (June 2008): 346. See also Trevor Norris, *Consuming Schools: Commercialism and the End of Politics* (Toronto: University of Toronto Press, 2011), 8–9.
4 Alex Molnar, Faith Boninger, and Joseph Fogarty, "The Educational Cost of Schoolhouse Commercialism: The Fourteenth Annual Report on Schoolhouse Commercializing Trends: 2010–2011, 9, nepc.colorado.edu; Maude Barlow and Heather-jane Robertson, *Class Warfare: The Assault on Canadian Public Education* (Toronto: Key Porter Books, 1994), 79; Deron Boyles, *American Education and Corporations: The Free Market Goes to School* (New York: Garland, 1998), 60.
5 A. Fisher and R. Gottlieb, "Who Benefits When Walmart Funds the Food Movement?" *Civil Eats*, December 18, 2014, cited in Marion Nestle, *Soda Politics: Taking on Big Soda (and Winning)* (New York: Oxford University Press, 2015), 232.
6 Carlos Frias and David A. Markiewicz, "Searching for a Star: Major Companies Latch on to Top High School Athletes by Offering Free Shoes and Equipment for Their Teams," *Atlanta Journal-Constitution*, March 7, 2004, 1A, cited in Alex Molnar, *School Commercialism: From Democratic Ideal to Market Commodity* (New York: Routledge, 2005), 32.
7 Nestle, *Soda Politics*, 232–34; Heather-jane Robertson, "The Many Faces of Privatization," *Our Schools, Our Selves* 14, no. 4 (Summer 2005): 52.
8 Scott Davies and Neil Guppy, *The Schooled Society: An Introduction to the Sociology of Education*, 2nd ed. (Don Mills, ON: Oxford University Press, 2010), 181.

9 David Harvey is writing specifically about neoliberalism but his words are equally applicable to this context. See Harvey, *A Brief History of Neoliberalism* (Oxford: Oxford University Press, 2005), 3, 62. See also Mayssoun Sukarieh and Stuart Tannock, "Putting School Commercialism in Context: A Global History of Junior Achievement Worldwide," *Journal of Education Policy* 24, no. 6 (November 2009): 769–86. For the difficulty of promoting alternative views in Canadian schools, see, for example, Myriam Dumont, "Not Everyone Loves the Olympics: Critical Thinking Meets Olympic Enthusiasm," *Our Schools, Our Selves* 20, no. 1 (Fall 2010): 93–100, and Judith Stamps, "Consumer Education and the Philosophy of Competitive Individualism in British Columbia," *BC Studies* 83 (Autumn 1989): 68–93.

10 For these arguments see also Deron Boyles, "Uncovering the Coverings: The Use of Corporate Supplied Textbook Covers to Further Uncritical Consumerism," in *The Corporate Assault on Youth Commercialism, Exploitation, and the End of Innocence*, ed. Deron Boyles, 174–86 (New York: Peter Lang, 2008), 182, and Trevor Norris, "The Illusory Solution: Is Commercialization the 'Future' of Education at the Toronto District School Board?" *Our Schools, Our Selves* 19, no. 1 (Fall 2009): 50–51.

11 Norris, "The Illusory Solution," 51–52.

12 Juliet Schor, "The New Politics of Consumption," *Boston Review: A Political and Literary Forum* (Summer 1999), bostonreview.net. See pages 3, 5–6, 11, respectively.

13 Craig Desson, "As Google for Education Tools Enter Classrooms ...," June 11, 2018, cbc.ca; Natasha Singer, "How Google Took Over the Classroom," *New York Times*, May 13, 2017, www.nyti.ms/2raVLDR.

14 Jane Kenway and Elizabeth Bullen, "Globalizing the Young in the Age of Desire: Some Educational Policy Issues," in *Globalizing Education: Policies, Pedagogies, and Politics*, ed. Michael W. Apple, Jane Kenway, and Michael Singh, 31–43 (New York: Peter Lang, 2005), 41–42.

Index

Italic page numbers indicate photos.

accountability, 33, 34
acid rain, 78
Active Healthy Kids Canada, 70, 180n18
Adopt-a-School programs, 38, 71
advertising: and consumption, 124; and donations, 133, 134; electronic scrolls, 76; exposure to, 3, 22, 133; justifications, 75, 76–77; outcomes of, 4; percentage of schools accepting, 73–74; as powerful for children, 3–4, 101; on school buses (*see* school bus advertisements); on school property, 72–74, 76, 81–83, 108, 181n26, 192n32; on school television, 88, 89, 90–93, 93–95, 96–97, 102–3; screen savers, 72, 83, 181n26; shaping necessities, 3; in teachers' magazines, 10, 15, 16; in yearbooks, 13, *14*, 15, 164n21. *See also* branded products; films/videos; logos
advertising, limiting: and Alliance for American Advertising, 195n80; banned in other countries, 184n67; guidelines for, 22–24, 25, 42–43, 83; junk food/fast food, 120, 124; in Quebec, 184n67; on Youth News Network, 97, 99, 102
Advisory Educational Group, 12
African Americans, 33
Akin, David, 58

Alberta Department of Education, 19, 50, 176n25
Alberta High School Curriculum Committee, 20
Alberta Home and School Councils' Association, 78
Alberta Ministry of Education, 90–91
Alberta Teachers' Association (ATA), 81, 91
alcohol, 19–20, 44
Aliant, 59
Alliance for American Advertising, 195n80
Alm, John, 110
American Association of School Administrators (AASA), 23
American Beverage Association (ABA), 120, 196n92
American Business and the Public School . . . (report), 33
American Can Company, 11
American Federation of Teachers, 88–89
American Library Association, 67
Anglophone East School District, 125
Anglophone West School District, 197n95
Annual Canadian Education Industry Summit, 37
anti-consumerism, 23
anti-corporate activism, 79–81, 83–84, 102, 183n55. *See also* social critics

anti-Semitism, 94
AOL Canada, 56
Apple, 47, 50–51, 57, 76, 78, 177n43
Apple Canada Education Foundation, 51
Archer, Douglas, 53
Ardrossan Junior Senior High School, 123
artwork, 39
Astra Credit Union, 40
Athena Educational Partners Inc. (AEP), 93–94, 99. *See also* Youth News Network
auctions. *See* lotteries/auctions
awards, 27
Aymong, Michael, 76

baby boom, 28
Baldwin-Cartier School Board, 90
Bank of Montreal (BMO), 16, 68
banks, 13, 68, 75, 77. *See also* credit unions; school banks
Barkley, Liz, 91
Barlow, Maude, 38, 81
Barrett, Ian, 38–39
Bateman, Lisa, 130
BC Credit Union League, 24
B.C. Hydro, 43, 173n77
B.C. Ministry of Education, 37
BC Teacher (magazine), 24, 43
BC Teachers' Federation (BCTF), 43, 184n63, 191n26
Beckley, Murray, 75
Bell Canada, 56
Bell Mobility, 40
Bell Northern Research, 39
Benton High School, 191n23
Bernice MacNaughton High School, 121–22
Bessborough Drive Elementary and Middle School, 141
Big Food: advertising on radio, 22; and health (*see* health); kiosks, 110, 191n24; opposition to, 113–14; Real Food Trips, 71; revenue from exclusivity contracts, 111–12. *See also* Coca-Cola; contracts; junk food/fast food; McDonald's Restaurants; Pepsi-Cola

Bigum, Chris, 61
Bill and Melinda Gates Foundation, 57
bingo nights, 136
"Bionic Beaver," 52–54, *53*
Bishop Grandin School, 137
Bliss Carman Middle School, 73, 147
Bluefield High School, 115–16
Boniface, Dale, 108–9
books, 67–68, 74, 135, 184n73. *See also* libraries; textbooks
Borden, Betsy, 21
Bosetti, Reno, 90–91
bottled water, 69, 117, 124
Brand, David, 87–88
branded products: books, 67; chocolate maps, 7, *8*, 151, 162n1; clothing, 133, 134; Crest maze puzzles, 1; early teaching aids, 10–12, 19, 165n36; extracurricular activities, 13; from government, 19, 165n36; hammers, 133; and Home Depot playground, 1; newer forms of, 125; as pervasive, 74; posters, 69, 70; sports-related, 70; tattoos, 133; textbook covers, 13; timetables, 13. *See also* advertising; logos; prizes; teaching aids
Brandon School Board, 23–24
Brewers Association of Canada, 44
Briar Hill Elementary School, 141
Brilliant Labs, 147–48
Bristol-Myers, 10–12
Britannia Public School, 71
British Columbia Teachers' Federation (BCTF), 81, 140
Brockie, Jack, 25
Buckingham, David, 61–62
Bullen, Elizabeth, 156
Burger King, 89, 125
Burnaby Central High School, 189n3
Business Council of British Columbia, 37
business lessons, 22, 115, 144
Butterfield, Holly, 112

cafeterias: history of, 189n3; McDonald's proposal, 82–83; as naturally unhealthy, 117; problems facing, 113;

Index

promoting healthy eating, 105–8, 117–18, 123, 197n95. *See also* contracts; healthy food; junk food/fast food
Caise populaire, 15, 44–45. *See also* banks; credit unions
Les Caisses populaires Desjardins, 44–45
Calgary Board of Education, 181nn25–26
Calgary Catholic School Board District, 137, 138
Calgary Educational Partnership Foundation, 138, 141
cameras, 39
Cameron, Mike, 115
Campbell, Cassie, 69–70
Campbell, Louise, 75
Campbell Soup Company, 73, 74, 82
Canadian Advanced Technology Association (CATA), 52
Canadian Airlines, 41
Canadian Association of Media Education Organizations (CAMEO), 98
Canadian Association of Media Organizations, 91
Canadian Broadcasting Company (CBC), 19, 49
Canadian Cellucotton, 11, 12
Canadian Centre for Policy Alternatives (CCPA), 81, 94, 96, 98
Canadian Conference of Catholic Bishops, 91, 94
Canadian Dairy Industry Suppliers' Association, 106
Canadian Education Association (CEA), 24, 60
Canadian Educational Microprocessor Corporation (CEM Corp.), 52
Canadian Federation of Students, 81–82
Canadian Imperial Bank of Commerce (CIBC), 15
Canadian Industries Limited (CIL), 11, 12, 20
Canadian Jewish Council, 94
Canadian Manufacturers' Association, 165n38
Canadian Nuclear Association, 66, 78
Canadian Olympic Committee, 69
Canadian Pacific Railway, 15
Canadian Sugar Factories, 11
Canadian Teachers' Federation, 61, 81, 98, 165n38
Capital City Savings and Credit Union, 69, 77
Carleton Board of Education, 42
Carlyle Elementary School, 132
Carnahan, Doug, *14*
casinos, 136–38, 199n26, 200n35
catering companies, 119
Catholic schools, 136–38, 199n26, 200n35. *See also individual Catholic schools*
Celms, Julian, 92
Center for Science in the Public Interest, 107
Center for Study of Responsive Law, 23
cereal, 10–11, 21, 70. *See also* Kellogg Company
Change Your Future, 143
Channel One, 88–89, 99, 101, 187n33
Charest, Jean, 120
charitable foundations, 138, 140–41, 148, 200n37
Charles E. London Secondary School, 41
charter schools, 34
Chartwells, 118, 197n95
Chevreau, Jonathan, 52–53, 176n24
child labour, 79, 80
childhood, 9, 10
children: advertising powerful for, 3–4; as consumers, 3, 8–9, 179n1, 180n13; and eating habits, 4–5; families of, 9, 21, 26 (*see also* parents); sentimentality of, 10. *See also* students
chocolate bars, 7, *8*, 129, 132, 151, 162n1; removal from school vending machines, 105, 107
chocolate milk, 106, 189n7
Choosing Free Materials for Use in the Schools (AASA), 23
Chrétien, Jean, 80
Church Street Public School, 135
Cindrich Elementary School, 69
curriculums: corporations' involvement

in, 35, 37, 40, 44, 140–41; and lobby groups, 67; relevant, 34–35
Clarkson Public School, 129
class (social), 33, 101, 141, 151
Class Warfare (Barlow and Robertson), 38, 81
Classroom Connections (magazine), 53
classrooms, for corporations, 41, 42
Clearasil, 89
clothing industry, 9, 79–80. *See also* Eaton's
CMT (Country Music Television), 95
Coal Association of Canada, 66, 78
Coalition for Public Education, 81–82
Coca-Cola: and bottle deposits, 196n92; branding, 74; and Channel One, 89; Coke Education Day, 115; competing with Pepsi, 116–17; exclusivity contracts, 108–9, 111–12, 183n56, 190nn16–17, 192n30, 192n32; as most prominent, 108; and physical education, 180n15; removal from schools, 121, 196n81; on school signs, *109*; secret contracts, 110, 114–15, 183n56; university protests, 80. *See also* junk food/fast food
coding lessons, 147
Coding Quest, 146
Coffin, Steve, 133
Cohen, Michael, 75, 77
Colgate, 10, 21
Colorado Springs District, 192n32
Colpitts Developments, 73
commercialism: conference about, 81–82; and early school projects, 20–21; vs. healthy food, 124; history of, 2–3; limited information about, 81; overview, 151–53; as pervasive, 3, 84; policies against overuse, 82–83; and privatization, 161n3; rethinking, 154–58; teachers critiquing, 22; tied to benefits, 2. *See also* corporate partnerships
Commercialism in Canadian Schools (survey), 81
commercials, 3–4, 88, 89
Commission scolaire des Découvreurs, 192n30

Committee for Economic Development, 33
commodification, 46
Commodore Business Machines, 50–51
computers: and achievement outcomes, 59–61, 178n58; adequate access to, 102; artificial interest in, 61–62; coding lessons, 146, 147; computer labs, 151; Computers in Education, 51–52; drawbacks to funding, 61; early use in schools, 50–51; and economy, 47–48, 52–53; Ednet, 53–54; in exchange for teacher's expertise, 39; families purchasing in 1983, 50; fundraising for, 54, 131–32, 140; ICON, 52–53, 175n22, 176n24; laptops for kids, 57–59, 60–61, 177nn43–44, 178n48; Max 20E, 175n20; as obsolete, 54, 148; operating costs, 58, 177–78nn47–8; per student, 47; price and access, 52–53; as prizes, 73; replacing schools, 49; and school banks, 74–75; SchoolNet, 55–57; School Technology Plan, 54; software, 50, 53, 54, 175n20; specifications of, 175n21. *See also* Apple; Internet
Comterm-Mantra, 175n20
Concerned Children's Advertisers (CCA), 76
Conference Board of Canada, 37, 40, 43–44, 48
Consolidated Mining and Smelting Company (Cominco), 15
consultants, 34–35, 43, 44, 46
consumer education courses, 16–17
consumerism, 8–9, 23, 156, 157. *See also* consumption
Consumers Union, 81
consumption: and advertising, 124; children as consumers, 8–9, 13, 179n1, 180n13; history of, 3; and human flourishing, 156; and identity, 4, 79–80; power of, 3; and soft drink revenue, 116; students as consumers, 77, 145, 180n13
contests, 15–16, 69–70, 144

contracts, 50–51, 108–9, 111–13. *See also* Big Food; Coca-Cola; Pepsi-Cola
co-op education, 35, 38
Copp Clark, 7, *8*, 15, 162n1
Coppertone, 66, 77
Coquitlam Credit Union, 24
Coquitlam School Board, 105, 112–13, 116, 124
Coquitlam Teachers' Association, 113
Corporate-Higher Education Forum, 36
corporate partnerships: adopting schools, 71; as beneficial, 2, 38–39, 41–42; in building schools, 34; condemnation of, 25; and Conference Board of Canada, 37; coordinators of, 43, 46 (*see also* principals); Corporate-Higher Education Forum, 36; corporate instruction, 41; as family, 155; and government agencies, 19–20, 165n38; growth in, 27–28; history of, 2; image of corporation, 12–13; increasing, 33; justifications, 17–22, 42, 74–78, 151; as linking learning elements, 36–37; as more than sponsorship, 41–42; questioning, 42–43, 44, 45, 78–84; refusal of, 23–25; regulating (*see* guidelines/regulations); samples financing classrooms, 16; school advisory committees, 39; as school projects, 20–21; students planning parties, 39–40, 41; students working for credits/money, 39; testing boundaries, 25; as unequal, 155–56. *See also* commercialism; school boards
corporate social responsibility (CSR), 154–55. *See also* social responsibility
corporations: denying self-interest, 21–22, 75–76, 135, 155; endorsement of, 155; framing activities, 155; language of, 38, 68, 146; perception of leadership, 46; primary obligations, 154; reforming schools, 32, 33; restructuring of, 29; shaping curriculums, 35, 37, 40, 44, 140–41
Corporations in the Classroom (film), 82
Council of Canadians, 94

Council of Ministers of Education, 37–38
coupons/vouchers, 17, 67
Courtney, Joan, 121
Cowling, Joan, 91–92
Cow's Paradise Lotto, 129–30, 131
Cranson, Lori, 143
Cream of Wheat, 21
Creative Arts Learning Partnership, 143
credit unions: Les Caisses populaires Desjardins, 44–45; refusal of, 24; school banks, 15; in schools, 69; student-driven partnerships, 40. *See also* banks
Cressy, Gordon, 143
Crest, 1
Critical Mass Promotions, 70
Cuba, 96
Cuban, Larry, 48, 50, 61
culinary arts programs, 118–19

Dark, Ian, 40
Davies, Scott, 155
Davis, Darryl, 131
Davis, Sarah, 131
Dedicated Notebook Computer Research Project, 58–59, 178n48
Deer Park Public School, 71
deindustrialization, 79
Dell, 177n43
depression, high consumer involvement and, 4
deschooling, 49
Devon Middle School, 181n24
dieticians, 70, 71, 118
Dietitians of Canada, 70
Director of Community Services (Coquitlam), 40
discounts, 16, 47, 51, 53, 136
displays, 18, 76
distance learning, 93
Dodds, Nicholas, 114–15
Doer, Gary, 94
dolls, 9
Dominion Department of Agriculture, 19
Dominion Penny Bank Act, 15
Don Mills Collegiate Institute, 70

Douglas, Mary, 20
Dube, Francine, 44
Dufferin-Peel Roman Catholic School Board, 67

Earl of March Secondary School, 39
Earth Day Canada, 135
East Chilliwack Elementary School, 111
Eastman, Jan, 61
Eastwood Public School, 111
Eaton, Donna, 65
Eaton's, 12–13, *14*, 21–22, 25
Ebbern, Jane, 76
École Maurice-Lavallée, 69
École St. Angela Merici, 133–34
Economic Council of Canada, 36
economics lessons, 21
economy, 28–29, 34–37, 47–48, 52–53
Edison, Thomas, 48
Edith Cavell Elementary School, 134
Edmonton Catholic School Board, 41
Edmonton Catholic Schools Board of Trustees, 83
Edmonton Public School Board, 83, 91, 91–92
Edmonton Public Teachers' Local, 31
Ednet, 53–54
education: as important, 28; purpose of, 61; quality questioned, 32–36; special, 29; universal, 29
Education Act, 96–97
Education and Learning Department, 37
Educational Review (magazine), 19
EducationMatters, 141
educators. *See* teachers
EFundraising.com, 131
elementary schools. *See* schools; students; *specific schools*
Empress Public School, 21
energy crisis, 28
English Montreal School Board, 75
Entrepreneurial Adventure, 144
entrepreneurship, 144, 147–48, 149, 154. *See also* workplace preparation
environmental destruction, 78, 79
environmentalism, 78, 89

Erika, Shaker, 43
ESL (English as Second Language), 29
"Ethical Guidelines for Education-Business Partnerships" (report), 43–44
ethics, 135, 135–37, 141, 149
Etobicoke Board of Education, 27–28, 38–39, 107, 110, 113. *See also* Toronto District School Board
Evoy, B. C. C., 18
exclusivity contracts, 107, 108–9, 111–12, 183n56, 190nn16–17, 192n30, 192n32
expectations: of consumption, 4; of schools, 2, 29, 31
extracurricular activities: advertising to fund, 76; and Bell Northern Research, 39; corporate partnerships, 12–13, 39; and Eaton's, 13
Eyre, Linda, 44

Fédération des commissions scolaires du Québec, 90
Fédération des syndicats de l'enseignement, 73, 81
Federation of Women Teachers' Associations of Ontario, 113
Fellows High School, 117–18
Field Trip Factory, 71, 76–77
field trips and extramural learning: early, 15, 27; forestry, 40; justifications, 76–77; local chain stores, 21, 71; mining, 40
films/videos: Coal Association of Canada, 66; early use of, 12, 21; government sponsored/endorsed, 19, 20; links to books, 68; McDonald's Restaurants, 17; refusing, 24; replacing textbooks, 48; SilverCity, 77; survey of usage, 50
financing of schools: critique of, 22; decrease in (*see* fiscal restraints); and equity (*see* inequities); increase in, 16, 28, 29; protests for, 82, 184n63; and provinces, 168n11
Finkelstein, Paul, 118–19
First Nations, 89, 95, 143
fiscal restraints: 1960s to 1980s, 168n10; in 1990s, 29–30, 169n15; and com-

Index

mercialism, 2–3, 17; and financing of schools, 169n18; and libraries, 30, 31, 168n9; real costs, 168n9; and Youth News Network, 92, 93
Fisher, John, 151
food. *See* Big Food; cafeterias; Coca-Cola; healthy food; junk food/fast food; nutrition; Pepsi-Cola; sugar
Foothills School Division, 181n25
forestry, 40
Fouchard, Steven, 92
Fox, Roy, 101
Francis, Diane, 92
Fraser, John, 92
Fraser Valley Tourist Association, 16
Fred Thompson Sales Ltd., 130
free labour, 39, 41, 43, 45
Freenets, 55
free speech, 87–88, 97–98, 115
Free the Children, 80
French courses, 38, 39
Froese-Germain, Bernie, 43, 124
Fry-Cadbury Company, 21
fundraising: casinos, 136–37; charitable foundations, 138, 140–41, 200n37; companies, 130–31; for computers, 131–32; corporate grants, 133–36; description of, 127; early versions of, 128–29, 132; and funding shortfalls, 129, 131, 137; inequities of, 140, 141–42; large-scale, 129–32; Learning Partnership, 142–48; percentage of schools fundraising, 198n15; professional fundraisers, 130–31, 139–40
Fundstream Inc. of Montreal, 131
Future Shop, 75, 151

gambling, 136–38, 199n26, 200n35
games, 68
Geary Elementary School, 121
Generation Y, 2
George S. Henry Secondary School, 27
Gidney, R. D., 10
Glenview Senior Public School, 106, 123
global warming, 78
Globe essay competition, 15–16

Goldstein, Mark, 98–99
Gomes, Mary, 21
goodwill. *See* social responsibility
Goodwin, Bryan, 60–61
government agencies, 2, 19–20, 42–43, 165n38. *See also* financing of schools
Grande Prairie and District Catholic Schools, 138
Grand Manan Elementary School, 108
grants, 30, 133–36
Green, Joan, 144–45
Greenan, Bill, 119
Greenbrier High School, 115
Gregory, John, 43
Grocery Manufacturers Association, 122–23
Grossman, Larry, 52
Le Groupe Jeunesse, 65
Grovenor Elementary School, 132
guidelines/regulations, 22–24, 25, 42–44, 82–83, 97
Guiding Stars school nutrition kit, 72
Gulf Canada, 27
Guppy, Neil, 155

Haider, Jörg, 95
Halton Board of Education, 47
Hamilton School District, 181n25
hands-on activities, 19, 20, 147
Harcourt Brace, 39
Harris, Mike, 30, 169n15
Hartmann, Norbert, 111
Harty, Sheila, 23
Harvey, David, 155
health, 4–5, 116–21, 156, 194n59, 195n73, 195n80
health education, 12, 18, 21, 95–96. *See also* physical education
healthy food: cafeterias, 105–8; vs. commercialism, 124; costs of, 123–24; funding of, 197n94; protests against, 121–23; protests for, 106–8, 115–16, 189n7, 190n15. *See also* nutrition
Hellman's, 71
Henry, Fred, 137–38
Heritage Canada, 76

Heritage Mountain Elementary School, 130, 132
"Heroes of Canada" (radio program), 19
Hewlett-Packard, 39, 43, 59, 60, 177n43
Hicks, Dawn, 40
The Hidden Persuaders (Packard), 22–23
high schools, 20, 29, 36. *See also* schools; students; *specific schools*
Highland Secondary School, 123
Hill and Knowlton, 94
Ms. Hilts (cafeteria manager), 117–18
Hispanics, 33
Hissink, Bob, 76
history lessons, 44–45
Holden Elementary School, 118
Holender, Allan, 139
home and school associations: fundraising, 106, 128–30, 131–32; regulations/guidelines, 42; and vending machines, 108; and Youth News Network, 91, 94. *See also* school boards
Home Depot, 1, 82, 127, 133–34
Horbay, Brian, 118
Horizons West Marketing, 130
hot dog days, 106, 113, 117, 121
"How To Catch a Cold" (educational film), 12
Hucksters in the Classroom . . . (report), 23
Hull, Quebec, 44–45
human flourishing, 154, 156, 157–58
human rights abuses, 79–80
Huron County School Board, 31

I Cubed, 144
IBM, 53–54
ICON computers, 52–54, *53*, 175n22, 176n24
IdeaBook (Conference Board of Canada), 37, 40
identity and consumption, 4, 79–80
Illich, Ivan, 49
Imperial Bank of Canada, 15
Imperial Oil, 12, 15, 20, 144, 201n56
Inco, 78
Indigenous Peoples, 89, 95, 143
Indigo, 135, 136

Industry Canada, 55
inequities: and donations, 156; of fundraising, 140, 141–42; and higher commercialism, 101, 151; real costs, 168n9; schools helping schools, 141; and technology, 48; and urban schools, 30
inflation, 28, 29–30
Information Technology Association of Canada (ITAC), 55, 176n36
Ingenia Communications Corporation, 55
Internet, 55–57, 58, 102, 131. *See also* computers
Investing in Our Children . . . (report), 33
Ipana tooth paste, 11–12, *11*
Ivey, Charles, 37

J. D. Irving Ltd., 40
Jarvis, Anne, 116–17
junk food/fast food: advertising, 4–5, 21, 74, 89; close to schools, 113, 116, 120, 192n39, 197n94; field trips to companies, 17, 21, 71; government bans on, 119–22, 195nn73–75, 196n88, 196n92; and health studies, 194n59; history in schools, 105–7, 189n6; kiosks, 110, 191nn23–24, 191n26; legitimizing, 156; and literacy, 67; in math examples, 23; naturalizing, 125; and physical education, 69–70; protest for, 121–22; protests against, 23, 113–16, 117–19; taxes on, 107. *See also* Big Food; Coca-Cola; McDonald's Restaurants; Pepsi-Cola; sugar; vending machines

KaBOOM!, 133
Kealey, Betty-Ann, 92
Kellogg Company, 21, 70, 73, 82, 180n18, 181n28, 195n80
Kendall, Bruce, 130
Kendall, Perry, 119
Kenway, Jane, 156
Kessler, David, 194n59
Keuhn, Larry, 184n63
Kidder, Annie, 82

Kielburger, Craig, 80
Kielburger, Marc, 80
Kildonan-East Collegiate, 187n30
Killarney Secondary School, 111
Kimberly-Clark, 20, 165n38
Kincheloe, Joe, 4
King, Angus, 57–58
King's County District School Board, 54
Kipling Collegiate Institute, 39–40
Kirkpatrick, Aubrey, 125
Kitsilano Secondary School, 111
Klein, Naomi, 79
Klein, Ralph, 30, 31
Knob Hill School, 129
Kostex, Rod, 130
Kowalewski, Christina, 84
Krispy Kreme Doughnuts, 122

Lalonde, Marc, 107
Langford Junior Secondary School, 70
LaPointe, Louis, 91
Laurenval School Board, 90, 92
lawsuits, 99, 195n80
Learning Partnership, 142–48, *145*, 201n56
Lefaivre, Peter, 139
Legault, François, 82, 96–97
Leo Hayes High School, 109
Lester B. Pearson School Board, 96–97, 177n44
Lev, Gerry, 110
Lévesque, René, 175n20
Levins, Jim, 144
libraries: and cost cutting, 30, 31, 168n9; films for, 20; funding of, 16; Indigo's Love of Reading Foundation, 135; resources for, 17; and Scholastic Corporation, 68; TD giveaway books, 184n73. *See also* books; textbooks
Lifebuoy, 10
lifelong learning, 49, 146–47
Liquid Candy (report), 120
literacy: financial; programs, 67; rates, 36
Lively District Secondary School, 98
lobby groups, 67, 122–23
Loblaws, 71

local businesses, 38, 41, 61. *See also* credit unions
logos: on books, 67, 83, 184n73; guidelines for, 43, 83, 97; in gym, 72, 80; and Olympic Day Run, 70. *See also* advertising; branded products
Long, Gayle, 51
Long and McQuade, 95
Lord, Bernard, 57–58, 59
Los Angeles United School District, 119
lotteries/auctions, 129–30, 131
Lounds, Margaret, 91–92
Love of Reading Foundation, 135, 136
Lynn Valley Elementary School, 1, 133

MacDonald, Roderick, 88, 89–90, 93, 94, 98, 102–3. *See also* Youth News Network
Maine, USA, 57, 60, 61
Majesta, 134–35
maker education, 147
Maple Ridge-Pitt Meadows school district, 109, 111–12, 114
maps, 7, *8*, 17, 18
Marchi, Sergio, 37
Mark R. Isfeld Secondary School, 123
Martin, Robert, 74–75
Martingrove Collegiate Institute, 115, 191n24
Masih, Iqbal, 80
Mathematics Around Us (resource series), 23
Matsushita Electrics Company, 39
Mattel, 79
Max 20E, 175n20
McArthur, Andrew, 87
McDonald's Restaurants: bullying presentations, 70; Environmental Action Pack, 78; field trips to, 17, 21; grad dinner, 122; hot-lunch program, 191n23; makeover, 69, 180n16; protests about, 82; running cafeterias, 82–83; screen savers, 181n26; social responsibility, 66, 76; Vancouver Olympic Committee sponsorship, 84
McDougald, Janet, 97
McEachern, Ron, 112

McGuinty, Dalton, 127
McKenna, Frank, 58
McKernan Elementary and Junior High School, 118
McLean, Les, 94, 95, 101–2
McLean's Instant Chocolate, 130
Meadowvale Secondary School, 87, 93–94, 97, 98
Meech Lake Accord, 89
Meharg, Jeremy, 48
Meridian Technologies, 52
Me to We, 80
Metropolitan Life Insurance, 12
Microsoft, 56, 59, 71
Microtel Ltd., 175n22
milk, 106, 189n7
Milner, Brian, 50
mining, 15, 40, 66–67
Mining Association of B.C., 40
Mining Matters program, 66–67
Ministries of Health and Education, 107
Ministry of Education, 42–43
Mission School District, 109
Moll, David, 112
Molnar, Alex, 81, 83
Montreal Catholic School Commission, 90
Montreal Island School Council, 90
movies. *See* films/videos
music programs, 30. *See also* schools: bands in

Nashwaak Valley School, 135
A Nation at Risk (report), 32–33
National Association of State Boards of Education, 88–89
National Commission on Excellence in Education, 32
National Education Association, 88–89, 165n38
National School Lunch Act, 189n7
National School Lunch Program, 191n23
National War Finance Committee, 19
necessities, advertisers shaping, 3
Neely, Susan, 120
neighbourhoods, 141

Neilson's Chocolate, 7, *8*, 151, 162n1
neoliberalism, 32
New Brunswick Department of Education, 40, 44, 58, 82, 108
New Brunswick Department of Health, 44
New Brunswick Federation of Home and School Associations, 108
Newman, Dale, 77
news. *See* Youth News Network
Nike, 72, 79, 80, 154
Nikiforuk, Andrew, 102
No More Teachers, No More Books . . . (Robertson), 81
Nonspi, 11
Norman Cook Junior Public School, 129
Norris, Trevor, 155–56
Northern Telecom, 67
Northern Vocational School, 13
Notebook Initiative, 59, 60
nutrition: biased information, 22; cafeterias, 105–7, 119–20; field trips for, 71; by force, 121; Guiding Stars kit, 72; and Kellogg Company, 70; and McDonald's Restaurants, 69, 180n16; and revenue drop, 123–24; and Slush Puppie Plus, 197n102; and Youth News Network, 90. *See also* health; healthy food

Oakwood Collegiate Institute, 13
O'Connor, Naoibh, 190n15
Old Scona Academic High School, 116–17
Ontario Department of Education, 20, 49
Ontario Institute for Studies in Education, 94
Ontario Liberal Party, 94
Ontario Medical Association, 119–20
Ontario Ministry of Education, 47, 51–52, 91, 122
Ontario Ministry of Industry and Trade, 52
Ontario NDP (New Democratic Party), 94
Ontario Public Schools Teachers' Federation, 129

Ontario Secondary School Teachers' Federation (OSSTF), 81, 91, 98, 145–46
oppositions. *See* protests/oppositions
Oromocto High School, 110
Orpwood, Graham, 34–35
Osborne, Ken, 1
Ottawa-Carleton Learning Foundation, 138
Ottawa Secondary School Board, 90
Ottawa Separate School Board, 92
Ozvoldik, Betty, 27

P3 schools, 30
packaging, 73, 181n28
Packard, Vance, 22–23
Palmerston Elementary School, 82
Papert, Seymour, 49
parents: and advertising for children, 9, 21, 23; computer adaptation pressure, 61; critiquing school quality, 34; paying for resources, 132; protests/oppositions, 22, 82, 84, 98–99, 121, 137–38; supporting corporate partnerships, 2, 122, 125. *See also* fundraising
Parents Against Commercial TV in Schools, 91
parent-teacher associations. *See* home and school associations
Parker, Carol, 42
Partners in Education (Coquitlam schools), 41
Peace Action League, 24
Peace River North School District, 59
Pearson, Nancy, 68
pedometers, 70
Pedwell, Laurie, 98–99
Peel District School Board/Peel Board of Education: and AEP/YNN, 90, 93–94, 97, 99, 101; exclusivity contracts, 107, 111; screen savers, 181n26; secret soft drink contracts, 110, 114–15
peer culture, 9
People Against Commercial Television in Schools, 99
People for Education, 82, 141, 198n15

Pepsi-Cola: advertising in schools, 74; and Carleton Board of Education, 42; competing with Coke, 116–17; exclusivity contracts, 108, 111–12, 190nn16–17, 192n32, 193n43; and human rights, 80; Old Scona Academic High School, 116–17; physical education, 180n15; protests/oppositions to, 113, 114; removal from schools, 121; and Toronto Board of Education, 108. *See also* junk food/fast food
Peters, Betty-Lorraine, *14*
Peterson, Robert, 200n35
Petro-Canada, 27
PetSmart, 71
physical education, 69–70, 76, 84, 180nn15–16. *See also* sports
Pielsticker, Charlie, 142
Pitt River Middle School, 105, 116
pizza days, 106, 117, 119
Pizza Hut, 67, 74, 82
Pizza Pizza, 115, 191n24
play, 65, 69
Player, Doug, 139
playgrounds, 1, 82, 127, 133, *134*
political education, 1
polls, 35
Popkin, John, 23–24
popular culture and identity, 4
Porter, Lindsay, 97
postsecondary school preparation, 33–34, 35
poverty, 22, 96, 141
power of consumption, 3
principals: and Fraser Valley Tourist Association contest, 16; at partnership forefront, 42, 83, 94, 98, 114, 130, 134. *See also* teachers
private schools, 34, 41
privatization, 32, 34, 161n3
prizes: cash, 15–16, 134, 135; computers, 54, 73; Cream of Wheat package, 21; pedometers, 70; pizza, 67; ranch lotto, 129–30; technology, 135. *See also* branded products

problem solving, 19
productivity, 32–33, 48
professional development, 39, 140–41, 173n77
Progressive Conservative (PC) party, 30, 31, 169n15
Project Business, 17
promotional products. *See* branded products
property taxes, 28, 168n11
Prospectors and Developers Association of Canada (PDAC), 66–67
Protestant School Board of Greater Montreal, 90
protests/oppositions: advertising, 195n80; anger in, 83–84; and anti-corporate activism, 79–80, 83–84, 102, 183n55; Big Food/junk food, 113–15, 117–21; and casino/bingo fundraising, 137–38; computer donations, 78, 151; corporate culture, 80–81; credit unions in schools, 24; curriculum content selection, 44; early, 22–26; environmental destruction, 78, 79; free labour/advertising, 45; against healthy food, 121–23; for healthy food, 106–8, 189n7, 190n15; about Learning Partnership, 145–46; parents involvement in, 22, 82, 84, 98–99, 121, 137–38; school board involvement in, 82–83; school financing, 82, 184n63; school television, 88–89, 96–99, *100*, 101–2, 103; teacher involvement in, 22, 113, 118, 145–46, 184n63; union involvement in, 81–82; Youth News Network, 90–91, 94. *See also* guidelines/regulations
provincial governments, 29–30
psychology manipulation, 22–23
public-private partnerships schools, 30

Quebec Consumer Protection Act, 82
Queen Mary Elementary School, 141
quotas, 115, 117

radio, 19, 22, 48–49
Rainbow District School Board, 98

Rainsberry, Linda, 42
RCS Netherwood School, 177n44
Real Canadian Superstore, 71, 72–73, 76, 78
Real Food Trips, 71
real life teaching, 19, 40, 42, 144, 145
receipts, 73
recessions, 28–29
Red Cross, 19
Reese, William, 33
Refreshments Canada, 120, 195n79
regulations. *See* guidelines/regulations
Reichl, Fred, 144
Reisman, Heather, 135
religion, 21. *See also* Catholic schools
Report of the Committee on Propaganda in the Schools (NEA), 22
revenue: from casino/bingo fundraising, 136–37; from exclusivity contracts (*see* Coca-Cola; Pepsi-Cola); nutrition and revenue drop, 123–24; from school bus advertisements, 181n25, 192n32; and soft drinks and consumption, 116
Rideau High School, 42
River Oaks Public School, 47, 51
Riverside Secondary School, *125*
Robert J. Clegg Ltd., 16
Robertson, Heather-jane, 38, 61, 81
Rollwagen, Katharine, 13
Rona Home & Garden, 71, 75
Ronald McDonald, 69, 70, 82, 180n16. *See also* McDonald's Restaurants
Rosedale Public School, 21
Rosemont Community School, 134
Rother, Lee, 92
Rubadeau, Ron, 76
Rubin, Joe, 114
rural schools, 17–18, 56, 105

Salada, 11
samples, 16, 19, 20–21
Samsung Canada, 135
Sarafinchan, Gord, 77
Sargent, Barbara, 113
Saskatchewan Department of Education, 20

Index

Saskatchewan Federation of Home and School Associations, 42
Scarborough High School, 189n3
scavenger hunts, 54
Schering-Plough, 77. *See also* Coppertone
Scholastic Corporation, 68, 72, 74, 180n11
The School (magazine), 21
school advisory committees, 39
school banks, 15, 21, 24, 69, 74–75
school boards: consolidation of, 16; and co-op education, 38; coordinating partnerships, 43, 112; and corporate guidelines, 82–83; and ESL programs, 29; justifying advertising, 76–77; justifying contracts, 112; and nutrition, 105; raising funds, 127; refusal of credit unions, 24; running cafeterias, 118; salaries, 169n15; supporting corporate partnerships, 2; and Youth News Network, 91–92, 94, 96–97. *See also* contracts; home and school associations; *individual school boards*
school bus advertisements: experimenting with, 72; justifying, 75, 76, 77; revenue generated from, 181n25, 192n32; schools as last frontier, 65; schools using, 181n25
school dances, 13
school newspapers, 41
SchoolNet, 55–57, 56, 176n36
schools: adoption of, 38, 71; age segregation, 9–10; attendance, 9, 163n9; bands in, 27, 39, 45, 87–88, 137, 181n24 (*see also* music programs); building, 34; charter, 34; class sizes, 29, 30; competition for grants, 136; as compulsory, 10; condemnation of public schools, 32–34; co-op education, 35, 38; cutting costs, 30–31, 168n9 (*see also* fiscal restraints); diversity of, 29; efficiency of management, 34; enrolments, 29, 30, 31; expanding programs, 30; expectations, 2, 29, 31; funded by property taxes, 28; and human flourishing, 154, 156, 157–58;

increasing costs, 30 (*see also* teachers: salaries); and local businesses, 38, 41; as marketing opportunities, 2; and modernity, 48–49; P3, 30; payment for promo distribution, 1; and political education, 1; as powerful, 1; private, 34; reforming, 32, 33–34, 36; as social centres, 9, 163n9. *See also* principals; students; teachers
Schools Helping Schools Fund, 141
Schor, Juliet, 4, 5, 156
Screaming Avocado Café, 118–19
Screen Ad Billboards Inc., 83
secret contracts, 109–10, 114, 117
Seddon, Cindi, 105
Select Standing Committee on Health, 195n73
Sentinel High School, 139–40, 142
Shaker, Erika, 37, 98, 102, 124
Shapiro, Jack, 42
Sharpe, Jill, 82
Shaver, William, 106
Shaw Cable, 70, 76
Shell, 12, 15
Shoup, Chris, 119
Shredded Wheat, 10–11
SilverCity, 77
Simeon, Peter, 115
Simon, Michele, 69, 122
Simpsons, 12, 13
Singer, Susan, 76–77
Sir Wilfrid Laurier Annex Elementary School, 1
Slush Puppie Plus, 124–25, 197n102
Smith, Gerry, 47
social class. *See* class (social)
social critics, 22, 24, 33, 83–84, 154. *See also* protests/oppositions
social responsibility, 75–76, 135, 144, 147, 154–55
soft drinks/soda. *See* Coca-Cola; Pepsi-Cola; sugar
songs, 1, 133
Southern Baptist Convention, 88–89
Southern Victoria High School, 58
Spears, Tom, 77

special education, 33
Spectrum Marketing, 108–9
sponsored talks, 70
sports: branding on uniforms, 83, 112; children as consumers, 9; earning equipment, 69, 84; electronic ads for funding, 76; and junk food/fast food, 112, 121, 123; logos in gym, 72, 80; TSN merchandise, 70. *See also* physical education
Sports Network (TSN), 70, 75
standardized testing, 34, 60
Staples, 135
St. George School, 132
St. James Collegiate, 40
St. Monica Catholic School, 21
St. Stanislaus Catholic Elementary School, 68
STEAM (science, technology, engineering, art, and mathematics), 147
Steinberg, Shirley, 4
STEM (science, technology, engineering, and mathematics): and Conference Board of Canada, 48; in educational television, 174n9; improved learning of, 36; and Internet, 55; Learning Partnership focus, 144, 146; and privatization, 34; Solve for Tomorrow challenge, 135. *See also* technology
Stentor, 55
Stephenson, Bette, 51, 52
"The Story of Menstruation" (educational film), 12, 20
"The Story of the Tea Plant" (Salada), 11
"The Story of Wheat" (Shredded Wheat), 11
Stratford Northwestern Secondary, 118–19
Stronck, David R., 173n77
student councils, 193n43
students: and alcohol, 44; as captive audiences, 25–26, 91, 114; and clothing industry, 9; as consumers, 77, 145, 180n13; Eaton's clubs, 12–13, *14*; Indigenous students, 143; pitching to, 10; planning corporate parties, 39–40, 41; preparation for workplace (*see* workplace preparation); preparation for postsecondary school, 33–34, 35; product development, 1, 5; selling junk food/fast food, 121–22; working for credits, 39, 69. *See also* children
Subway Developments, 110
sugar, 117–21, 189n7, 190n15, 194n59, 195n79
Superintendent of Education for Nova Scotia, 128
Superstore. *See* Real Canadian Superstore
swag. *See* branded products
sweatshops, 79–80, 183n56

Take Our Kids to Work, 143, 146
Tannock, Stuart, 66
taxes, 28, 107, 156, 168n11
Taylor, Alison, 140–41
TD Grade One Book Giveaway, 74, 184n73
teachers: advertising teachers and samples, 16; Cominco dinner, 15; computer adaptation pressure, 61; computers and teaching, 178n58; encouraging commercialism, 13, 20–21, 26, 43, 140, 166n44; Imperial Oil exchange training, 15; magazines for, 19; paying for resources, 132; protests/oppositions, 22, 113, 118, 140, 145–46, 184n63; reasons for sponsorship use, 17–22; reduction in support services, 31; salaries, 16, 18, 30, 34, 132, 169n15; using school television, 101–2; Shell Merit Fellowships, 15; summer jobs for, 41; teaching time, 58; unions (*see* unions); volunteering, 43. *See also* principals
teaching aids: advertising for, 16; early forms of, 10–12, 22, 163n12; and environmentalism, 78; increase in, 29; as tried and true, 66
technology: boom as burden, 2, 33, 148; economy of, 34–38, 55, 61; and entrepreneurship, 148; history in schools, 48–49; industry and graduates, 36. *See*

also computers; Internet; STEAM; STEM

teenagers. *See* children; students

Telescene Film Group, 93

television, 3–4, 48–49, 68, 76, 174n9. *See also specific media companies*; Youth News Network

Terry Fox Secondary School, 72, 80, 110, 111

textbooks: film replacing, 48; as outdated, 17, 18, 20, 31; sponsored covers, 13; testing, 39. *See also* books

Thomson, Kathleen, 113

Thorncliffe Elementary School, 71

Thyme Savers Catering, 119

Tim Hortons, 191n24

Toronto Association of Student Councils, 193n43

Toronto District School Board/Toronto Board of Education: and chocolate milk, 106; and Eaton's, 25; and Future Shop computer labs, 151; and junk food/fast food, 107, 123; and soft drink contracts, 108, 111–12, 114

Toronto Dominion (TD) Bank Financial Group, 67, 74, 184n73

toys, 68

trade associations, 10–11

Tree Canada, 134–35

trees, 71, 134–35

Trout, Jennie, 95

Tsallas, George, 45

Turning Points, 144

tutoring, 45

Tymoschuk, Gary, 77

unemployment, 29

unions, 79, 81, 91, 113–14, 146

United Students Against Sweatshops, 80, 183n55

Université du Québec à Montréal, 183n56

universities, 36, 80–81, 183n55

University of British Columbia (UBC), 109–10, 183n56

University of New Brunswick, 44

urban schools, 30

US National Education Association (NEA), 22

Vaccaro, Sonny, 154

Valentine, Peggy, 75

VanCity Credit Union, 69, 180n13

Vancouver Olympic Committee, 84

Vancouver School Board, 190n15

vending machines: and advertising, 74, 83; banning, 108, 119, 195n75; and Channel One, 101; and healthy options, 105, 107, 116, 118, 122; history of, 106, 189n6; limiting access to, 118, 123; Refreshments Canada and, 195n79; Riverside Secondary School, 125. *See also* junk food/fast food

Vezina, Guy, 69

Vigilance in Public Education, 23

vocational schools, 33, 172n62

vouchers/coupons, 17; 67

VS Services Ltd., 107

W. P. Wagner High School, 123

Wal-Mart, 71, 75–76, 79, 181n24

Walt Disney productions, 12, 20, 79

Walter Murray Collegiate, 114

Walton, Dawn, 31

War Savings Stamps, 19

Wealthy School Revolution, 131

Welcome to Kindergarten, 143–44, *145*

welfare state, 28, 32, 52–53

Wellington County Board of Education, 181n25

Wente, Margaret, 97, 136

West Island Educational Foundation, 138–39

West Vancouver School Board, 139

Westmount High School, 140

White Spot, 1

Whitney Public School, 130, 141

Winson, Anthony, 116–17, 192n39

Withrow Public School, 17

workplace preparation: classroom extensions, 42; I Cubed, 144; *IdeaBook*, 40–41; maker education, 147; *Partners in Education*, 41; school as marketplace, 147; Take Our Kids to Work, 143, 146; technology economy, 34–38, 55, 61. *See also* entrepreneurship

Wrigley's Company, 181n26

York Region District School Board/York Region Board of Education, 39, 76, 83, 110, 111, 181n25

York Region Roman Catholic Separate School Board, 181n25

Youth News Network (YNN), 87–88, 89–99, *100*, 101–2, 187n30, 187n32

Zechel, Bob, 132